Mark

INTERPRETATION
A Bible Commentary for Teaching and Preaching

INTERPRETATION
A BIBLE COMMENTARY FOR TEACHING AND PREACHING

James Luther Mays, *Editor*
Patrick D. Miller Jr., *Old Testament Editor*
Paul J. Achtemeier, *New Testament Editor*

Old Testament: *Genesis* by Walter Brueggemann
Exodus by Terence E. Fretheim
Leviticus by Samuel E. Balentine
Numbers by Dennis T. Olson
Deuteronomy by Patrick D. Miller
Joshua by Jerome F. D. Creach
Judges by J. Clinton McCann
Ruth by Katherine Doob Sakenfeld
First and Second Samuel by Walter Brueggemann
First and Second Kings by Richard D. Nelson
First and Second Chronicles by Steven S. Tuell
Ezra–Nehemiah by Mark A. Throntveit
Esther by Carol M. Bechtel
Job by J. Gerald Janzen
Psalms by James L. Mays
Proverbs by Leo G. Perdue
Ecclesiastes by William P. Brown
Song of Songs by Robert W. Jenson
Isaiah 1–39 by Christopher R. Seitz
Isaiah 40–66 by Paul D. Hanson
Jeremiah by R. E. Clements
Lamentations by F. W. Dobbs-Allsopp
Ezekiel by Joseph Blenkinsopp
Daniel by W. Sibley Towner
Hosea–Micah by James Limburg
Nahum–Malachi by Elizabeth Achtemeier

New Testament: *Matthew* by Douglas R. A. Hare
Mark by Lamar Williamson Jr.
Luke by Fred B. Craddock
John by Gerard S. Sloyan
Acts by William H. Willimon
Romans by Paul J. Achtemeier
First Corinthians by Richard B. Hays
Second Corinthians by Ernest Best
Galations by Charles Cousar
Ephesians, Colossians, and Philemon by Ralph. P. Martin
Philippians by Fred B. Craddock
First and Second Thessalonians by Beverly Roberts Gaventa
First and Second Timothy and Titus by Thomas C. Oden
Hebrews by Thomas G. Long
First and Second Peter, James, and Jude by Pheme Perkins
First, Second, and Third John by D. Moody Smith
Revelation by M. Eugene Boring

LAMAR WILLIAMSON JR.

Mark

A Bible Commentary
for Teaching and Preaching

WJK WESTMINSTER
JOHN KNOX PRESS
LOUISVILLE · KENTUCKY

Nth edition
Published by Westminster John Knox Press
Louisville, Kentucky

09 10 11 12 13 14 15 16 17 18—10 9 8 7 6 5 4 3 2 1

Scripture quotations are from the Revised Standard Version of the Holy Bible, copyright © 1946, 1952, 1971, and 1973 by the Division of Christian Education of the National Council of the Churches of Christ in the U.S.A., and are used by permission.

Library of Congress Cataloging-in-Publication Data
Williamson, Lamar.
  Mark / Lamar Williamson, Jr.
      p. cm. — (Interpretation, a Bible commentary for teaching and preaching)
  Originally published: Atlanta, Ga. : J. Knox Press, c1983.
  Includes bibliographical references.
  ISBN 978-0-664-23434-8 (alk. paper)
  1. Bible. N.T. Mark—Commentaries. 2. Bible. N.T. Mark—Homiletical use. I. Title.
  BS2585.53.W55 2009
  226.3'07—dc22

                                                              2009012007

PRINTED IN THE UNITED STATES OF AMERICA

∞ The paper used in this publication meets the minimum requirements of the American National Standard for Information Sciences—Permanence of Paper for Printed Library Materials, ANSI Z39.48-1992

Westminster John Knox Press advocates the responsible use of our natural resources. The text paper of this book is made from 30% post-consumer waste.

SERIES PREFACE

This series of commentaries offers an interpretation of the books of the Bible. It is designed to meet the need of students, teachers, ministers, and priests for a contemporary expository commentary. These volumes will not replace the historical critical commentary or homiletical aids to preaching. The purpose of this series is rather to provide a third kind of resource, a commentary which presents the integrated result of historical and theological work with the biblical text.

An interpretation in the full sense of the term involves a text, an interpreter, and someone for whom the interpretation is made. Here, the text is what stands written in the Bible in its full identity as literature from the time of "the prophets and apostles," the literature which is read to inform, inspire, and guide the life of faith. The interpreters are scholars who seek to create an interpretation which is both faithful to the text and useful to the church. The series is written for those who teach, preach, and study the Bible in the community of faith.

The comment generally takes the form of expository essays. It is planned and written in the light of the needs and questions which arise in the use of the Bible as Holy Scripture. The insights and results of contemporary scholarly research are used for the sake of the exposition. The commentators write as exegetes and theologians. The task which they undertake is both to deal with what the texts say and to discern their meaning for faith and life. The exposition is the unified work of one interpreter.

The text on which the comment is based is the Revised Standard Version of the Bible. The general availability of this translation makes the printing of a translation unnecessary and saves the space for comment. The text is divided into sections appropriate to the particular book; comment deals with passages as a whole, rather than proceeding word by word, or verse by verse.

Writers have planned their volumes in light of the requirements set by the exposition of the book assigned to them. Biblical books differ in character, content, and arrangement. They also differ in the way they have been and are used in the liturgy, thought, and devotion of the church. The distinctiveness and use of particular books have been taken into account in decisions about the approach, emphasis, and use of space in the commentaries. The goal has been to allow writers to develop the format which provides for the best presentation of their interpretation.

The result, writers and editors hope, is a commentary which both explains and applies, an interpretation which deals with both the meaning and the significance of biblical texts. Each commentary reflects, of course, the writer's own approach and perception of the church and world. It could and should not be otherwise. Every interpretation of any kind is individual in that sense; it is one reading of the text. But all who work at the interpretation of Scripture in the church need the help and stimulation of a colleague's reading and understanding of the text. If these volumes serve and encourage interpretation in that way, their preparation and publication will realize their purpose.

Series Editors

CONTENTS

Dedicated to my wife and colleague, Ruthmary
Offered to Jesus Christ and his contemporary disciples

Introduction

Mark is a gospel.

First gospel or not, Mark is surely the only New Testament book which calls itself a gospel. "The beginning of the gospel of Jesus Christ, the Son of God" is the title of this work, and its self-designation ought to shape any interpretation which respects the text.

"Gospel" can signify a literary genre, or a particular theological message, or a canonical writing normative in the life of the church. The Gospel of Mark is all three: a collection of traditions about Jesus presented in story form, a narrative constituting good news about God and his kingdom, and a writing which occupies a place of fundamental importance in the Scriptures of the church.

Literary Genre: Gospel as Story

The purpose of Mark's Gospel is to bear witness to Jesus Christ as proclaimer and embodiment of the Kingdom of God, and to challenge readers to follow him in anticipation of his final coming as Son of man.

The Gospel of Mark presupposes that the best way to bear witness to the coming Kingdom of God and to challenge readers to faithful discipleship is to tell the story of Jesus. The first part of this introduction will review that story briefly, since no individual unit can be rightly understood apart from its place in the whole.

Much of the power of Mark's witness lies in the cumulative effect of the story in its entirety. The structure and flow of the narrative and the relationships among its parts are important. The table of contents of this commentary offers a convenient summary of the elements in the story and serves as an outline of the Gospel. Occasional reference to the contents pages will

1

clarify the following analysis of the whole as well as the detailed comments on individual passages.

After the evangelist's own title for his work (1:1), the story is introduced by a prologue set in the wilderness of Judea (1:1–13), a place of indeterminate geographical location but profound theological significance. John the Baptist appears Elijah-like to prepare the way. Jesus is introduced at verse 9 to be baptized and tempted. These two brief scenes establish his identity and his authority; they also hint at the trials which lie ahead.

That Jesus came into Galilee preaching the gospel of God (1:14–15) serves as transition from the prologue to the body of the narrative. His coming also announces the central theme of the Galilean ministry and of the entire Gospel: "The time is fulfilled, and the kingdom of God is at hand; repent, and believe the Good News" (author's trans.).

The Galilean ministry, dominated by the question of the identity of Jesus (e.g., "Who then is this?" 4:41), occupies the first half of the Gospel (1:16—8:21). The question is raised by a series of remarkable demonstrations of Jesus' authority in word and deed. Different groups and individuals respond in a variety of ways ranging from enthusiasm to misunderstanding to rejection. Jesus never declares his own identity. He imposes silence on the demons who alone see and confess clearly that he is the Son of God. He simply offers himself and his teachings, appealing for individual decision and commitment: "Whoever has ears to hear, let him hear!"

The kingdom Jesus announces is not only an individual matter. It also creates a community. Jesus calls, names, and sends out disciples whom he associates with himself in his mission. These decisive actions mark the beginning of each of three major parts in the Galilean ministry which can be identified by transitional passages and summary formulas. Each of these parts ends with an inadequate response to Jesus: hostility, unbelief, and misunderstanding.

The first part, from the call of the first four disciples (1:16–20) to the plot of the Pharisees and Herodians to kill Jesus (3:6), includes a series of five passages about healing (a demoniac in the Capernaum synagogue, Simon's mother-in-law, a crowd at evening, a leper, and a paralytic) followed by a series of five controversy stories (about forgiving the paralytic's sins, eating with tax collectors and sinners, not fasting, plucking grain on the sabbath, and healing on the sabbath). The passage about the paralytic (2:1–12) is the hinge of this part of the Gospel: as miracle story it belongs to the first section, and as controversy it belongs to the second. The first section uses preaching, teaching, and healing interchangeably as means of announcing the Kingdom of God. The response is immediate and spectacular. Jesus' fame spreads throughout Galilee, and clamoring crowds finally make it impossible for him even to enter a town openly (1:28, 33, 37, 39, 45). The second section, on the other hand, reports growing hostility to Jesus on the part of the religious leaders, from the scribes' murmuring (2:6–7), through hostile questions (2:16, 18, and 24), to the plot to kill Jesus (3:6).

After a transitional passage (3:7–12), part two opens with the naming of the Twelve, a group of disciples who would enjoy intimate fellowship with Jesus and share his ministry of preaching and healing (3:13–19). This part of the Galilean ministry begins (3:20–35) and ends (6:1–6) with the response to Jesus by his own people. The misunderstanding by his mother and brothers at the beginning (they think he is crazy, "beside himself," 3:21, 31–32) is underscored by the insertion of an accusation by the scribes that he performs exorcisms through the power of Satan himself (3:22–30), and by the replacement of his blood kin by "whoever does the will of God" (3:33–35). At the end, rejected by his neighbors and kinspeople in his home town, Jesus marvels because of their unbelief (6:1–6).

These units about the blindness of Jesus' own people bracket the first great discourse of Jesus in Mark, the parables of the kingdom told beside the sea (4:1–34). They are understood neither by those outside nor by the disciples (4:10–13). This discourse is followed by what may well have been the first four in a pre-Marcan cycle of miracle stories: a sea miracle (the stilling of the storm) and three healing miracles (the Gerasene demoniac, Jairus' daughter, and the woman with a hemorrhage). The healing of the woman is inserted into the story of the raising of Jairus' daughter so that each can interpret the other, a technique which is characteristic of the Gospel of Mark. The series ends with the charge "that no one should know this," a significant Marcan trait.

Part three begins with the sending of the Twelve to heal, preach, and teach (6:7–13, 30–32). In another Marcan insertion (6:14–29), the death of John the Baptist is reported at the time the Twelve begin their ministry, just as John's arrest marked

3

the beginning of Jesus' ministry (1:14). Two feeding stories enclose the remainder of this part of the Galilean ministry: the five thousand (6:30–44) and the four thousand (8:1–10). Between these brackets lies another miracle cycle: a sea miracle (walking on water) and three healings (the crowd at Gennesaret, the Syrophoenician woman's daughter, the deaf-mute of Decapolis). A second block of controversy material (7:1–23) continues the theme of rejection while at the same time constituting a collection of Jesus' teachings concerning tradition for the guidance of the early church. The Pharisees' demand for a sign and the disciples' discussion about bread bring this part of the Gospel to a close. Pharisees and disciples alike are blind to the meaning of the feedings and of all the mighty acts and teachings of Jesus. His enemies plot to kill him (3:6), his family and friends disbelieve (6:1–6), and his disciples misunderstand (8:14–21). The last word in the Galilean ministry is Jesus' question to his disciples, "Do you not yet understand?"

Part four (8:22—10:52) shows Jesus trying to heal the blindness of his disciples. The limits of this part of the Gospel are set by the only two healings of blind people in Mark: the blind man of Bethsaida (8:22–26) and blind Bartimaeus (10:46–52). The theme of these chapters is discipleship, depicted as the way of Jesus. Although Jesus does not physically leave Galilee till chapter 10 (v. 1), from verse 31 of chapter 8 onward he looks and moves toward his suffering, death, and resurrection in Jerusalem. Crowds continue to follow him and his disciples throughout these chapters (e.g., 10:46) but the accent shifts from public demonstrations of authority and the question of Jesus' identity to instruction of the disciples on the true nature of Jesus' messiahship and what it means to follow him.

The shift occurs right at the middle of Mark's sixteen chapters (8:27—9:1). This passage serves as the Gospel's major turning point. By confessing Jesus to be the Christ (8:29), Peter answers the "Who is Jesus?" question of chapters 1—8. Jesus then introduces a reinterpretation of what the Christ (Messiah) must do (8:31) and what following him means (8:34–35), themes that dominate the rest of the Gospel. Martin Kähler, observing in 1892 that from this point on the story of Jesus falls under the shadow of his impending death, called Mark and the other Gospels "passion narratives with extended introductions" (*The So-called Historical Jesus and the Historic, Biblical Christ*, p. 80, note 11).

4

Three passion prediction units determine the structure and express the central thrust of the discipleship section. Each unit consists of a prediction of the passion and resurrection (8:31; 9:31; 10:33–34; the last virtually a table of contents for chaps. 11—16), a misunderstanding on the part of the disciples (8:32–33; 9:32; 10:35–41), and teaching about discipleship (8:34 —9:1; 9:33–37; 10:42–45).

By means of these prediction units the Marcan Jesus, challenging his disciples' understanding of messianic kingship as national and personal glory, reinterprets that kingship in terms of a Son of man rejected, suffering and dying, and vindicated by resurrection. If this is the way of Jesus, it must also be the way of his disciples. Between the first and second prediction units the transfiguration confirms the hidden glory of Jesus' kingship as Son of God, while the story of the epileptic boy adds impotence and failure to the theme of the disciples' misunderstanding. Between the second and third prediction units, Jesus' teachings about divorce and remarriage, children, and possessions give specificity to the demands of discipleship. The third prediction unit is followed immediately by the closing restoration-of-sight story in which Bartimaeus, appealing to Jesus as Son of David (Messiah), is healed and follows Jesus "on the way."

While parts one through three depict the Galilean ministry and part four tells of Jesus and his disciples on their way to Jerusalem, from verse 1 of chapter 11 onward the action occurs in or near Jerusalem itself. The entry to the city (11:1–11), which some view as the beginning of the passion narrative, hints at Jesus' kingship but does not declare it. Jesus enters the Temple, looks around it, and withdraws.

With the second entry into Jerusalem on the next day, Mark introduces Jesus' confrontation with the Temple and its authorities, the theme which dominates part five (chaps. 11—13). Mark presents this theme by inserting Jesus' "cleansing" of the Temple (more aptly, his opening the Temple to the Gentiles) into the account of the withering of a fruitless fig tree. The fig tree thus becomes a symbol of the barren Temple.

Upon Jesus' third entry into Jerusalem (11:27), his controversy with the religious authorities becomes overt. The basic issue, stated boldly in the question of authority put to Jesus by the chief priests, scribes, and elders, precedes the parable of the wicked tenants which Jesus tells against them (12:1–12).

The controversy is continued in a series of questions put to

5

Jesus by his opponents. In each case the unit takes the form of a pronouncement story; that is, a memorable and authoritative saying (pronouncement) of Jesus, preceded by a brief setting. In this series each setting consists of the naming of the adversaries and a trick question turning upon the interpretation of Scripture. The Pharisees and Herodians approached, hostile and confident, "to entrap him in his talk" (12:13); the Sadducees simply "asked him a question" (12:18); and one of the scribes "seeing that he answered them well, asked . . ." (12:28), and then on hearing Jesus' answer responded, "You are right, Teacher" (12:32). Having won this duel of wits ("after that, no one dared to ask him any question"), Jesus turns the tables on his opponents by a question about the son of David (12:35). Jesus' question is also about the interpretation of Scripture and is set in a pronouncement story. To this story directed against the scribes is appended a saying which warns against the scribes "who devour widows' houses" (12:40). A vignette about a poor widow (12:41–44) contrasts her dedication and generosity with the hypocrisy of the scribes and closes this third set of controversies in Mark.

Chapter 13, Jesus' discourse about the destruction of the Temple and the end-time, is so different in tone and style from the rest of Mark that some commentators hold it to be a late insertion which is foreign to the basic structure of the Gospel. Others find in it the clue to the intention of the entire Gospel. Chapter 13 in fact concludes part five because it records Jesus' departure from Jerusalem (13:3), echoing his arrival there (11:1–11), and because it presents the last word in his polemic against the Temple (13:1–2). Jesus' discourse about the end-time, delivered from the Mount of Olives opposite the Temple, is closely attached to this prediction of the destruction of the Temple. The Temple now lies behind; the discourse points forward to the coming of the Son of man.

Mark 14:1–11 marks the beginning of the passion narrative proper (chaps. 14 and 15). This passage is the beginning of the end of Mark's drama, which is the end of "the beginning of the gospel of Jesus Christ, the Son of God." In another Marcan insertion pattern, the priests and scribes seek to kill him (14:1–2), a woman anoints his body for burial (14:3–9), Judas seeks to betray him (14:10–11). The Son of man is about to die.

This last part of the story gathers up the major themes of the Gospel into a drama of growing intensity, punctuated by

6

frequent time notices: the days preceding Passover, the watches of the night in which Jesus was betrayed, the hours of the day he died. Time is marked in smaller units and events are reported in greater detail as the drama builds in intensity and significance. The movement is linear and inexorable, from upper room to garden and betrayal, to Jewish trial and Peter's denial, to Roman trial and condemnation, to crucifixion, death and burial. Along the way Jesus is betrayed by Judas, let down by the inner three in the garden, forsaken by all the disciples after the arrest, and on the cross seemingly abandoned by God. Three times Jesus is mocked: at the Jewish trial (14:65), at the Roman trial (15:16–20), and on the cross (15:29–32). Only the women stand by him throughout, though at a distance. They witness his death "from afar," see the place where he is buried, and go to anoint him when the sabbath is past (15:40, 47; 16:1).

Many themes converge in the passion narrative; notably Jesus' rejection by his enemies, the failure of his friends, and the unfolding revelation of his true identity and mission. Jesus' prophecies are fulfilled: He is rejected, mocked and killed by the authorities, betrayed by Judas, and denied by Peter. As Son of man he gives his life as a ransom for many (10:45). The action toward which the drama has been moving has reached a climax and seems to be complete, with a stone rolled against the door of a tomb to mark the end (15:46). The burial, however, is not the end; it is a void from which bursts a new beginning.

The darkness and silence are broken in the first eight verses of chapter 16. This unit is more than an epilogue and other than a conclusion. The resurrection of Jesus reverses the tragedy, vindicates the suffering Son of man as Christ and Son of God, and makes of the story "the gospel of God." The passage may be called an "envoi," for the message of the young man in white is a renewed call to follow Jesus who goes before his disciples into Galilee; "there you will see him, as he told you" (16:7; cf. 14:28).

Here the original Gospel of Mark ends, to be completed in the lives of its readers. Some of its early readers, knowing how the story came out in the mission of the apostolic church, apparently felt compelled to round off the abrupt conclusion. Two different endings were written, the longer of which appears as verses 9–20, chapter 16 in the RSV. It belongs to the canonical Gospel of Mark and will be treated as an appendix.

Mark, like all the New Testament Gospels and like good

7

narrative in general, communicates at more than one level. At the narrative level, characters in the story interact within an assumed framework of relationships, attitudes, and knowledge that becomes evident as the plot unfolds. At another level, the evangelist interacts with the reader within a different assumed framework of attitudes and knowledge. For example, the evangelist tells the reader at the outset that Jesus is the Christ, the Son of God (1:1). Characters within the story are assumed not to know this, however, and much of the drama is built upon gradual discovery of and reaction to the identity of Jesus.

Two-level communication often appears in Mark in the form of ambiguity (e.g., the centurion's confession that Jesus is a son of God or the Son of God, 15:39) and of irony (e.g., the title "king of the Jews," used in mockery, but really true, chapter 15 *passim*). Paradox is also a feature of Mark, especially notable in the parabolic teaching of Jesus which both reveals and conceals (4:10–12, 21–22, 33–34).

Awareness of these literary characteristics of Mark may save the interpreter from trying to answer literary questions by historical means as in the "messianic secret" debate (see pp. 12–13 below). Such awareness can also illumine the interpretation of many Marcan passages, as noted in the body of the commentary. (This literary perspective on Mark is helpfully amplified in Donald Juel, *An Introduction to New Testament Literature,* Chap. 8).

Theological Message: Gospel as Good News

"Gospel" means "Good News." In this sense, Mark is a Gospel because of its basic message.

The Kingdom of God

The Galilean ministry begins in Mark with the notice that "Jesus came . . . preaching the gospel of God" (1:14), or "Jesus went to Galilee and preached the Good News from God" (TEV). The Good News is about the Kingdom of God: "The time is fulfilled, and the kingdom of God is at hand" (1:15).

This news dominates the entire Gospel of Mark. The longest discourse in the Galilean ministry is the collection of parables of the kingdom (4:1–34). The Kingdom of God is also a recurrent theme in Jesus' teachings on discipleship (e.g., 9:1, 47; 10:14–15, 23–25). Jesus enters Jerusalem to the acclamation, "Blessed is the coming kingdom of our father David" (11:10,

8

author's trans.), and there he commends the scribe whose wise response to Jesus shows that he is "not far from the kingdom of God" (12:34). In the passion narrative, Jesus at the last supper states solemnly that he will not drink again of the fruit of the vine until he drinks it new in the Kingdom of God (14:25). He then dies as Christ, the Son of God, and King of the Jews (see 14:61; 15:2, 9, 12, 18, 26, 32, 39) and is buried in the tomb of a respected man "who was also himself looking for the kingdom of God" (15:43).

The foregoing references suggest the extraordinary range and depth of teachings about the Kingdom of God in the Gospel according to Mark. This rich and varied message clusters about two major foci: Jesus as king and his disciples as subjects in the Kingdom of God. Jesus not only announces the kingdom's coming but also, by his authoritative words and deeds, incarnates its hidden presence. Disciples are those to whom the secret of the kingdom is given; they are those who receive it, enter it, and share Jesus' mission of announcing it. Christology and discipleship are two basic concerns in the proclamation of the Kingdom of God in Mark.

Christology

The question of who Jesus is has already been noted in Mark's unfolding story. Patterns are discernible in the way Mark presents the person and work of Jesus. The threads in these patterns are several christological titles, including the two which appear in the opening words, "The beginning of the gospel of Jesus Christ, the Son of God."

1. Christ, or Son of David

Christ, the Greek form of the Hebrew title "Messiah," means literally "the anointed one." Although priests as well as kings were anointed in ancient Israel, in Mark "Christ" refers to God's anointed king, and in particular to the messianic figure whom Jews expected to restore the throne of David and to consummate the age. Jesus comes to announce and to inaugurate the Kingdom of God, but the nature of that kingdom and the form of Jesus' kingship contrasts with contemporary expectations. This disparity accounts for a certain reticence in the use of the term *Christ* in Mark.

After verse 1 this title is not used at all until Peter's confession of Jesus as the Christ (8:29). Jesus never refers to himself as Christ in the entire Gospel. However, during his trial before the

9

Jewish authorities the high priest asks Jesus point-blank if he is the Christ, and Jesus replies "I am." Although Jesus affirms that this claim will be vindicated when the glory of the Son of man is revealed, the high priest views it as self-evident blasphemy (14:61–64).

These three uses of the term *Christ* establish a significant pattern. From the title the reader knows that Jesus is the Christ, the messianic king of the Jews. This is not evident to participants in the story, however. They must decide who he is on the basis of what they see and hear. By mid-point, Peter, the first among the apostles, and representative of the later Jewish church, comes to recognize that Jesus is the Christ. Jesus rejects what Peter means by that title and begins to teach that the Son of man must suffer, die, and rise again. Near the end of the narrative, the highest authority in Judaism elicits from Jesus a confession that he is the Christ, only to reject his claim out of hand. Jesus, while acknowledging the title, "Christ," uses "Son of man" to point to his coming vindication.

Of the four remaining uses of "Christ" in Mark, three are on the lips of those who abuse or misunderstand the term (12:35; 13:21; 15:32). Only after the death and resurrection of Jesus can anyone rightly and unambiguously call him Christ. Post-resurrection usage of this title in the early church is reflected in the predictive word of Jesus, ". . . whoever gives you a cup of water to drink because you bear the name of Christ . . ." (9:41).

A closely related title, "Son of David," is used in Mark as a synonym for "Christ" (see II Sam. 7:12–13; Jer. 30:9; Hos. 3:5). "Son of David," probably implicit in the acclamation of the crowd at the entry to Jerusalem (11:10), appears explicitly in the healing of blind Bartimaeus (10:46–52) and in Jesus' question about scribal teaching (12:35–37). In all three cases, the text shows the same reticence and ambivalence toward "Son of David" that it does toward "Christ." According to Mark, only after the resurrection could anyone fully understand how the crucified one can be the Christ, the Son of David.

2. Son of God

The most probable Greek text of Mark 1:1 calls Jesus Christ the Son of God, introducing a theme whose development throughout the Gospel also presents a striking pattern. In this case, the terminology varies somewhat: *Son of God, my beloved Son, Holy One of God, Son of the Most High God, Son of the*

10

Blessed. These terms all refer to the same concept, and some passages convey the idea without explicit use of a title. As in the case of "Christ," Jesus never refers to himself as "Son of God." One possible exception is the allegorical use of "son" in the parable of the wicked tenants (12:6). Others refer to Jesus as "God's Son" in various and significant ways.

God calls Jesus his Son through the divine voice at the baptism (1:11), when only Jesus hears, and at the transfiguration (9:7), when Peter, James, and John are addressed.

Meanwhile, the demons have recognized and openly proclaimed Jesus' divine sonship (1:24; 3:11; 5:7), but the text informs us in a summary statement that Jesus silenced the demons on such occasions (3:12).

This title is combined with "Christ" in the high priest's question, "are you the Christ, the Son of the Blessed?" (14:61). "Son of the Blessed" is a pious circumlocution for "Son of God," and on the lips of the high priest it is another synonym for Messiah.

Finally, at the crucifixion a gentile army officer, seeing how Jesus dies, exclaims, "Truly this man was a/the Son of God!"

The ambiguity of "Son of God" in Mark comes to a head in this final reference. To Jews, "Son of God" was a title used of Israel's kings in general and of the messianic king in particular (II Sam. 7:14; Ps. 2:7; Ps. 89:26–27). This seems to be the intended sense at the baptism, the transfiguration, and the trial. In the Hellenistic world, however, "Son of God" could be a term of respect for a heroic person, or it could designate one who in some way participates in deity. The "Son of God" confessions by the demons are to be understood in the latter sense. The centurion's confession should probably be understood initially as a form of respect ("a son of God"); but at a second level of communication the evangelist is telling the reader, who stands this side of the resurrection, that Jesus is in fact *"the* Son of God." Understood in this way, the centurion's word at the cross is the climactic expression of the Son of God theme in Mark.

3. Son of man

The one christological title used unambiguously in Mark is "Son of man." This phrase had been used variously in Jewish writings, sometimes as a generic term for humankind (e.g., Ps. 8:4), sometimes in apocalyptic literature to refer to a more-than-human figure of the end-time (e.g., Dan. 7; I Enoch 37—

11

71; cf. "man" in II Esdras 13), and throughout Ezekiel as the Lord's term of address for the prophet. Unlike "Christ," "Son of David," and "Son of God," all of which were titles associated with the king in Jerusalem, "Son of man" was a somewhat fluid term, in no way identified with the civil or religious institutions of Judaism. According to Mark, Jesus preferred this self-designation. His person and work as Son of man defines, corrects, and completes our understanding of him as Christ, the Son of David, and Son of God.

When Jesus corrects Peter's erroneous understanding of Christ, he does so by changing terminology and predicting the suffering, death, and resurrection of the Son of man (8:31). When Jesus acknowledges before the high priest that he is the Christ, the Son of the Blessed, he shifts terms immediately and points to the future exaltation and glorious coming of the Son of man (14:62). When Jesus seeks to teach the Twelve the meaning of discipleship, he does so by three solemn predictions of the passion of the Son of man (8:31; 9:31; 10:33–34; cf. 9:12). When Jesus states in a single word the meaning of his death, it is a word about the Son of man who "came not to be served but to serve, and to give his life as a ransom for many" (10:45). When Jesus teaches about the consummation of the age (13:4), it is in terms of "the Son of man coming in clouds with great power and glory" (13:26; cf. 8:38). When Jesus on other occasions uses "Son of man" as a substitute for "I," it is in texts that reveal his person and his word at a profound level: "The Son of man has authority on earth to forgive sins" (2:10); "the Son of man is lord even of the sabbath" (2:28); "he charged them to tell no one what they had seen (the transfiguration), until the Son of man should have risen from the dead" (9:9); "the Son of man goes as it is written of him, but woe to that man by whom the Son of man is betrayed!" (14:21; cf. 14:41). In Mark, the Son of man is one who has authority, who dies and rises again, and who will at the end come in glory. Jesus is that Son of man. His authority governs our relationship to God. His death and resurrection are God's work on our behalf. His coming in glory is the vindication of God's way with us and the world.

4. The "messianic secret"

12   Mark announces (1:1) that Jesus is Christ and Son of God, then is extremely reticent in the use of those titles while giving prominence to the Son of man title. This fact has always struck

careful readers as peculiar, and many attempts have been made to explain it. One of the most brilliant and influential explanations was that of William Wrede in *The Messianic Secret*. Wrede believed that commands to silence about his messiahship were attributed to Jesus by the early church (some later critics would say the evangelist) in order to veil the fact that according to the earliest traditions Jesus himself never claimed to be Messiah. Since this claim became fundamental in the church's proclamation after the resurrection, the church needed to ground it in the life of the historical Jesus, while respecting the traditions about Jesus which were silent on the subject. The church's stories about Jesus therefore had others affirm that Jesus was Messiah and Son of God, while Jesus himself commanded all who recognized this to say nothing about it till after the resurrection. Wrede used this hypothesis to explain not only the commands to silence, but also texts about Jesus' search for privacy, about his use of parables to reveal truth to disciples but to conceal it from others, and about the misunderstanding of the disciples despite private instruction.

Whereas Wrede constructs an elaborate explanation of "the messianic secret motif" on the basis of the hypothesis that in the earliest traditions Jesus himself never claimed to be Messiah, the more plausible explanation seems to be that in the development of Mark's narrative no full and appropriate understanding of Jesus is possible except in the light of his passion, death, and resurrection. Jesus seeks neither to conceal nor to deny that he is Christ and Son of God, but rather to correct and complete all inadequate understandings of those terms.

Furthermore, communication at several levels is characteristic of good narrative (see pp. 7–8). Although Jesus' identity is a mystery for the characters in Mark's story, readers of Mark know who Jesus is from the beginning. The term *messianic secret* is appropriate only to communication within the narrative framework. From the perspective of the reader, what is communicated is not a gradual revelation of who Jesus is, but an unfolding clarification of what he must undergo and what that implies for those who follow him. Indeed, Mark's Gospel seems to assume that readers are believing Christians who know of Jesus' death and resurrection but who need further instruction in the meaning of Messiahship and the requirements of discipleship.

13

INTERPRETATION

Discipleship

If Jesus is one major focus of the gospel message in Mark, the disciples are the other. Mark depicts the way of Jesus as the way his disciples are called to follow. Only a clear and correct understanding of Jesus can produce a clear and correct understanding of what it means to be a disciple. This intimate relationship between Jesus and his disciples forms the underlying structure of many a passage in Mark, and it also provides a basic link between this ancient writing and our lives today. This Gospel is written for disciples of every age, and a concern for disciples pervades the entire Gospel from the call of the first four (1:16–20) to the final message to the disciples and Peter (16:7). While even the most frequently used christological title, Son of man, appears fourteen times in Mark, the term *disciples* is used more than forty times, and *the Twelve* another ten times. In Mark, the disciples often stand for the evangelist's church or simply the Christian community. Similarly the Twelve represent church leaders in any age.

How the disciples are portrayed is far more significant than the frequency with which they appear. Their initial presentation is highly favorable: The first five disciples respond immediately to the call of Jesus, moved only by the power of his word (1:16–20; 2:13–14). Throughout the early chapters of Mark the disciples (or the Twelve) accompany Jesus (2:15; 3:7, 14; 6:1; 8:10), assist him (3:9; 6:41; 8:6), are identified with Jesus in attacks from his opponents (2:16, 18, 23; 7:2, 5) and share in his ministry of healing, preaching, and teaching (6:7–13, 30).

However, early on the disciples fail to understand the teaching of Jesus (4:10–13), although he repeatedly gives them private instructions (4:34; 7:17–19). Their misunderstanding becomes increasingly evident in their response to his mighty works (4:41; 5:31; 6:52; 8:4) and is summarized in Jesus' word to them at the end of the Galilean ministry, "Do you not yet understand?" (8:21).

Misunderstanding dominates the discipleship section (8:22 —10:52). Peter understands that Jesus is the Christ, but rebukes him when he speaks of suffering and death (8:32). The disciples not only misunderstand Jesus' second passion prediction (9:32), but their discussion about who is the greatest (9:34) shows they have not understood Jesus' teaching about denying self and taking up one's cross (8:34–35). James' and John's request to sit

14

at Jesus' right and left hand in glory (10:35–41) demonstrates their misunderstanding or rejection of his teaching that if anyone would be first he must be last of all and servant of all (9:35). When Jesus teaches about divorce, the disciples later ask him again about this matter (10:10). When people bring children to Jesus, the disciples rebuke them, incurring Jesus' indignation (10:13–14). When Jesus teaches how hard it is for the rich to enter the Kingdom of God, the amazement (10:24) and astonishment (10:26) of the disciples are signs of their misunderstanding and resistance to his teaching.

In addition to misunderstanding Jesus, the disciples fail in other ways. The theme of failure is introduced by the story of the boy the disciples could not heal (9:14–29). It becomes prominent in the passion narrative when Judas, "one of the Twelve," betrays Jesus (14:10, 20, 43). The inner group of three, asked to watch in Gethsemane, falls asleep three times (14:32–42). Peter, despite all his protestations (14:29, 31), denies him (14:66–72), and all the disciples forsake him and flee (14:50, cf. 51–52). No friend or disciple stands at the foot of the cross in Mark. The women, who in Mark are distinguished from the disciples, witness his death from afar (15:40); but even they fail at the end. Entrusted to tell his disciples and Peter that Jesus is risen from the dead, they are so afraid that they flee from the tomb and say nothing.

How are we to understand this downward pattern in the Marcan theme of discipleship, with its ignominious and incomplete ending at 16:8? If Mark 16:8 is not the original and intended end of the Gospel, the answer is evident (see the Appendix, pp. 286–88). Answers based on the assumption that 16:8 is the original ending of Mark fall into two general categories: Some presuppose that readers are intended to distance themselves from the disciples; others assume that we are expected to identify with them.

According to some recent interpreters, the disciples represent the apostolic Jewish-Christian community in Jerusalem headed by the Twelve and erroneously waiting for the Lord to appear there in the Temple. The evangelist, writing after the fall of Jerusalem and the Temple, shows that the disciples and the Twelve never understood Jesus' teaching on the Kingdom of God, or on suffering and service, or on the dissociation of the coming of the Son of man from the fate of the Temple. The purpose of the Gospel of Mark, according to this view, is to show

15

the misunderstanding and failure of the Twelve so that the original readers would turn away from the apostolic church based in Jerusalem and await the coming of the Lord in Galilee. (This view is spelled out, with differences of detail and emphasis, in T. J. Weeden, *Mark, Traditions in Conflict* and W. Kelber, *The Kingdom in Mark* and *Mark's Story of Jesus*.)

Such theories are attractive, but they do not take into account either the historical fact that the apostolic church canonized this Gospel or the psychological fact that readers almost universally identify with the disciples. The present commentary assumes that a more traditional view is probably correct. The disciples in Mark reflect the enthusiasms, misunderstandings, and failures characteristic of the Marcan community and of each succeeding generation of Christians. As the grumbling of Israel in the wilderness was written down for the instruction of succeeding generations, so the misunderstanding and failure of the disciples is "written down for our instruction, upon whom the end of the ages has come" (I Cor. 10:11; cf. Rom. 15:4). When Jesus calls disciples to follow him (1:17, 20; 2:14; 8:34; 10:21, 49–52), he calls us. When Jesus rebukes obtuse disciples, relatives, and friends (4:13, 40; 6:4–6; 8:21, 33; 10:14; 14:21, 37–38), we stand convicted. When, even after the disciples have contradicted, betrayed, denied, and abandoned him, Jesus promises to go before them into Galilee and reveal himself to them there (14:28; 16:7), we are confronted by his forgiveness and offered the hope of another chance to follow him.

All theories of the ultimate rejection of the disciples in Mark are undone by Jesus' final promise to meet precisely those flawed and failed disciples in Galilee, even if—especially if—that promise remains unfulfilled within the text of the original Gospel. The open-endedness of the Gospel is the climactic invitation to readers to identify with those first disciples. They and we, in spite of failure, are still invited to follow him as he goes before us to Galilee. Whoever has ears to hear may still hear (4:9, 23), repent (1:4), believe (1:15), receive the Kingdom of God as a child (10:15), and follow Jesus on the way (10:52). This element of invitation and of promise turns the otherwise disastrous story of the disciples in Mark into gospel; that is, good news. That we must be like Jesus is not good news. On that score disciples always fail. The good news is rather that, despite our failure, Jesus constantly renews the call to follow him and that he has authority on earth to forgive sins.

16

As gospel, then, Mark proclaims a message that includes two foci: Jesus and the disciples. Of these two, however, one has clear priority. The good news is about Jesus. The final message to disciples is true in more ways than one: *"He goes before you."*

Canonical Writing: Gospel as Scripture

Although it is possible to study the Gospel of Mark as an interesting example of first-century narrative and to analyze its message as a particular case in the history of religions, these approaches are incommensurate with the intention revealed in the text and with the function which has kept it alive for two millennia. Like all the writings of the New Testament, Mark grows out of the traditions of a community of faith and is written for use in and by that community to awaken, challenge, and nurture faith. Written by and for disciples of Jesus Christ, Mark occupies a prominent place in the canon of the church's Scripture. Users of this commentary who are entrusted with the interpretation of Scripture in the church will encounter the text in its own natural habitat. This can facilitate a vital reading and hearing of Mark, provided the interpreter takes seriously the implications of the fact that this Gospel is Scripture.

Scripture and History

For most of the first eighteen centuries of church history, few readers perceived any tension between reading the Gospels as Scripture and reading them as history. In the nineteenth century, however, major challenges to the historicity of the gospel traditions emerged. Scholars sought to strip away myth and legend in order to recover the historical Jesus, who, presumably, could be discerned beneath and behind the text. During this same period, careful study of sources and of the relationship among the Gospels produced a growing consensus that Mark is the earliest of the Gospels and therefore the most reliable historical source. Despite the eclipse of the quest for the historical Jesus early in the twentieth century, the concern for history (What really happened?) dominated most commentaries on Mark until about 1950. Since then, a growing consensus has held that the writer of Mark, like all the evangelists, was a theologian of the Christian community. His purpose is not primarily to write history, but to announce a message.

17

INTERPRETATION

The relatively slight concern for history in Mark is evident in the absence of any account of Jesus' ancestry, birth, or early years, as well as the absence of any account of the results of his resurrection (the original Gospel ended at 16:8). Within the segment of Jesus' life treated in Mark, geographical references are sometimes so jumbled as to make a sequentially accurate account impossible (e.g., the absence of any time reference between 4:35 and 6:2; the date of the last supper, 14:12, conflicting with that given in John 13:1–2; 19:14). Finally, time and again Mark is either ambiguous or silent on some detail important to anyone who wants to know exactly what happened (e.g., Whose house in 2:1; in 2:15? And how were the loaves and fish multiplied in 6:41?). The evangelist is either a very careless historian, or else he was not trying to write history. This commentary will assume, with a large current consensus, that history is not the primary interest of the Gospel of Mark.

This does not mean that Mark is irrelevant for historical research on Christian beginnings or that historical study is irrelevant to the understanding of this Gospel. Indeed, three levels of history played a part in shaping the present text and are reflected in it. The most recent of these, for which the canonical text is a primary source, is the history of the evangelist and his community. Behind that lies the history of the earlier community which, for approximately four decades (A.D. 30–70) preserved the traditions about Jesus in oral form. At the base of the tradition, accessible only through the corporate memory of Christian believers, lies the history of Jesus and his first disciples. Historical certainty becomes increasingly problematical as one moves back through these three levels.

Many Christians today still read Mark in a pre-critical fashion, seeing no tension between history and gospel, reading every text as a literal and reliable historical account of what Jesus and those around him said and did. Others read critically, preoccupied by the question of historicity; they ask constantly and often skeptically, "What really happened?" The position of the present commentary is neither of the above, but rather one which treats Mark as Scripture.

To treat this first-century writing as holy Scripture for a twentieth- or twenty-first-century community of faith presents certain interpretive and pastoral problems. One which recurs frequently in Mark is the question of miracle and faith healing.

MIRACLES IN MARK

I. Specific Miracles of Jesus	TEXT	KIND
A. Healings		
1. Man in Capernaum Synagogue	1:21–28	Exorcism
2. Simon's Mother-in-law	1:29–31	Fever
3. Leper whom Jesus touched	1:40–45	Leprosy
4. Paralytic healed and forgiven	2:1–12	Paralysis
5. Man with withered hand	3:1–6	Deformity
6. Gerasene demoniac	5:1–20	Exorcism
7. Jairus' daughter	5:21–24a, 35–43	Death
8. Woman with hemorrhage	5:24b–34	Hemorrhage
9. Canaanite woman's daughter	7:24–30	Exorcism
10. Deaf-mute of Decapolis	7:31–37	Deafness
11. Blind man of Bethsaida	8:22–26	Blindness
12. Boy the disciples couldn't heal	9:14–29	Exorcism
13. Blind Bartimaeus	10:46–52	Blindness
B. Other		
1. Stilling the storm	4:35–41	Sea
2. Feeding of 5,000	6:35–44	Feeding
3. Walking on water	6:45–52	Sea
4. Feeding of 4,000	8:1–10	Feeding
5. Cursing the fig tree	11:12–14, 20–23	Curse

II. General Accounts of Healings

A. By Jesus		
1. Simon's door at sundown	1:32–34	Diseases/demons
2. Crowd by the sea	3:7–12	Diseases
3. Crowds at Gennesaret	6:53–56	Sick people
B. By the Twelve		
Preaching mission in Galilee	6:7–13	Demons/the sick

III. Brief References to Healings

A. Jesus' preaching tour in		
Galilee (summary)	1:39	Exorcism
B. No mighty work in Nazareth	6:5–6	A few sick people
C. The strange exorcist	9:38–39	Exorcism
D. Signs accompanying	16:17–18,20	Demons, sick,
mission (long ending)		tongues, poison

Special case: Resurrection of Jesus 16:1–8 Death
(Not a miracle of Jesus; not "miracle story" in form but "angelophany.")

INTERPRETATION

Miracles and Healing

More than any other Gospel, Mark emphasizes the miracles, healings, and exorcisms of Jesus. Of the hundreds of verses in Mark (678), approximately one-third (198) recount miracles. About one fourth of the Gospel (18 units) belongs to the literary type "miracle story": a problem, a solution, and evidence of cure or resolution, sometimes with a note of the observers' reaction. Thirteen of these eighteen specific miracles of Jesus are healings, and four of the thirteen are exorcisms. The chart on the preceding page shows where miracles appear in Mark and organizes them into types for ready reference.

The prevalence of miracle in Mark raises for modern readers such questions as these: "Did those events really occur because of supernatural intervention?" "Do demons really exist?" "Do miracles happen today?" These were not questions for the original readers, so the text does not address them. Supernatural intervention in human affairs was viewed as extraordinary, yet it was a feature common to Hellenistic religions. Demonology, which attributed certain illnesses to demons, was characteristic of apocalyptic thought.

Jesus undoubtedly did remarkable deeds, as his friends and foes all recognized. To understand their meaning in the text, the interpreter must assume the text's world-view regardless of questions about its adequacy. The appropriate question is not, "What really happened?" but "What did this happening really mean?" In seeking the significance of the text for life today, the interpreter must assume the world-view of hearers or readers in a given audience, remembering that any current world-view is likely also to be inadequate and is subject to revision. Basic questions about miracle and demons, then, cannot be resolved by exegesis, but a humble and open dialogue with the text can help to inform theological and philosophical discussion of these issues.

Among believers the miracle stories in Mark raise questions about the relation of faith and healing. Is the absence of miracles in our experience due to our lack of faith? Does faith heal? Whose faith is essential, the sick person's, the healer's, or that of an interested third party? Is there any hope for patients who push the healer away? Careful study of the healings listed in the previous chart on "Miracles" offers helpful guidance about these and related questions.

Faith is usually associated with Jesus' healings, but only twice is reference made to the faith of the sick person (5:34; 10:52). Sometimes the faith of friends or a parent is significant (2:5; 5:36; 9:23–24), and sometimes that of the healer (11:22–24; 9:23?). Three times lack of faith is deplored (4:40; 6:5–6; 9:19), and in other passages where faith is not explicitly mentioned it is present by implication. Faith, in Mark, is not simply an inward disposition but in several cases is a quality demonstrated in visible acts (1:40; 2:4–5; 2:11–12; 3:5; 5:28–34). Some wonder stories, however, while saying nothing about faith, attest to the authority of Jesus (1:21–28; 5:1–20; 6:35–44; 8:1–10) or of the disciples (6:7–13).

Whose faith comes into play seems to depend on the type of miracle or kind of illness involved. Nature miracles (I, B on chart) relate solely to the faith of the miracle-worker. The faith of helping persons figures in every case of paralysis and blindness. In no case is any demon-possessed (mentally ill?) person said to have faith; their healing is always related either to the faith of a parent (7:24–30; 9:14–29) or solely to Jesus' authority over demons (1:21–28; 5:1–20).

To approach Mark as Scripture implies letting the text raise its questions and express its concerns, not always imposing our questions and our understanding of the world and history. Miracles function theologically in Mark, and how this occurs is important for interpretation.

First, the majority of Jesus' healings and other miracles appear during his Galilean ministry, chapters 1—8 (see chart). They function as demonstrations of Jesus' power, raising the question of his identity to which the Gospel shows various responses.

Second, the two accounts of Jesus healing blindness (8:22–26; 10:46–52) delimit and interpret the discipleship section, while the story about the boy the disciples could not heal (9:14–29) underscores the disciples' impotence.

Third, the one remaining miracle (the cursing of the fig tree (11:12–14, 20–23) reinforces the main point of the Jerusalem section of the Gospel: Jesus' confrontation with the Temple and all it represents.

Finally, redaction criticism has shown that whereas the other Synoptics and later Christian writings tend to magnify the miraculous element when retelling Marcan stories of Jesus, the writer of Mark, by editorial changes and additions, challenges

21

the idea in the earlier tradition, that Jesus is just another miracle worker or "divine man." (See P. J. Achtemeier, *Mark*, chapter 8, for fuller development of the use and interpretation of miracle stories in Mark.)

A proper understanding of miracle in Mark begins by hearing the miracle stories as proclamations of the Kingdom of God. Immediately after the announcement that "the kingdom of God is at hand" (1:15), Jesus begins to teach, exorcise demons, and heal sick people. All three are apparently viewed as ways of preaching the Kingdom of God. Jesus' wondrous works manifest God's merciful, mighty presence and governance, thereby proclaiming God's Kingdom.

That realm is accessible only to those who repent and believe the message about it, hence the great emphasis on faith in the miracle stories. It is the reign of a God who is compassionate, hence the emphasis on pity in many of them. Yet the central message of the gospel is about a realm in which the will of the king is sovereign and decisive, hence the freedom of God both to work in the absence of faith and to respond in the negative to requests which may seem legitimate to us. God's Kingdom encompasses the natural order and means wholeness in that order, hence Jesus' opposition to disease and the validity of our use of medical science.

The miracles in Mark bear witness to a kingdom that is greater than the natural order, however. Mark invites us to repent, believe the gospel, and follow Jesus. Insofar as we respond to that invitation, we live in the Kingdom of God and may expect experiences of strength beyond our own. That strength is never simply at the service of our desires; Gethsemane and the cross attest the costliness of submission to God's rule and will. The power of God to save is not limited to the horizons of our expectations; Jesus was raised despite the expectations of his disciples, and the risen Lord will go before and meet his followers despite their flight and fears.

The mighty acts of Jesus offer no method for manipulating providence, but they do invite disciples of every time and place to expect the unexpected.

Preaching and Teaching

Since many users of this commentary will probably be preachers or teachers in the church, or both, a consideration of the relationship between teaching and preaching in Mark may be useful.

In Mark preaching seems always to refer to the announcement of news, usually in order to elicit a faith commitment from hearers. John the Baptist preaches repentance for the forgiveness of sins (1:4, 5). Jesus comes into Galilee preaching the gospel of God (1:14–15), and his preaching is associated with casting out demons (1:38–39). The Twelve preach during Jesus' earthly ministry (3:14; 6:12), and after his resurrection disciples are to preach the gospel everywhere (13:10; 14:9; also 16:15, 20). Three healed persons "preach" (*kēryssō,* proclaim) in the sense of announcing news, without reference to a response of faith: the leper (1:45), the Gerasene demoniac (5:20), and the deaf-mute of the Decapolis (7:36).

The fourteen uses of "preach" in the foregoing texts, with "speaking the word" in 2:2 (which might equally well be understood as teaching, see 4:33 and 8:32) exhaust the instances of this idea in Mark. Other words of the same family (herald, *kēryx;* the preaching, *kērygma*) and the related verb "to evangelize" do not appear in Mark at all, nor does Mark say that Jesus "preached" after 1:39.

In contrast, Mark uses "to teach" seventeen times, refers to Jesus as "teacher" twelve times and as "rabbi" four more, speaks six times of "the teaching," and presents Jesus as the teacher par excellence.

"Teaching" vocabulary figures prominently in the Capernaum synagogue scene (coupled with healing, 1:21–28), the parabolic discourse about the Kingdom of God (4:1–34), the passion predictions (8:31; 9:31; 10:32), and the controversies in the Temple (11:15–19; 11:27—12:44). Examination of these passages and others suggests that "to teach" in Mark includes at least the following:

1. By word or deed to elicit thought that leads to new or deeper understanding (e.g., 4:1–9, 13, 21–25, 33–34; 11:15–19).

2. To give authoritative instruction in a given situation, often by interpreting Scripture (e.g., 1:22; 11:17–18; 12:14, 18, 32; and 8:31; 9:31; 10:23–24 where the teaching is authoritative prediction without reference to Scripture).

3. To elicit commitment from a group of followers ("disciples" or "learners") in a religious movement or "teaching" (e.g., 1:27; 4:9, 23).

23

INTERPRETATION

In Mark, as throughout the New Testament, the distinction between preaching and teaching is not crystal clear. The difference lies not simply in content, for the Kingdom of God may be either preached or taught; nor in the speaker, for both Jesus and his disciples sometimes preach and sometimes teach; nor in the audience, for both preaching and teaching are addressed to the crowds (though preaching in Mark is never addressed to disciples gathered apart). The two cannot be distinguished by setting, for both preaching and teaching occur in the synagogue as well as in public places like the street or the countryside or beside the sea; nor by the form of the message, for both may occur through dramatic deeds (e.g., healings) or through words.

Yet there is a distinction between preaching and teaching in Mark. Teaching, for instance, draws upon a much wider variety of literary types than preaching. Preaching, on the other hand, is always characterized by urgency while teaching may or may not be. Perhaps the basic distinction lies in the intentionality of the speaker or in the function of the message relative to its hearers. Preaching is discourse which intends to win a faith commitment from the hearers, while teaching intends to provoke rational reflection leading to a new understanding. Even this distinction is not fully satisfactory, however, for teaching may also intend to lead past understanding to decision or to action, as in the "Hear!" of Mark 4, or the teaching on the occasion of cleansing the Temple.

In Mark preaching is in one sense the basic category. Structurally it brackets the entire Gospel in its traditional canonical form, with the preaching of John the Baptist and Jesus' programmatic announcement in 1:14–15 at the beginning and the two references to the missionary preaching of the church in the longer ending, 16:15, 20. From this perspective, the pervasive teaching throughout the Gospel simply spells out the content of the message and serves as vehicle for its ultimate intention to make disciples out of hearers and readers.

In another sense, however, teaching is the basic category. While preaching is limited to announcement in situations in which the kingdom message is news, teaching occurs throughout the Gospel in widely diverse situations and forms. Besides its distinctive functions of interpretation, instruction, and argument appealing to the mind, teaching may also appeal to the heart and will. Teaching, as well as preaching, serves the basic

24

intention of the Gospel to make faithful disciples out of hearers and readers.

These reflections should remind interpreters of Mark who are preachers that Jesus and his disciples engaged in far more teaching than preaching; that preaching belongs in the public forum as much or more than in assemblies of believers; and that teaching offers a rich variety of vivid and effective ways to communicate the good news of God as well as its implications for discipleship. Teachers, on the other hand, will be reminded that their function is not limited to the classroom, nor to believers, nor to words; that their role in the Christian community is a responsible extension of the Master Teacher's authority; and that Jesus' teaching, while focused on processes of the mind, was also an open-ended, sometimes indirect but always powerful, appeal to the will.

Of the Jesus who confronts us in Mark, one much later disciple wrote, "Thy touch hath still its ancient power, no word from thee can fruitless fall (Henry Twells' hymn, "At Even, When the Sun Was Set"). Both preaching and teaching at their best are vehicles of that power, agents of that healing.

Scripture and Commentary: The Shape of This Book

The decision to approach Mark as Scripture has several implications for what the reader may expect to find in the present commentary and how the material is organized.

Focus and Format

"Scripture" means "what is written," so this commentary will focus on the text, not the history behind it. When insights from historical-critical research seem pertinent to the interpretation of Mark as the church's Scripture, they will be noted in comments on the text. In principle, however, matters of purely historical interest will not be treated in these expository essays.

The comments presuppose no particular judgment about the identity of the evangelist or the place and time of writing or the special character of the community that is addressed. This commentary, although it draws upon the insight of redaction critics, does not seek primarily to discover the intention of the evangelist or to reconstruct his situation and that of his readers. For this reason "Mark" will mean the Gospel, not the evangelist, except where the latter is stated explicitly.

"Scripture" also means a writing that is fundamental and

normative for a religious community, so this commentary will focus on the meaning of the text for the life of the church.

This understanding of Mark as Scripture determines the general format of the commentary. In most passages, an introductory statement will be followed by notes on the *text* (what is written) which call attention to the meaning of the passage in its own context and on its own terms. A section on *significance* then seeks to indicate some of the ways in which the passage may function as source, resource, and norm for the life of Christians today. Sometimes this format is laid aside in favor of another suggested by the particular passage, and the distinction between "then" and "now" is not followed rigidly in dealing with "text" and "significance." The concern for Mark as Scripture, however, is constant.

Lectionary References

This commentary focuses on Mark as Scripture; that is, on its use in the life of the church. For this reason the amount of attention given to a passage, the nature of the expository notes, and sometimes the delimitation of units has been influenced by the lectionary now commonly used, with minor variations, in five different communions or denominational clusters: Roman Catholic; Episcopal; Lutheran; Presbyterian, United Church of Christ, Christian; Methodist and the Consultation on Church Union. Variations among these five forms of the lectionary are slighter in the Gospel readings than in the Old Testament or Epistle lessons. References to "the lectionary" in the body of this commentary will indicate that with regard to the text under discussion the five forms of the common lectionary are the same. When they differ, this commentary will use the Presbyterian form of the lectionary unless another form is specified.

In the three-year cycle of the common lectionary, Mark is the source of Gospel readings for Year B. Unless otherwise specified, therefore, references to any specific Sunday in the liturgical year will mean the Gospel reading for that Sunday in Year B.

Scripture References

26

References to biblical texts will either be written in full or will follow standard abbreviations, with one exception. Chapter and verse references to texts in Mark will give only the numerals when the context makes clear that Mark is intended. Any undesignated chapter and verse notation refers to Mark.

All references are to the Revised Standard Version (RSV) unless otherwise noted. Other English versions will be referred to by the following abbreviations:

King James (Authorized) Version - AV
Jerusalem Bible - JB
New American Bible - NAB
New English Bible - NEB
New International Version - NIV
Today's English Version
    (The Good News Bible) - TEV

Prologue

Mark 1:1-13

Mark 1:1
The Title

Mark 1:1 stands alone, as most but not all editions of the Greek text and modern versions recognize. As a title, the Greek phrase has no verb. Whether by the evangelist himself (as is likely) or by a scribe who thereby may have become Mark's earliest interpreter, this title belongs to the canonical text and correctly designates the content of the writing. The superscription "According to Mark," on the other hand, was added in the second century.

TEXT

The title alerts readers to the basic nature of what will follow: Good News! The word "gospel" here refers primarily to the message about Jesus, those words and events in which Christians saw and heard the good news of God's salvation. However, the very use of the term in the title of this book was doubtless a major factor in the later use of "Gospel" to designate the specifically Christian literary genre of which Mark is probably the earliest example.

The title also names the central character of the Gospel: Jesus Christ. It attributes to him the christological designation "Son of God," though the manuscript evidence for these words is divided. The fact that Jesus Christ is used here and nowhere else in Mark as a proper name, that "Son of God" is a doubtful reading, and that Mark clearly prefers the title "Son of man" all

28

caution against the familiar use of verse 1 as a key to the structure of Mark's Gospel.

This warning, however, should not blind the interpreter to the fact that either the evangelist or a perceptive scribe chose precisely these titles to designate Jesus in the book's heading. Both titles appear often throughout this Gospel: Christ—8:29; 9:41; 12:35; 13:21; 14:61 and 15:32; Son of God or its equivalent —1:11, 24; 3:11; 5:7; 9:7; 12:6; 13:32; 14:61 and 15:39. These numerous texts serve to shape, correct, and clarify the reader's understanding of these basic christological titles (see Introduction, pp. 9–12).

SIGNIFICANCE

In Mark the poor performance of the disciples is often linked to their erroneous or inadequate understanding of the person and work of Jesus (see Introduction, pp. 14–17). This relationship still holds true, and interpreters today may appropriately prepare a series of sermons or lessons on the Christology of Mark, using this first verse and adding the title "Son of man." Paradoxically, in no Gospel is the humanity of Jesus more transparent, nor his divine authority more striking. Mark's emphasis on the costly service, rejection, and death of the Son of man, vindicated only by his resurrection and coming in glory, serves as a healthy corrective to the doctrine of cheap grace that pervades many churches and individual Christian lives.

Additional help with the Christology of Mark may be found in Taylor, *The Gospel According to St. Mark* (pp. 117–24) and in Achtemeier, *Mark* (pp. 41–50).

Mark 1:2–8
The Preaching of John

The common lectionary proposes for the second Sunday in Advent a reading (1:1–8) from a Gospel which has no account of the birth of Jesus Christ. The choice seems odd at first. Advent, however, marks the coming of Jesus Christ into human history, and Mark 1:1–8 begins the gospel of Jesus Christ with a clear announcement of the coming (advent) of the Lord.

INTERPRETATION

The unit under consideration (1:2–8) includes only the second of four elements in Mark's prologue (see Contents). The major emphases of this unit—expectancy, repentance, and the coming one—offer points of contact for faith today to anyone willing to look beyond shepherds, angels, wise men, and a manger. This passage speaks at any season to those who can hear a voice crying in the desert. It addresses us as a compelling announcement: Now hear this!

TEXT AND SIGNIFICANCE

The preaching of John the Baptist comprises the longest of the subdivisions in Mark's prologue. Beginning with a composite Scripture quotation (vv. 2–3), the text shows how John's preaching fulfilled the Scripture by calling people to repent and to be baptized (vv. 4–5) and by pointing ahead to the coming one (vv. 6–8). From God's promises in the past the text moves to John's call for his hearers to respond in the present and to his announcement of what God is about to do in the future. Three major themes correspond roughly to this movement in the passage: expectancy rooted in the scriptural promises, repentance (what the hearers are to do), and the coming one (what God will do).

Expectancy

The mood of expectancy is created in the text by the pattern of promise and fulfillment ("as it is written . . . John the baptizer appeared") and by the hyperbolic description of the crowd ("there went out to him all the country of Judea and all the people of Jerusalem"). New Testament allusions to followers of the Baptist (e.g., Mark 2:18; Luke 3:15, 11:1; John 1:6–8, 15, 20 by inference) and a reference in Josephus' *Antiquities* 8,5,2 (ca. A.D. 94) attest the deep impression John made. Judaism was longing for a revival of prophecy (I Macc. 4:46; 14:41; Matt. 11:9), so John's appearance and message caused great excitement.

How can readers today recover that excitement? One way might be to follow Mark in presenting old scriptures in new combinations. Mark did this by skillfully combining Malachi 3:1 (influenced also by Exod. 23:20) and Isa. 40:3. Today's interpreter might use musical settings of the Old Testament lesson (Isa. 40:1–5, 9–11) such as "Prepare ye the way of the Lord"

30

from the musical *Godspell* or "O, thou that bringest good tidings to Zion" from Händel's *Messiah*.

The second lesson in the lectionary, II Peter 3:11–14, with its repeated "wait," calls readers to eager expectation of the Lord's return, picking up a major theme of the Gospel of Mark. If John the Baptist looked forward to the coming of Jesus Christ, Mark's Gospel looks forward just as eagerly to his coming again. In a world where the apocalyptic vision is debased by sensational books that make doomsayers rich, Mark 1:2–8 dares us still to look to the coming of Jesus Christ with a steady expectancy, a sustained and sober excitement.

The annual recurrence of the Advent season invites us to expect not only some far-off event, but also to expect that the one who came into Galilee preaching a kingdom near at hand may come to baptize us with the Holy Spirit this year . . . soon . . . now.

Repentance

The participial phrase, "preaching a baptism of repentance for the forgiveness of sins" (1:4), seems simple enough, but a comparison of several versions will show that it bristles with questions for the interpreter. First, in the case of every action word, who is doing what? The context makes it plain that John preaches and baptizes, the hearers sin and repent, and God forgives.

Second, what is the meaning of repentance? The question is important, for John's hearers then and for readers now. The Greek word means "to change one's mind." Behind it lies the Hebrew verb, "to turn around;" that is, to change one's heart, will, and conduct. Since in verse 5 John's hearers respond to his call by "confessing their sins," repentance seems also to imply recognizing one's sins, being sorry for them, and admitting them publicly. The TEV translates John's call to repentance by "Turn away from your sins," underscoring the practical, behavioral element in repentance. Other translations retain the more ambiguous but richer term, "repentance." The wealth of the traditional word will escape most contemporary hearers unless the interpreter shows its central thrust, its nuances, and the way it relates to the problem of guilt.

31

Third, what is the exact relationship between repentance, baptism, and forgiveness? The NEB suggests that baptism is a *sign* of repentance (" . . . proclaiming a baptism in token of repentance"), while the NIV could suggest that both repentance and baptism are effective *means* of forgiveness (". . . **preaching repentance and baptism for the forgiveness of sins**"). The latter possibility is stoutly rejected by Calvin who writes,

> Repentance is not placed first, as some ignorantly suppose, as if it were the ground of the forgiveness of sins, or as if it induced God to begin to be gracious to us; but men are commanded to repent, that they may receive the reconciliation which is offered to them (*Harmony*, I, 179).

Repentance, no less than the heavenly kingdom, is the gift of God.

The text makes clear that repentance, baptism and forgiveness of sins belong together. Those who wish to develop the content of repentance had better work from the parallel passage in Luke 3:1–14 which identifies specific sins of particular groups. The Marcan text focuses on repentance as preparation for the Lord's coming. Western liturgical tradition has understood: the Advent color is violet and the purple candle of the Advent wreath is for penitence.

The Coming One

In verses 6–8 John, dressed as a prophet (II Kings 1:8; Zech. 13:4), foretells God's intervention in the immediate future. As a herald, he proclaims *(kērysso)* the coming of the king. He is the awaited Elijah (Mal. 4:5; Mark 9:11).

He appears in the wilderness or desert (v. 4) and lives on desert food (v. 6b). This wilderness is neither a virgin forest nor an empty landscape. Usually an uninhabited place, the wilderness where John preaches is crowded with penitents. In Mark the wilderness functions as a symbol of that time and place in the life of God's people when God, through rigorous discipline, was preparing them for their promised salvation, entrance into the promised land (see Ulrich Mauser, *Christ in the Wilderness*, pp. 77–102). In the wilderness a voice cries, "Prepare the way of the Lord, make his paths straight . . ." (v. 3).

The major emphasis in verses 6–8, however, is neither on the place nor on the prophet, but on the Lord whose way John prepares, on the one who is coming. Of him John affirms two things. First, he is greater than his herald. John says he is not worthy even to perform the slave's task of removing the sandals of the coming one. The analogy may allude to the crowds who were taking off their own sandals and wading into the Jordan humbly to receive baptism from John. By pointing to the surpassing greatness of the one who comes after him, John suggests but does not define who Jesus is.

Second, John announces what the coming one will do: "He will baptize you with the Holy Spirit." To what event does this prophecy allude? The Holy Spirit descends on Jesus at his baptism (1:9–11) and drives him into the wilderness to be tempted (1:12–13). Jesus casts out demons by the power of the Holy Spirit (3:22–30) and promises his disciples that the Holy Spirit will tell them what to say when they are brought to trial (13:11). Nowhere, however, does Mark offer anything like Luke's Pentecost account or John's report of the risen Lord breathing the Holy Spirit into his disciples. In Mark this word about baptism with the Holy Spirit stands expectantly, still pregnant with promise.

That is why the text can still encounter every hearer in the emptiness of his or her own wilderness, why the voice of a rough and roaring prophet can still call the hearer to turn around, accept the greater baptism offered by a risen Lord, and thus experience his coming as a powerful, personal advent.

The promise of this text is not only for unbelievers or lukewarm Christians. Gregory the Great (d. A.D. 604) saw its relevance for John's followers, the heralds of every generation:

> Whoever preaches right faith and good works prepares nothing other than a road for the Lord to come into the hearers' hearts so that this gracious power might penetrate and the light of truth illuminate them. Thus may the preacher make straight paths for God, while forming pure thoughts in the soul by the word of good preaching" (quoted by Bede, *Corpus Christianorum,* CXX, 439).

Mark 1:9–11
The Baptism of Jesus

Why does baptism matter?

Baptism does matter quite a lot in the liturgy of the Eastern Orthodox Churches whose Feast of the Epiphany celebrates the baptism of Jesus. Epiphany means "manifestation." The

Eastern emphasis on the baptism of Jesus as his prime manifestation, commemorated in one of the three great festivals of the church year, corresponds well with the role the baptism (1:9–11) plays in the Gospel of Mark and the role baptism can play in the life of a believer.

TEXT

In Mark the baptism narrative is placed not within the public ministry of Jesus, but rather in the prologue. Coupled with the temptation, the baptism performs a function important for the entire Gospel: It establishes the identity and authority of the story's central character, Jesus of Nazareth (see Introduction, p. 2).

A glance at the structure of the text shows that this, and not the imparting of information about the historical event, is its primary function. Verse 9, the setting, tells of the *event* and identifies Jesus as being from Nazareth in Galilee. The *epiphany* (vv. 10 and 11) consists of two parts, a vision (10) and a voice (11).

The vision is more vivid in Greek than in most English translations. "As he (Jesus) was coming up out of the water he saw the heavens in the process of being ripped apart" (author's trans.). The passive voice here implies an act of God, and the verb is the same used of the Temple curtain which was "torn in two from top to bottom" when Jesus died (15:38). In both cases, what had long been sealed is suddenly flung open. Jesus' ministry answers to the long-deferred hope, "O that thou wouldst rend the heavens and come down" (Isa. 64:1). The content of the vision is the descent of the Spirit as a dove. "As a dove" may appropriately be understood to refer either to the form Jesus saw in the vision, "the Spirit like a dove" (AV; Luke 3:22, RSV; and Bratcher, *Mark,* p. 29), or to the kind of movement "descended like a dove" (RSV, TEV, NIV, NAB and Gen. 1:2, where "brooded" expresses the bird-like movement suggested by the Hebrew verb). In either case, the descent of the dove on Jesus at his baptism shows that he is the one greater than John. Jesus, empowered by the Holy Spirit, will baptize his followers with the Spirit (1:7–8).

34

The voice from heaven attests that Jesus is the Son of God, a basic theme in Mark (see Introduction, pp. 10–11). This divine revelation echoes, but does not quote, certain Old Testament texts (Ps. 2:7; Isa. 42:1; Gen. 22:2). These allusions invite and at the same time frustrate efforts to discover the Old Testament figure or figures that define who Jesus is. Is he the king of Israel, the servant of God, or the one to be sacrificed? Most lectionaries stress the servant image by choosing Isa. 42:1–7 as the Old Testament lesson to accompany Mark 1:4–11, and the Presbyterian choice of Isa. 61:1–4 concurs with this understanding. According to Mark, Jesus will qualify by his own words and deeds any Old Testament representation of the Son of God. These point to him, but the story of his life, death, and resurrection will determine the sense of the Old Testament witness.

In Mark, unlike Matthew and John, both the vision and the voice are intended for Jesus alone. Nothing in the text suggests that others present saw or heard anything. Although the reader has been informed of the true identity of Jesus in the title (1:1) and now in the baptismal epiphany, at the narrative level that truth so far is known only to Jesus. This is a secret epiphany. Jesus knows who he is by means of an experience that is not accessible to objective, public verification. Others must discover this truth by listening to what Jesus says and by watching what he does. The centurion who watches Jesus die (15:39) will confess publicly what here is revealed privately: Jesus is the Son of God.

SIGNIFICANCE

The basic significance of the baptism passage is still its witness to the identity of Jesus. The text tells of a particular past event which, for all its similarity with thousands of other baptisms of its time and since, was unique. The split heavens point to the cosmic significance of this baptism. The voice from heaven, like John's preaching, affirms that Jesus is radically different. John the baptizer continues the line of prophets in the pattern of Elijah, but Jesus is of another order of greatness. He is the beloved Son of God, whose relationship with the Father is altogether right and pleasing. Through him the heavens and the Temple curtain are split (15:38). The entire story which will follow is above all the story of Jesus and of what God did through him. That is why the baptism of Jesus matters. As a secret epiphany, it tells the reader the true identity of Jesus.

Alternatively, interpretation could focus on the act of baptism. In Mark the baptism of Jesus establishes his identity. In Paul (Gal. 3:26–29; Rom. 6:3–11) the baptism of believers establishes our identity. Jesus is who God says he is. So also we are

35

who God says we are, and in Christ Jesus we are sons and daughters of God, "for as many of you as were baptized into Christ have put on Christ" (Gal. 3:26–27).

This alternative interpretation, combining Mark with Paul, answers the question, "Why does baptism matter?" It matters because we are who God says we are. The identity declared at baptism, however, is only a word until it is revealed with convincing power in the unfolding story of our life and death . . . and resurrection.

Mark 1:12–13
The Temptation of Jesus

As soon as Jesus was attested Son of God at his baptism, "the Spirit immediately drove him out into the wilderness." This literary context is a key to interpretation: Commissioning means conflict; sonship means struggle.

TEXT

In comparison with Matt. 4:1–11 and Luke 4:1–13, Mark's account of the temptation of Jesus is very brief. The most familiar elements in the story are not found in Mark: no fasting or hunger, nothing about the nature and content of the temptation, nothing about the outcome of the struggle. Yet Mark's lean text offers much for exposition if one reads the passage theologically, with attention to clues in the text.

One clue is the wilderness setting which links the temptation of Jesus to the ministry of John the Baptist, holds verses 1–13 together and situates all of this material theologically (see pp. 2, 32). This clue points to conflict and struggle as basic to a true understanding of the temptation passage. Jesus' forty days in the wilderness (1:13) parallel Israel's forty years in the wilderness (Num. 32:13), Moses' forty days on Sinai (Exod. 34:28), and Elijah's forty-day trip to Horeb (I Kings 19:8). In addition to the number forty, the common denominator in all these allusions is the crisis induced by a sense of the absence of God. The wilderness is the dwelling place of forces hostile to God, the residue of the primeval chaos that menaces human life. Despite appearances and feelings, God is present in the wilderness in

36

the Old Testament traditions (Deut. 2:7; 32:10) and in the Marcan Gospel accounts (e.g., 1:2–4, 35; 6:31–44). The discovery of this presence and this providence, however, grows out of struggle and testing. In the Old Testament, Israel tests God in the wilderness (Exod. 17:7; Deut. 6:16); in Mark, Satan tests Jesus in the wilderness.

A second clue is the verb *peirazō* (to tempt or test) from which this passage derives its traditional name, "the temptation." Of the various possible meanings of the term the two viable options in this context are enticement to sin and putting to the test. The Arndt-Gingrich Greek lexicon lists Mark 1:13 under the former meaning, which may apply correctly to the parallels in Matthew and Luke, but in Mark the meaning is the latter: Jesus "stayed in the wasteland forty days, put to the test there by Satan" (NAB). Every other use of the verb "to tempt" in Mark (8:11; 10:2; 12:15) clearly speaks of putting to the test without reference to enticement to sin. This is almost surely the intention of 1:13 and of Mark's one use of the noun (14:38) as well. The present passage is about a test of strength between Jesus and Satan.

A third clue to the theological significance of this text is its structure. In addition to Jesus, the only human being in the scene, four other figures appear in this passage: the Spirit, Satan, the wild beasts, and the angels. Though some see in these wild beasts allusion to the peaceful coexistence of Eden, the more likely sense of the passage is that the beasts, like Satan, belong to the realm of the wilderness. Thus Mark frames Jesus' struggle against hostile powers (Satan/beasts) by mentioning the divine providence that sends him to the wilderness at the beginning (the Spirit) and sustains him in the testing at the end (the angels). In Matthew and Luke the temptation comes only after the forty days of fasting, and Matthew mentions the ministry of angels only after the devil has left Jesus. In Mark, however, the testing clearly lasts throughout the forty days; and it would appear that both the beasts (hostile powers) and the angels (divine providence) are present throughout. Satan is never reported to have left Jesus, and the scene may well be viewed as a paradigm of the cosmic struggle which underlies the entire Gospel of Mark. The ensuing drama portrays the nature of Jesus' testing (e.g., 8:11; 10:2; 12:15), the authoritative way he engaged in conflict (e.g., 1:21–28; 2:1–12; 12:35–37), and the evidence of his victory over Satan and all evil powers (e.g., 3:27;

37

INTERPRETATION

15:37–39; 16:1–8). Although the present text does not announce the defeat of Satan, it does say enough to indicate, for those who have ears to hear, that the victory of Jesus Christ is already secured in principle. Satan's power is real but limited. It is bracketed in this text by the commanding Spirit and the sustaining angels of God.

SIGNIFICANCE

The temptation narrative tells us something about God, about Jesus, and about ourselves.

About God: "The Spirit immediately drove him (Jesus) out into the wilderness." The verb in Mark is unequivocally harsh: not "led him" or "drew him" but "drove him out." How can a God who "cannot be tempted with evil and himself tempts no one" (James 1:13) inflict such treatment upon one to whom the divine voice has just said "Thou art my beloved Son; with thee I am well pleased"? This seeming contradiction may be resolved by two observations. First, in James 1:13 "tempt" means "entice to sin," while in Mark 1:13 it means "test." Second, according to Hebrews 12:6, "The Lord disciplines him whom he loves." Temptation, understood as testing, is part of the divine pedagogy. In Mark, to be sure, God himself does not do the tempting. The text in Mark states that whereas the Spirit drove Jesus out, Satan tempted him. Furthermore, the divine intent to preserve and not to destroy is shown by the fact that angels served him (v. 13). Reflection on Mark 1:12–13 in the context of the whole New Testament suggests that God uses harsh means, including the very powers of hell, to accomplish redemptive purposes.

About Jesus: "He was in the wilderness forty days, tempted by Satan." The divine sonship attested by his baptism does not exempt Jesus from struggle or from testing. Gregory the Great (ca. A.D. 600) commented, "He dwelt among beasts as a man; he was ministered to by angels as God" (Bede, *Corpus Christianorum*, CXX, 445). Though this interpretation reflects a later, developed form of christological dogma, it nevertheless contains a sound intuition of one dimension of the text. This Son of God is truly human. He is tempted by Satan. Yet his struggle with Satan is not simply an example of the common human condition. Falling between God's announcement, "Thou art my beloved Son," and Jesus' announcement, "the kingdom of God is at hand," the temptation of Jesus represents a unique conflict

38

having cosmic import. In Mark his single combat with Satan is the ordeal which validates the man Jesus as the bearer of God's banner throughout the coming battle.

About ourselves: Besides its once-for-allness, the temptation of Jesus also possesses the quality of perpetual contemporaneity. Interpreters of every age have used this text to warn new Christians that the onslaught of Satan is strongest just after the exhilaration of a moment of revelation. Although the emphasis in the text is clearly on Jesus and not on his disciples (they have not yet been introduced), the secondary application of the text to followers of Jesus is not wrong. As through identification with the Son of God we are children of God, so with him we may expect to be driven into the wilderness, caught up in the cosmic battle between God and Satan. The text contains for us, as it does for Jesus, warning ("forty days tempted by Satan") and promise ("the angels were ministering to him").

The lectionary directs interpreters to this text on the first Sunday in Lent, an apt choice since the forty days of Lent commemorate Christ's forty days in the wilderness. However, the liturgical link includes fasting, which does not appear in the Marcan account.

The pericope is defined as Mark 1:9–13 in the Episcopal lectionary. This combination of Jesus' baptism and temptation is appropriate to certain redactional clues in the text and facilitates the use of several of the foregoing interpretive suggestions. The other four lectionaries in the common family (see Introduction, p. 26) list Mark 1:12–15, which combines the temptation with Jesus' thematic announcement of the Kingdom of God. This combination allows the interpreter to underscore the preparatory nature of the time in the wilderness (Lent), and to point to the death and resurrection of Jesus (Holy Week) as the realization of Christ's victory over Satan and the basis of the coming Kingdom of God. In Western tradition Lent prepares for the baptism of catechumens on Palm Sunday; in Mark, however, the temptation does not prepare for but follows the baptism of Jesus. The interpreter treating this text before baptism may well point to the times of testing which are likely to follow.

The sacrifice or binding of Isaac (Gen. 22:1–14), which is the Old Testament lesson for the day in the Lutheran and Episcopal lectionaries, is tied to the temptation passage by the words "God tested (tempted) Abraham" and to the baptism

39

passage by the words "your son, your only son Isaac, whom you love." The father-son typology which links Gen. 22:1–14 with the baptism and temptation of Jesus invites reflection on the function of life's trials or tests in the light of God's parental love.

Mark 1:14–15
Theme: The Gospel of God

The introduction to this commentary uses twenty-five pages to lay out the meaning of "gospel." The evangelist takes just two verses, almost as if he had been challenged to say what Jesus' message was while standing on one foot. While Mark as a whole presents the gospel about Jesus (1:1), this particular unit summarizes the gospel Jesus preached. What is this gospel? How is it still significant, now that the proclaimer has become the proclaimed?

TEXT

The unit functions as a transition from the prologue in the wilderness (1:1–13) to Jesus' public ministry in Galilee (1:16—8:21). Mark 1:14–15 is a summary, because it gathers up in a brief statement the activity characteristic of Jesus over a period of time (compare 1:39; 3:7–12; 6:6*b*, 53–56). The combination of a brief setting (v. 14) and an important saying of Jesus (v. 15) makes this particular summary resemble a pronouncement story as well.

Verse 14 states that Jesus came into Galilee, thereby establishing the geographical setting for the first half of the Gospel of Mark. The unit gives the theme of Jesus' preaching during his Galilean ministry, but in a broader sense it is the theme of the entire story. The motifs of fulfillment and kingdom are particularly prominent in the passion narrative, while the call to repent and believe underlies the communication between text and reader throughout the Gospel.

"Jesus came . . . preaching" establishes Jesus as herald of the Kingdom of God. Proclamation is basic for Mark, which makes no clear distinction between preaching and teaching (see Introduction, p. 24) and which presents the authoritative deeds of Jesus as ways of proclaiming the arrival of the Kingdom of God (see Introduction, pp. 19–22).

What Jesus preaches is "the gospel of God." The difference between this phrase and "the gospel of Jesus Christ" in the title is significant. Mark 1:1 uses "gospel" in the sense that Paul and the earliest Christian tradition (I Cor. 15:1–6) did: the good news about Jesus Christ. In Mark 1:14, however, "gospel" is what Jesus preached about the Kingdom of God. (The AV states this explicitly, based on a variant reading in some Greek texts of v. 14).

The content of Jesus' preaching (v. 15) is symmetrically structured:

A. Announcement
   1. The time is fulfilled.
   2. The Kingdom of God is at hand.
B. Appeal
   1. Repent.
   2. Believe in the gospel.

"The time is fulfilled" includes at least three dimensions of meaning. Most broadly, the coming of Jesus fulfills God's plan for the grand sweep of history. At that time ("after John was arrested") and in that place (Galilee) God stepped into human history in a unique and decisive way. The time is fulfilled, and ours is an invaded planet. Second, Mark links the time of John's arrest with the time when Jesus starts preaching the gospel. The time of John the prophet is over; the time of Jesus and fulfillment has come. A different era begins in God's dispensation: It is the gospel time. Third, and most precisely, Mark ties the turning point in time to the preaching of Jesus. When the good news of God is preached, it is decision time: The time is fulfilled.

"The kingdom of God is at hand," or "has drawn near." Does this mean that the kingdom is about to arrive, or that it is already here? Other Gospels have Jesus speak of a kingdom that is present or realized (e.g., Luke 17:21; John 3:36). In Mark, however, Jesus proclaims that the Kingdom of God is about to appear. John the Baptist announced the imminent appearance of Jesus (1:4–8) and Jesus appeared (1:9–11). Jesus announces the imminent appearance of the Kingdom of God (1:14–15) and the kingdom appears (1:16 through 16:8, and beyond). For Jesus in 1:15 the kingdom lay in the immediate future. As the narrative unfolds, those who are confronted by the power of God in the words and works of Jesus experience the kingdom as present, yet hidden; its full manifestation still lies in a future that has drawn near.

41

INTERPRETATION

To this two-part announcement in the indicative Jesus adds a two-part imperative appeal: "Repent, and believe in the gospel."

"Repent" is the same message John had preached (1:4, see pp. 31–32). Calvin points to the two dimensions of repentance as changing our lives for the better ("turn away from your sins," TEV) and as conversion and newness of life (*Harmony*, I, 145). The latter, deeper dimension of the term is the primary meaning of "repent" in this verse. Jesus calls his hearers to turn around, to shift the direction of their lives, to look, listen, and give their full attention to the kingdom which is arriving.

The climax of the appeal and of the unit is "Believe the Good News!" (TEV). Jesus calls his hearers to believe the good news that the Kingdom of God is arriving. Where Jesus Christ is, there the rule, power, and Kingdom of God is actively at work. But for hearers then, just as for hearers today, this truth is not self-evident. To be seen, it must be believed. The relationship between faith and sight will be elaborated at important points later in the Gospel (e.g., 8:22–26; 10:46–52).

SIGNIFICANCE

When Jesus appears, God's time is fulfilled. Patristic writers (Jerome, Victor) interpreted this to mean the end of the time of the law and its replacement by the principle of the gospel. Bede, referring to Gal. 4:4–5, heard "the time is fulfilled" as a call to renounce dead works and believe in the living God. More recent interpreters (Lohmeyer, Lightfoot), taking Galilee as a symbol for the Gentiles, have understood the opening of the kingdom to Gentiles as a turning-point in time. All these interpretations represent serious listening to the text in ever-new situations, yet each focuses on the transition from John to Jesus and each bears the marks of its own time.

Interpretation that focuses on the link between the preaching of Jesus and the arrival of the kingdom facilitates a fresh hearing of the message in every new time. In Galilee, Jesus was present in the flesh. For us, Jesus is present in the word of proclamation. Whenever the gospel is faithfully preached (whether by preachers or teachers, see p. 24), the kingdom of God draws near to the hearers. For them, "time's up"; decision time has come.

Jesus preached the Kingdom of God and today's heralds preach Jesus, but the essential dynamic is the same. Confronted

42

by the message, we are confronted by the Kingdom of God. The appropriate response is also the same: Repent, and believe the good news.

A modern analogy may capture some (not all) dimensions of this summary of the preaching of Jesus. In a crowded airline terminal, hundreds of persons are scurrying in dozens of directions. Above the steady buzz of noise a voice booms through a loud-speaker, "Flight 362 is now arriving at gate 23. Will passengers holding tickets for New York please check in at gate 23; you will be boarding soon." Some people, of course, never hear the announcement and continue on their way. Others hear it but, having reservations on another flight, pay no attention. Some, however, who want to go to New York and who have been nervously awaiting such an announcement, look up expectantly, check their ticket for the flight number, gather their baggage, turn around and set out with some urgency for gate 23.

PART ONE

From the Call
of the First Disciples
to the Plot
of Jesus' Opponents

Mark 1:16—3:6

Mark 1:16–20
The Call of the First Disciples

It is hard not to answer a ringing telephone.

The compelling urgency of a call is at least part of the undiminished power of the call narrative in Mark 1:16–20. Jesus' call of his first four disciples had evidently long been treasured in the communal memory of early Christians. The direct and vivid style, the stringing together of clauses with "and," and the repeated point about leaving all to follow Jesus suggest the use of this story in the earliest preaching of the church.

In Mark, as the very first incident in Jesus' public ministry, this passage introduces the group which, after Jesus himself, will be the second major concern of the entire story: the disciples. As soon as Jesus announces the Kingdom of God, he calls persons to enter it ("Follow me") and to invite others to enter it, too ("I will make you become fishers of men"). Although Mark lacks the strong church emphasis of Matthew, here too, the kingdom is corporate. Mark offers no solo salvation, no individualist reign or rule of God.

44

TEXT

The remarkable number of sharp details in this brief story makes it easy to visualize. The five personal names, the Sea of

Galilee, the nets, the boats, the hired servants, the action of casting, mending, following—all of these elements give the reader a sense of participation in the scene. They also heighten the atmosphere of unspoiled freshness which attends this first encounter between Jesus and his disciples.

In Mark it *is* the first encounter. No prior contact serves to explain the immediacy of the fishermen's response; no earlier failures cloud its spontaneity.

The only words are those of Jesus. He calls, they follow. We are not told whether these fishermen had previously enjoyed their work or detested it, whether they were prosperous or impoverished. We do not know how the two pairs of brothers got along with each other, nor how the sons of Zebedee related to their father. The sun may have been bright and the breeze off the lake fresh, but Mark does not say so. The absence of details that interest us pushes us to remember the primary interest of the Gospel: the authority of Jesus, and the response of disciples.

In two successive encounters (1:16–18 and 1:19–20) Jesus appears to four ordinary men who are engaged in routine activities. He calls and they follow. Later they will calculate the effect of their obedience and admire their own virtue (10:28); they will perceive where Jesus is going and tremble (10:32). But in this first encounter the interaction is reduced to the essentials: What does Jesus say, and how will they respond?

The answers to these questions appear in each panel of this diptych. "Jesus said . . . 'Follow me . . .' and immediately they (Simon and Andrew) left . . . and followed him" (1:17–18). "And immediately he called them (James and John); and they left . . . and followed him" (1:20). Here the two basic foci of the entire Gospel stand forth clearly: the presence and word of Jesus on the one hand and response to his call to discipleship on the other. In this interaction the Kingdom of God is actualized in the present. Where Jesus is, there is the kingdom, for he is king. His authoritative presence is manifested in his word, and his effective reign appears in the response of the four. They hear—really hear—his word. The call of the four, then, not only prepares for the further preaching of the Kingdom of God; it exemplifies that kingdom in human experience.

45

The literal meaning of the words translated "Follow me" is "Come (plural) after me." The nuance is worth noting because the echo in a later text (8:33) might otherwise not be recognized and because this way of stating the call assures the permanent priority of Jesus and what he does. These men are not called to save the world by their heroic performance, but rather in their subordination to Jesus to bear witness to him.

In addition to the command to follow him, Jesus' word includes the promise which defines the content of this call: "I will make you become fishers of men." The figurative language is well adapted to the four fishermen.

Jesus himself offers the best example of what he calls these disciples to do. He acts here as the fisherman, and the four men by the sea are the fish. He casts his word; they are caught up into the Kingdom of God. He calls them in turn to become fishermen at this deeper level. After his death and resurrection they will spread the good news about Jesus and others will be caught up into the Kingdom of God.

Interpreters should be alert to the possibility that some children who think concretely and know nothing of net fishing may visualize an enormous hook piercing the mouth and head of a human being. For some who use the TEV, "I will teach you to catch men" may connote deception and menace. Others may reflect that whether caught by hook or by net, any fish removed from water is doomed, not saved.

Although these are misunderstandings due to inappropriate literalism, the last reflection contains an element of truth. Following Jesus entails a radical change of milieu which will in fact mean death of one sort or another for those first four and for all who hear the word of Jesus and are caught up into the Kingdom of God (see 8:34–35a and 10:39). Yet at the deeper level, to follow Jesus and to be with him means life. This is the only life that is finally significant (see 8:35b and 10:43–44; also 14:9).

In the remainder of Mark, the disciples will not fare very well. Seldom, if ever, will their performance match the brightness of this first response. Their failures tarnish the noun "disciple" in Mark, but the verb "to follow" is never impugned. The purpose of Mark's Gospel is to make of its faithful readers faithful disciples of Jesus Christ, and the fundamental quality of faithful discipleship is to be found here: "Follow me."

46

SIGNIFICANCE

Jesus' approach to strangers beside the sea functions first in the church's preaching to the world. At the root of all evangelistic outreach lies the invitation to follow Jesus. Every faithful use of the text, whether in preaching or in teaching, must take seriously this dimension of its purpose: to call to first commitment those who have no previous personal knowledge of Jesus Christ.

The story also functions in the community of faith as a means by which Christ continues to call men and women to ministry. The first four disciples left everything to follow Jesus. Like Abraham they went from their father's house (cf. 1:20 with Gen. 12:1), which was against all urgings of their cultural heritage and self interest. The narrative is appropriately used to invite members of the Christian community, and younger members in particular, to give themselves fully to the work of following Jesus and encouraging others to do so.

Besides awaking an initial commitment to church vocations, the text can function significantly for ministers and other church professionals throughout their training and career. By warning against cooly calculated professionalism and by helping to rekindle the flame of obedience to Christ's call, this Scripture can sustain the quality of vocation which makes ministry authentic and fruitful.

To restrict the force of the passage to clergy and to other church workers, however, is an abuse of its meaning. Jesus' "Follow me" confronts us all with a decision that lies deeper than the question of earning a living. His call to discipleship focuses on the question of life's ultimate loyalty, a question more basic than that of vocational choice. It speaks to Christians whose lives are humdrum, whose discipleship has degenerated into a preoccupation with things like nets and boats and hired servants.

The significance of the text can be appropriated by identification with the various personalities involved in this scene: Jesus, Zebedee, the hired hands, the disciples. The interpreter may invite hearers to imagine that they are, successively, one or another of these persons and to relive the scene from that perspective. Through empathy the hearers will gain a deeper understanding of the text and of themselves.

The perennial, lively power of this passage is rooted in its relationship to Jesus' proclamation of the Kingdom of God. In Mark, Jesus announces the kingdom, then calls four people to follow him. When the fishermen hear Jesus' word, they immediately turn their backs on their past and follow him. This obedience is the reign of God in one's life. This "immediately" marks the fullness of time. The story about the beginning of discipleship also conveys its essence. It is not only about four fishermen at that time, but also about us now. For us, as for them, the heart of discipleship and the actualization of the Kingdom of God in our lives lies in following Jesus.

This does not mean that failure in our attempts to follow Jesus bars us from the kingdom nor that salvation is the result of our obedience. Later texts in Mark will confront this issue (e.g., 14:27–28; 16:7). What saves us is Jesus Christ's obedience (14:36) and his death as a ransom for many (10:45). But if the cross is the basis for our salvation, following Jesus constitutes our life in the Kingdom of God.

The abiding significance of this text is attested by its echoes from the first century through the twentieth. If Luke 5:1–11 is a variant form of the same story, John 21:1–23 is its earliest sequel. There Simon Peter, failed, chastened, and restored, hears the words that renew his call: "Follow me" (John 21:19, 22).

In modern times the call of the first four disciples underlies the second stanza of Whittier's poem "Dear Lord and Father of Mankind," found in most protestant hymnals:

> In simple trust like theirs who heard
> > Beside the Syrian sea
> The gracious calling of the Lord,
> Let us, like them, without a word,
> > Rise up and follow thee.

The familiar words of Albert Schweitzer echo the Marcan text together with its Johannine sequel:

> He comes to us as One unknown, without a name, as of old, by the lakeside, He came to those men who knew Him not. He speaks to us the same word: "Follow thou me!" and sets us to the tasks which He has to fulfil for our time. He commands. And to those who obey Him, whether they be wise or simple, He will reveal Himself in the toils, the conflicts, the sufferings which they shall pass through in His fellowship, and as an ineffable mystery, they shall learn in their own experience Who He is (*The Quest of the Historical Jesus*, p. 40).

48

Mark 1:21–28
Exorcism at Capernaum

The above title is useful for identifying the unit, but it risks drawing attention to the problem of miracle rather than to the real subject of the passage: Jesus' authority in word and deed. For questions raised by the text as miracle story, see the Introduction, pages 19–22. Attention to these questions may recapture some of the force the story once had when it was repeated enthusiastically in the oral tradition, but it will only cloud the intention of this unit of Scripture. The heart of the text is revealed in the exclamation, "What is this? A new teaching!" (1:27).

TEXT

Focus on Jesus' teaching and authority is evident in the structure of the text.

General setting: Capernaum	21*a*
The teaching of Jesus	21*b*–22
Precise setting: Sabbath, synagogue	21*b*
Essential action: taught	21*c*
Response: astonishment, authority	22
The exorcism in the synagogue	23–28
Problem: unclean spirit	23–24
Solution: healing word	25
Evidence of cure: convulsion, shout	26
Response: amazement, authority	27
General conclusion: spreading fame	28

The repetition of "teaching" and "authority" in verses 22 and 27 ties the two sub-units on teaching and healing into a single passage, as do the general setting and conclusion. It is somewhat awkward to refer to an exorcism as "a new teaching" (v. 27), but this very awkwardness shows the intention to subordinate healing to teaching, linking Jesus' power in both word and deed as evidence of his amazing authority.

The setting (v. 21*a*) is significant in two ways. First, the

49

Greek verb is in the present tense: "They *come* into Capernaum." The gospel is about past events and includes future predictions, but it addresses the reader in her or his own circumstances, blending past, present, and future into an immediate confrontation with Jesus Christ and the Kingdom of God. Use of the historical present tense is one way the Gospel of Mark achieves this immediacy.

Second, the place is important, but not for geographical reasons. Just as the second or third century ruins on the north shore of Lake Galilee bear at best a secondary relationship to the Capernaum synagogue where Jesus taught, so the geographical reference in the text is secondary to its theological importance. Jesus first publicly confronted and defeated the powers of evil in the place of worship of the people of God. The scribes (v. 22) belonged there; the unclean spirit did not. In this unit Jesus is set over against both.

Three key terms carry much of the weight in verses 21*b* –22. *Teaching* is the subject of the sub-unit, yet the text says nothing about what Jesus taught. Emphasis falls not on the content of the teaching, but on its quality.

Authority can mean either the right or the power to do something or both. Although Jesus' teaching was undoubtedly powerful, his right to speak is underscored by the contrast between his teaching and that of the scribes. They taught with erudition, but Jesus taught with authority. Jesus interprets the Scripture as one who has the right to say what it means. Furthermore, his teaching has no need of external support, whether from Scripture or elsewhere; his word is self-authenticating, not like that of the scribes.

Scribes were more than copyists or secretaries. Spiritual descendants of "Ezra the scribe" (Neh. 8:1, 4; 12:26, 36), they were honored for their function of reading and interpreting the Scriptures. The scribes were the doctors of the law, the authorized biblical scholars of their time. Mark 1:22 distances Jesus from the scribes in a way that will later blossom into conflict.

The exorcism in verses 23–28 follows the basic form of a miracle story. The expansions of that form in the cry of the man with an evil spirit (v. 24) and in the lengthened response of the onlookers (v. 27) draw attention to the authority of Jesus. Again, several key terms merit comment.

Unclean spirit, evil spirit, and *demon* are used synonymously in Mark; that is, they have the same denotation (see

50

5:1–20) but different connotations. *Unclean* (or evil) *spirit* connotes ritual impurity, while *demon* connotes satanic power. *Unclean* or *evil* is a translator's choice, and each is open to misunderstanding. In this context, *unclean* does not mean physically dirty, and *evil* does not mean morally depraved. All three terms denote an invisible spiritual being, neither human nor divine, alienated from and hostile to God (see Introduction, p. 20).

"Holy One of God" is what the unclean spirit, speaking through the man, calls Jesus. The term can be understood in a weak sense as describing God's representative (see Ps. 106:16; II Kings 4:9 and "God's holy messenger" at Mark 1:24, TEV) or in a strong sense as affirming Jesus' unique relationship to God (see John 6:69; Acts 3:14; 4:27, 30; Rev. 3:7). This is one of many examples of two-level communication in Mark. Without defining his nature or precise relationship to God, the demons recognize Jesus and tremble (James 2:19). Readers, however, are expected to remember the title of the Gospel and to understand that this Holy One of God is Christ, the Son of God (1:1).

Rebuked (v. 25) is a term of censure, warning, or prohibition used characteristically in Mark to express Jesus' word of command to unclean spirits (1:25; 3:12; 9:25). It figures prominently in the exchange between Jesus and Peter at Caesarea Philippi (8:30, 32, 33) where it is also an expression of the authority of Jesus.

The absence of the learned term for *seizure* in verse 26 is significant. Where Hippocrates or Aristotle might have used the objectively descriptive word *epilēpsia* (whose literal meaning is simply "a seizure"), Mark attributes the man's seizure to an unclean spirit. The point of the story is that Jesus has authority over the demonic powers.

Three terms in the response of the observers need explanation. The word used for *new (kainos)* does not mean recent in time *(neos)* but refers to what is unprecedented or previously unknown. *Teaching* refers to the action of Jesus rather than his words, and the action is seen as a sign that a new religious leader has appeared (see Introduction, pp. 23–24). *Authority* in verse 27 has a nuance different from that in verse 22. Here the accent falls on authority as power: "He commands . . . they obey."

51

In both its parts, then, the text affirms the amazing authority of Jesus. This authority is evidenced through teaching which shows up the aridity of the authorized biblical interpreters of the day and through a special kind of healing which demonstrates Jesus' power over spiritual forces hostile to God. Although the text introduces conflict on two fronts, its primary emphasis is on the positive but puzzled response of the anonymous observers. "They were astonished . . . " and they were all amazed. . . ." "And at once his fame spread everywhere throughout all the surrounding region of Galilee."

SIGNIFICANCE

Mark's "not as the scribes" raises a question for all biblical interpreters. Does our teaching communicate the authority of Jesus Christ or obscure it? The text by its very brevity gives powerful expression to a lament over the sterility of biblical scholarship which is heard today, not only from obscurantists and anti-intellectuals, but also from members of the biblical guild and, most significantly, from ordinary church members.

The desire to be like Jesus and not like the scribes, however, can lead to consequences which violate the intent of the Marcan text and God's will for interpreters. Besides serving as an excuse to avoid the hard work of exegesis (confusing piety with laziness), a moralistic reading of the text can result in an arrogance that forgets our proper relationship to Jesus Christ. He is the one who can speak with direct authority. We interpreters remain essentially in the position of the scribes, dependent upon a prior authority and responsible to a scriptural tradition. We deceive ourselves and those we teach if we try to deny these limitations.

This text invites interpreters of Scripture to reflect on how we can both acknowledge our scribal limitations and at the same time be channels for the living, authoritative word of Jesus Christ. He exorcised an unclean spirit in the synagogue; he can purge and empower preachers and teachers today.

The entire passage raises a more fundamental question for all readers. One purpose of the Gospel of Mark is to allow us to participate with Jesus' first disciples in the gradual and growing recognition of who he is, until we reach the conclusion to which the demoniac already points. That recognition, here mediated by a disturbed personality, crashes through from the realm of ultimate reality, shatters the decorum of the synagogue, and generates astonished questioning among bystanders. We are invited to ask the same question ("What is this?") even though we already know the answer to which we shall be led. A simple

52

got up and prepared dinner for them" *(Living Bible)*. In another sense, however, this text like several others in Mark makes the role of women the model of discipleship. Here the mother-in-law's response to the healing of Jesus is the discipleship of lowly service, a model to which Jesus will repeatedly call his followers throughout this Gospel and which he supremely embodies in his own service (e.g., 8:34; 9:35; 10:43–45). Her action contrasts with that of her son-in-law, Simon, who calls to Jesus' attention the crowd clamoring for more healings (v. 37) but does nothing, himself, about them. This is the first of a series of incidents in which a woman represents a right response (the poor widow, 12:41–44; the woman with the ointment, 14:3–9; the women at the cross, 15:40–41; the women at the tomb, 16:1). In contrast, the insensitivity and misunderstanding of the male disciples will become increasingly evident. This text, then, can lead to a wider consideration of women in Mark, of discipleship, and of service. (This insight derives from a chapel talk by James L. Mays.)

Another interpretation of 1:29–31 is suggested by Jerome who, preaching on this text in Bethlehem about A.D. 400, said:

> O that he would come to our house and enter and heal the fever of our sins by his command. For each and every one of us suffers from fever. When I grow angry, I am feverish. So many vices, so many fevers. But let us ask the apostles to call upon Jesus to come to us and touch our hand; for if he touches our hand, at once the fever flees *(Corpus Christianorum,* LXXVIII, 468).

Prayer to the apostles is questionable, but this allegorical interpretation of "fever" may offer a link between the Gospel pericope and its accompanying Old Testament lesson (Job 7:1–7 in most lectionaries). Job complains of hard labor, sleepless nights, a dreadful disease, and the brevity of his hopeless life. For him, all of life is a fever (cf. J.H. Newman's familiar prayer, "O Lord preserve us all the day long . . . until the fever of life is over, and our work is done.") The healing of Simon's mother-in-law proclaims the power of Jesus to heal all sorts of fevers.

The Sick Healed at Evening (1:32–34)

The interpreter may choose to treat Jesus' healing of the sick at evening, when the Sabbath was over, at the door of Simon's house. The text would be appropriate for a sermon or lesson on the relationship between Christianity and healing, between demon possession and illness (see Introduction, pp.

55

19–22). A helpful resource for this line of interpretation is the hymn of Henry Twells based on this passage, "At Even When the Sun Was Set." It could serve equally well in connection with the Job-Jerome-fever interpretation suggested for the healing of Simon's mother-in-law.

Alternatively, interpretation might center on Jesus' silencing of the demons in verse 34, moving outward to a broader consideration of Christology in Mark (see Introduction, pp. 9–13 and notes on 3:12, pp. 77–79), then forward to reflection on what it means to know, confess, and serve Christ today.

Departure to a Lonely Place (1:35–39)

The interpretation of this incident might follow one of two paths or both: the theme of prayer and the theme of preaching.

If the prayer theme is chosen, it would be useful to relate this scene to the two others in Mark in which Jesus withdraws to pray alone (6:46 and 14:32). He exemplifies in his own life the rhythm of work, rest, and prayer. Although the theme of prayer is more prominent in Luke than in any other Gospel, it is also important in Mark. The Lukan parallel to this passage does not mention prayer explicitly and Matthew omits the incident entirely. In Mark, Jesus prays alone and often, revealing not only his Jewishness (see Ps. 5:3 and 88:13 for private prayer in the morning), but also his full humanity; in times of stress, temptation, and decision he turns to God for strength and guidance. Hebrews 4:14—5:10 and especially 5:7 offer an illuminating commentary on the role of prayer in the life of Jesus, serving as an invitation to us to "draw near to the throne of grace, that we may receive mercy and find grace to help in time of need" (Heb. 4:16). The mention of a "lonely place" in Mark 1:35, as in 1:45 and 6:31–33, is reminiscent of the wilderness setting of the prologue (1:1–13) and of the temptation narrative in particular. There Jesus encountered Satan directly. Perhaps here he faces the temptation to return with Simon and the others to curry the crowd's favor by working miracles.

The latter consideration opens the way to the second theme in this paragraph: the importance of preaching. In verse 38 we find on the lips of Jesus an expression of his own mission and destiny analogous to "for this I was born, and for this I have come into the world" in John 18:37. In Mark, the baptism is the narrative of the commissioning of Jesus, but the present text is Jesus' own expression of that commission: "Let us go . . . that I

56

may preach . . . for that is why I came out." This emphasis on preaching as the divine commission laid on Jesus is echoed in Paul's "Woe to me if I do not preach the gospel!" found in the Epistle lesson (I Cor. 9:16–23) which accompanies the present Gospel text in the common lectionary. The emphasis is particularly appropriate for any gathering of preachers or on occasions when youth (or older persons) are challenged by a call to the ministry of the Word. In any such use of the text, the final summary in 1:39 will surely be included.

Passage as a Whole

Instead of focusing on one or another paragraph, the interpreter might treat the pericope as a whole, using persons as a unifying element and noting the place of the passage in the unfolding drama of the Gospel.

The central person in that drama is Jesus, the proclaimer of the Kingdom of God. The full account of a day in Capernaum depicts him as teaching (1:21–28), healing and preaching. Though his name is not mentioned in verses 29–39 (it last appears in verse 25), he is nevertheless the center of attention. The preaching which dominates the announcement of his ministry (1:14–15) and the conclusion of this pericope (1:39) is intimately linked with teaching, healings, and exorcisms in this passage. All are ways in which the presence of Jesus proclaims and embodies the presence of the Kingdom of God (see Introduction, pp. 8–9). The faith of Jesus, the prayer of Jesus, and his steadfast obedience to his divine commission are qualities which disciples are called to emulate as they follow Jesus. Yet interpretation which says essentially, "Be like Jesus," is inadequate. By the dramatic healings and by the theme of secrecy the text draws attention to the unique identity of Jesus himself, calling us to recognize him without clamor (1:34) and to serve him without pretention (1:31).

The discipleship motif is anticipated in the way other personalities are presented in this passage. On the one hand, Simon's mother-in-law appears in a modest but favorable light (see above on 1:29–31). On the other hand, the mention of the inner circle of Simon, Andrew, James, and John, found in Mark only (cf. 1:29 with Matt. 8:14 and Luke 4:38), calls attention to their special role throughout the Gospel (the four in 1:16–20; 13:3; the three in 5:37; 9:2; 14:33; Simon Peter at 8:29–33; 9:5; 10:28; 11:21; 14:29, 37, 54, 66–72 and 16:7). When Simon and

57

those with him interrupt Jesus at prayer (1:35–38), their misunderstanding of his priorities introduces a tension which will become a major theme of the Gospel. Those who should know Jesus best seem so often to understand him least. The significance for disciples today is as painful as it is evident.

The fact that the whole city gathered together about the door (1:33–34) is concrete evidence of the spreading fame of Jesus (1:28) and the first appearance of the crowds that will surround Jesus throughout Mark. This crowd represents humanity with all its needs. Rembrandt's etching, "Christ Healing the Sick" (also called "The Hundred Guilder Print"), though based on the parallel in Matt. 19, expresses well the Marcan picture of desperation and hope with which we reach out to Jesus and the mixture of power and compassion with which he reaches out to us.

The demons complete the cast of actors in this day in the life of Jesus. Demons we encounter in our daily lives may be of different sorts. That Jesus "went throughout all Galilee, preaching in their synagogues and casting out demons" was—and is—good news.

Mark 1:40–45
The Leper Jesus Touched

On his first preaching tour throughout Galilee, Jesus encounters and heals a leper. This is the third account of an individual healing in Mark. Like all the healing narratives, it bears witness to the lordship of Jesus. More clearly than the first two (1:21–28, 29–31), this account also draws attention to the role of faith in healing. Although these two themes are common in Mark, their development in this particular passage offers special challenges and rewards to the interpreter.

TEXT

The passage is a clear example of the literary type "miracle story" depicting a problem (v. 40), a solution (vv. 41–42, beginning perhaps with the leper's request in 40*b*), and evidence of cure (vv. 43–44) with public acclamation (v. 45). The healing itself is reported concisely, while the concluding elements are unusually full and circumstantial, inviting special attention to their meaning.

The account includes a striking exchange between Jesus and the leper, stated in direct discourse: "If you will, you can make me clean. . . ." "I will; be clean." The sequence of healing narratives at the beginning of Mark's Gospel shows a growing emphasis on faith. The unclean spirit (1:24) expressed belief and fear, but not faith as trust and commitment. Faith is not mentioned in the case of Simon's mother-in-law, but the fact that others immediately told Jesus about her fever (1:30) suggests their faith that he could and would do something about it. Faith is still not explicitly mentioned in Mark 1:40–45, but the leper's statement, "If you will, you can . . ." clearly affirms a confidence and trust which is genuine faith. In contrast to the request of a distraught father in 9:22, " . . . if you can do anything . . . ," the present text underscores the leper's firm faith in Jesus' power. He can heal if he will.

The text also gives us a rare glimpse into the motivation of Jesus. "Moved with pity" seems to satisfy our desire to know how Jesus felt and why he acted as he did. The Greek text, however, is uncertain. Some ancient manuscripts read "anger" ("indignation") instead of "pity." Many recent critical commentators think this more difficult reading is correct (see "in warm indignation," NEB). "Indignation" would fit well with the harshness of verse 43 whose Greek verbal roots suggest "he snorted at him and cast him out." It would also explain why the other evangelists, finding "anger" in the Marcan text, omitted all references to Jesus' motivation (Matt. 8:3; Luke 5:13).

If "anger" is the original reading the text could be interpreted either of two ways. The term may express Jesus' hostility to the powers of evil, as in his rebuke of demons (1:25; 9:25) and his anger at hard-hearted religious leaders (3:5). The healing of the leper is then an example of Jesus' aggressive action against all that is unclean and destructive.

Alternatively, Jesus may have been indignant at this interruption of his primary mission of preaching. Jesus heals the leper, but foreseeing that crowds drawn by news of another healing would further impede his work (1:39, 45), he sends the leper away brusquely with a command to silence which the leper ignores.

59

"Moved with pity" is the usual reading. It accords well with the compassion which characterized Jesus (6:34; 8:2) and to which a sick boy's father appeals (9:22). Even if Jesus were "indignant" in the present instance, his compassion overcomes his irritation and he heals the leper. If "pity" is the correct reading, it explains why Jesus touched this untouchable. In an Old Testament parallel to this passage (II Kings 5:1-14), Elisha does not touch Naaman. To touch a leper is a compassionate and courageous gesture whose significance only an outcast can fully appreciate.

Both "indignation" and "pity" enjoy weighty support, and each bears witness to elements of truth about Jesus: his divine enmity against sickness, sin, and alienation; his human irritation in the face of an interruption; and his divine/human compassion for suffering human beings.

The expansions of the basic miracle story form in verses 43-45 raise certain questions. The question concerning Jesus' command to silence (the so-called "messianic secret") has been discussed (in the Introduction [pp. 12-13] and in comments on 3:12). The command to offer the sacrifices ordained in the Mosaic law for the cleansing of lepers seems at first extraneous to the story and irrelevant for non-Jewish readers today. It serves two useful functions, however.

First, the command to the leper prepares the reader to understand correctly the series of controversies between Jesus and the Jewish religious leaders (2:1-3:6). Though he will there break certain Jewish laws, the present text (like repeated references to his teaching in the synagogue) shows that he respects his Jewishness and does not lightly flout Mosaic law (see 7:9-13 and 12:29-31). The deeper issue here, as later (2:1—3:6), however, is Jesus' implied claim to divine authority.

Second, Jesus' command to offer sacrifice will allow the cured man to re-enter society. Even though healed of his leprosy, he is still ceremonially unclean until the prescribed ritual of cleansing has been accomplished. "Clean" appears four times in this passage. In the first three instances it refers to the actual healing of the disease, while the fourth use in verse 44 refers to ceremonial purification. The importance of this rite can be understood by reading Leviticus, chapters 13 and 14, from which the Old Testament lectionary reading accompanying Mark 1: 40-45 is taken. Leviticus is of no help in understanding the disease, but it does show that victims of leprosy were outcasts and it does prescribe how to achieve their reintegration into society. Jesus' concern was to restore this man physically, spiritually, and socially. The command to offer sacrifice and so to accomplish ritual purification and social reintegration shows once more the compassion of Jesus.

SIGNIFICANCE

Interruptions are usually irritating, and the interpreter may be tempted to take up the theme of pity that overcomes indignation. The theme of irritation at interruptions depends here on a particular interpretation of a variant reading seen in the context of the preceding passage; it will therefore be treated later in connection with 5:21–43 and 10:46–52 where it is more obvious.

The attitude of the leper is more clearly significant in the present passage. His request, "If you will, you can make me clean," is viewed positively in the text. It shows belief in the power of Jesus to heal, but not the confident trust which will elsewhere be called faith (5:34) and for which a sick boy's father will pray (9:24). Jesus, however, does not scold the leper for inadequate faith. Desperation may not be the noblest motive for seeking help, but Jesus does not scorn it. He recognizes it and is moved with compassion. The text is significant for desperate sufferers.

For such sufferers, as for all readers, the main point of the passage lies in the response of Jesus, "I will." By this reply Jesus shows he can in fact heal even the most dreaded diseases, such as leprosy or cancer. This word, which is grace to the leper, is also good news to the reader: God wills healing.

The healing of the leper confirms the impression given throughout Mark that Jesus is the great physician (see Introduction, pp. 19–22). The text is therefore significant for all who devote themselves to healing, whether physical healing as in this case, or psychological and spiritual healing as in other instances. By extension, the principle would apply to the healing of interpersonal, social, and international disorders as well. God is on the side of the healers.

However, to state the gospel of this passage in such a way is immediately to raise a serious theological and practical problem. If the ministry of Jesus on earth was a revelation of the will of God, and he willed to heal this leper who came to him, why does he not always heal those who in faith seek his healing

61

touch? Human experience makes it evident that either God cannot always do as he will or else God does not always will healing, at least not at the time and in the way that we beg for it.

Both experience and the text suggest that perhaps we have created the problem by stating the premise wrongly. We wish to hear: "God *always* wills healing," but this is justified neither by Scripture (e.g., Paul's "thorn in the flesh") nor by life. If this affirmation were true, the ultimate arbiter of events would be our will, not God's. The present text, however, affirms the lordship of Jesus Christ: "*I* will." And it appears in a Gospel in which Jesus himself, at the crucial hour, makes a prayer reminiscent of the leper's: "Father, all things are possible to thee; . . . yet not what I will, but what thou wilt" (14:36). The healing of the leper must be interpreted finally in light of Jesus' own submission to the will of God. Though the passage does not resolve the theological problem it raises, it does illumine the terrain for persons confronted by a struggle with unrelieved illness and the problem of prayer unanswered or denied.

Jesus' will to heal and his touching the untouchable offer a model for the ministry of healing today, in the church and through individual Christians in their daily work. Disregard of personal danger and an overriding concern to restore the sick person is seen in many doctors and nurses and should characterize every follower of Christ.

Jesus' stern command to the leper not to tell anyone is significant as a word of caution and rebuke to "faith healing" as it is sometimes practiced. Though Jesus does perform a miracle, he wishes to be known as more than a miracle worker. The crowds that gather in response to the leper's "preaching" (*kēryssō*, v. 45) attest Jesus' popularity but are viewed as an embarrassment and a hindrance to his mission. This scripture offers firm guidelines in this matter for the church and for individual Christians. Ministries of healing? Yes. Opposition to disease and efforts to eradicate it? Yes. Compassion for those who suffer? Yes. Campaigns to gather crowds, win converts, and boost personalities (including that of Jesus)? No. There is in the present text no warrant for using healing programs as a means of attracting converts or making them the central focus of a church's life. The text does, however, invite all readers, including the interpreter, to join the leper at Jesus' feet and pray, "If you will, you can make me clean."

Mark 2:1–12
The Paralytic: Forgiveness and Healing

What is the relationship, if any, between sickness and sin, between forgiveness and healing? Why should anyone be upset if Jesus forgives another person's sins? Such are the questions raised by this story which includes the first use of the term *Son of man* in Mark, the first rumblings of a conflict whose climax is the crucifixion, the first appearance of the scribes in an active role, and the first mention of faith as a noun.

TEXT

The setting of this passage is unusually detailed and vivid. The phrase "at home," the crowd that packs the room and spills out into the street, the paralytic carried by four men who make an opening in the roof (literally, "dig through") and lower him on his stretcher-bed, all of these elements in the text convey visual images that invite the reader to envisage the scene. Some commentators have found here evidence of a historical memory, perhaps that of Peter to whose eyewitness testimony Mark is linked by a second-century tradition. Eyewitness memory or not, the details in the passage enable us to feel our way into the text, to identify with persons in the scene, and thus to participate in the event so that the text becomes a living word. In this way the roof can be removed and we, too, can be let down right into the middle of the crowd surrounding Jesus.

More recent interpreters have noted the unusual combination of literary types in this passage. The unit begins like most miracle stories with a scene in which a severe problem (paralysis) is presented. Jesus, the healer, sees the problem and recognizes the faith of those who come to him. The reader expects a word or touch that will cure the paralysis, but instead Jesus says, "My son, your sins are forgiven." This word of forgiveness provides the setting for a controversy which issues in an authoritative word of Jesus: ". . . the Son of man has authority on earth to forgive sins." Then, as proof that this word is true, Jesus pronounces the healing formula expected earlier: ". . . rise, take

63

up your pallet and go home." From this point on, the narrative follows the usual pattern of miracle story. The man gives evidence of his cure by taking up his pallet and walking out, and the onlookers are amazed. The interruption of the miracle story and the insertion of a controversial pronouncement story can be represented schematically as follows:

Miracle Story	2:1–5a, 10b–12	
Setting	1–2	
Problem	3:5a	
Pronouncement Story		2:5b–10a
Setting		5b–9
Surprise solution		5b
"Your sins are forgiven"		
Controversy		6–9
Saying		10a
"Son of man has authority . . ."		
Expected Solution	10b–11	
"Rise . . . walk"		
Evidence of cure	12	
amazement		

This miracle story (2:1–5a, 10b–12) forms the fifth and last of a series of healing accounts in 1:21—2:12; the pronouncement story is the first of a series of five controversies in 2:1—3:6. The story thus marks a transition between two major clusters of material in Part One (see Introduction, p. 2–3).

The breaking of the miracle story form (v. 5), reinforced by a saying of the Lord (v. 10), underscores the forgiveness of sins as the main point of this story. This theme lies at the heart of the passage in more ways than one. These literary observations throw considerable light on the intention of the passage as gospel, and the interpreter's art as preacher or teacher can be well invested in enabling a congregation or a class to see this significance.

A third fascinating element in the passage is the relation of sin to paralysis, of forgiveness to healing, and of faith to both healing and forgiveness. The text does not specify any particular sin on the part of the paralytic, nor is guilt mentioned. Yet the point at which Jesus injects his word of forgiveness shows that he perceives sin to be the man's real problem. It would be a mistake to extrapolate from this case the general principle that all illness (or even all paralysis) is the result of sin, for sin is nowhere mentioned in connection with any of the dozen other healings and exorcisms in Mark. Indeed, the only other Gospel text in which sin is related to sickness is the healing of the paralytic at the Pool of Bethzatha (John 5:1–15). Furthermore, the connection between sickness (or other kinds of suffering) and sin is explicitly ruled out when this question is raised in John 9:2 and Luke 13:1–5. In Mark the only mention of sins (always plural, never singular as in Paul) outside of this passage is in connection with the preaching of John the Baptist (1:4–5), though Jesus' call to repent (1:15) includes the idea of turning away from sins.

The forgiveness and healing of the paralytic is but one among many Marcan examples of the good news that Jesus came to proclaim and that readers are invited to believe. A part of the gospel is that Jesus as Son of man (see Introduction, pp. 11–12) has authority to forgive and to heal; these are two dimensions of the wholeness that characterizes the Kingdom (reign) of God. A word of caution is in order. It is possible for a person to be healed and not forgiven, or forgiven and not healed. In this case, however, the two are treated together by Jesus, and one pathway open to the interpreter is to explore whether and how the two might be related to human experience today; that is, to examine the nexus between psychology and theology, between faith and wholeness.

SIGNIFICANCE

The final sentence above, growing out of the observation of the text from a theological perspective, is already a suggestion about one dimension of the text's significance. The interpreter could pursue the insights of psychosomatic medicine, showing how guilt is sometimes literally paralyzing ("hysterical paralysis") and how forgiveness, even on a human level (reading "Son of man" as "human being," with Ezekiel and Ps. 8:4), can heal such dysfunctions.

Similarly, one could interpret paralysis allegorically and treat the passage as a parable of the human condition. It is true that many an impasse in interpersonal or international relations can be understood as a kind of paralysis which only forgiveness can break.

65

Whereas such insights may be true, literary observations noted above warn that the text points in another direction. Psychological and allegorical interpretations move only at the level of human problems and their cure; that is, at the level of the miracle story. The text has broken that pattern by inserting a strong pronouncement on the authority of Jesus as "Son of man" (an apocalyptic, eschatological figure as in Dan. 7) to forgive sins on earth, an authority ultimately belonging to God alone. The text is primarily a witness to God's forgiveness and to Jesus' authority. That is where the emphasis must fall in interpretation, else integrity is forfeited to relevance.

Yet the text preserves the miracle story as well as the pronouncement story. It is about Jesus and about us. Exegesis cannot fully settle the question of whether or not the paralytic had faith, but it is clear that his four friends did, and their faith played an important role in his healing. By its very structure the text means that Jesus has the right and the power (authority, 2:10) to forgive sins and to heal sickness. When by our actions we give evidence of our faith that Jesus has this authority, miracles can still occur. When we forgive because Jesus has forgiven us, our faith is a faith that can be seen (2:5). Conversely, when we accept the forgiveness of others, thereby recognizing our own sickness and incapacity, we are in that very act borne into the presence of God, who alone has the power to forgive and whose forgiveness alone ultimately matters. Interpretation need not follow this particular line, but it should present a pattern that preserves the priority of God's gracious intervention in Christ and the real connection between faith, forgiveness, and healing.

The Old Testament reading which accompanies this text in the lectionary, Isa. 43:18–25, speaks of Yahweh's gracious forgiveness which does not depend on the worthiness of his people: "I, I am He who blots out your transgressions for my own sake." The relationship to Mark 2:10 is illuminating.

The association of forgiveness with God and with Jesus has become so commonplace that it is hard to recover the freshness and bite of the text. We are children of Voltaire: *"Dieu me pardonnera; c'est son metier"* ("God will forgive me; that's his business"). The scribes were not so flippant: They leveled against Jesus the charge of blasphemy, a capital crime (v. 7). Jesus understands the cost of forgiveness: He later speaks of the Son of man coming "to give his life as a ransom for many" (10:45). To claim the authority to forgive sins is no light matter and to forgive them is not cheap.

66

Mark 2:13–22
The Call of Levi and the Question About Fasting

The call of Levi is followed by four controversy stories in which opponents of Jesus chide his disciples, either by asking them to justify the way Jesus behaves (2:16) or by asking Jesus to justify the way his disciples behave (2:18, 24). In every case, the text answers with an authoritative word of Jesus. In such stories the early church found a response to her adversaries and guidance for her life in community. Today's acculturated church is challenged by the text at both levels.

TEXT

In the series of five controversy stories in Part One (see Introduction, pp. 2–3), the teaching scene beside the sea (2:13) marks a shift from the first confrontation with the scribes in Capernaum to a cluster of three controversies concerning eating. The present passage contains a provocative call and two of the controversies: on eating with sinners and on fasting. Each of these topics is the subject of a pronouncement story; that is, a memorable saying of Jesus preceded by a concise setting.

The Call of Levi and Eating with Sinners (2:13–17)

Jesus' call of Levi (vv. 13–14) gives rise to the controversy about Jesus' association with outcasts (vv. 15–17). The call story itself, essentially like that in 1:16–20, is reduced to the bare minimum and occupies only one verse (2:14). While walking along, Jesus sees Levi at his place of business. Jesus calls and Levi follows. The text gives no details about where Levi sat, what kind of taxes he collected, how much money he made, or why he followed Jesus. We are told nothing of this man's identity or subsequent importance. Mark's list of the Twelve (3:13–19) does not include Levi, nor is his name ever mentioned again in this Gospel. The lean and direct call story makes only two points: First, the person called was a tax collector and there-

67

fore a "sinner." Second, he became a disciple solely on the basis of Jesus' authoritative invitation, "Follow me."

The call of Levi fits its context in two ways. Not only does it provide the physical setting for the ensuing story of a dinner party in Levi's house (Luke 5:29 correctly interprets "his house") but it also shows Jesus' authority to forgive sins (2:10) as he associates freely with tax collectors and sinners (2:15). "Mark presents the call of Levi as an act of forgiveness and a crossing of the boundary that separates the sinner from God" (Schweizer, p. 64).

"Tax collectors and sinners" are linked three times (2:15–17). Both terms represent groups that were ostracized from pious Jewish society, the former for political and ethical reasons and the latter for more purely religious or cultic reasons. Both are spoken of in the NEB as "bad characters" and "this bad company." The TEV's translation for "sinners" expresses the essential issue in a single word: "outcasts." The note in verse 15 that "there were many (of these social and religious outcasts) who followed him" doubtless describes not only Jesus' associates during his earthly life, but also the early Christian community from which this Gospel emerged and for which it was written. Such a church would remember this story gratefully as its members answered their critics in the synagogue.

Those critics are described in the text as "the scribes of the Pharisees," that is, teachers of the law who belonged to the Pharisee party. All modern versions indicate correctly that only one group is in view here, not two (scribes and Pharisees," AV). These are the "righteous" to whom Jesus refers (v. 17). Their function in their own society was not unlike that of preachers and teachers today. Admirable in many ways, "virtuous" (JB, NEB) and "respectable people" (TEV) often cannot hear the call of Jesus Christ because they (and we) are "self-righteous" (NAB).

The issue centers in the fact that Jesus eats with outcasts. This question of table fellowship also foreshadows and reflects a concern among early Christians (see Gal. 2:12), which explains why the story was treasured. For pious Jews who kept a kosher table, indiscriminate association with those who did not was unthinkable.

68

Jesus answers his critics with a common-sense proverb about who it is that needs a doctor, then gives to it a pointed application: "I came not to call the righteous, but sinners."

On Fasting (2:18–22)

The second pronouncement story in this series turns on the question of fasting, a personal rather than social element in traditional piety. The opponents include not only the Pharisees, but also "John's disciples." Followers of John the Baptist may have comprised a sect in competition with the followers of Jesus. Though historical knowledge of this group is shadowy, their function in the text is quite clear. They, with the Pharisees, stand for a kind of rigor in piety which the disciples of Jesus did not practice.

Jesus answers his critics with a cluster of analogies. The first is that of bridegroom and wedding guests. The opponents' question is answered by another question: "Can the wedding guests fast while the bridegroom is with them?" To this question, common to the three Synoptic Gospels, only Mark has Jesus add, "As long as they have the bridegroom with them, they cannot fast." The image of Christ as bridegroom (cf. Matt. 25:1–13; John 3:28–30; Eph. 5:21–33 and Rev. 19:9) connotes in this Marcan passage joy in the presence of the Lord and celebration of the "already" dimension of the Kingdom of God. A second aspect of the bridegroom analogy unfolds in verse 20, which speaks of a coming time "when the bridegroom is taken away from them"; then the disciples will fast. This word of the Lord warrants the practice of fasting by Christians after Jesus' earthly ministry had ended. Fasting here connotes sorrow at the absence of the Lord and is appropriate to the "not yet" dimension of the Kingdom of God.

Jesus continues his answer in a pair of analogies showing the incompatibility of new and old: the new patch on an old garment and new wine in old wineskins. The two are parallel in form, but the second has one extra clause. The additional and final clause, "Fresh skins for new wine!" (NEB, TEV) makes the main point of the entire paragraph. Jesus' disciples do not fast because the message of the Kingdom of God is a fresh, new force which demands appropriate new forms.

Yet this single statement does not exhaust the meaning of Jesus' metaphors. It may be significant, for instance, that the reason one sews on patches is to preserve an old garment, while the reason one uses wineskins is to preserve new wine. Thus, while the major thrust of the text is parallel to Paul's "the old has passed away, behold, the new has come" (II Cor. 5:17), Jesus'

69

teaching here has the paradoxical quality of wisdom sayings. Just as one proverb may be true in a given situation while another proverb expressing a diametrically opposite principle may be true in another, so Jesus' sayings on fasting include an inner tension: Sometimes the old must be preserved. Interpretation includes discerning the times and occasions on which one or another of these sayings of Jesus may appropriately come into play.

SIGNIFICANCE

The early church found in this passage ammunition for her arguments with the synagogue and guidance for her own emerging institutional forms. Over against the synagogue, these stories about Jesus were used to justify the inclusion of ritually unclean Gentiles in the community of faith and at table, as well as the relaxation of other rules of Jewish piety. For their own guidance, some Christians may have taken the teachings of these verses (2:19, 21–22) to mean "no more fasting," but most (in line with 2:20) have practiced fasting (see Matt. 6: 16–18; Acts 13:2–3; 14:23; cf. the variant reading "and fasting" at Mark 9:29). The text functioned first in the setting of Jewish exclusivism and early Christian asceticism. How does it speak to the tolerantly inclusive Christianity of our time?

A sensitive interpreter may judge that the dominant problem today is not too much but too little spiritual discrimination and discipline. In a parish which admits virtually without question anyone who asks to join and which imposes few if any requirements of conventional piety on its members, to insist on Jesus' teachings about eating with sinners and not fasting so much may seem to be superfluous. Yet the text raises issues which, in various forms, are of perennial importance.

Exclusivism today is more likely to take the form of ethnic, economic, or social prejudice rather than religious intolerance. In circumstances where this is true, the social and economic barriers that made Levi an outcast may suggest a line of interpretation. Good news! Jesus and his first disciples called into fellowship and went home to eat with "tax collectors and sinners!" It was shocking then for poor disciples to eat with rich "sinners." In our time the roles may often be reversed, but the principle is unchanged.

Significantly, Jesus answers the question about eating with a proverb about healing (vv. 16–17). Relationships are healed when people eat together. What witness do meals in our congregations and homes bear to Jesus' teaching in word and deed about calling "outcasts" to himself through table fellowship? It takes nerve to pattern our eating habits after those of Jesus, for any challenge to exclusivism still produces controversy as well as healing.

Exclusivism may still take the form of religious or theological snobbery and self-righteousness, whether in charismatics or traditionalists, in "Jesus freaks" or those who look down on them. Wherever this is true, Jesus' word to his critics comes into play: "I came to call . . . sinners."

A second issue addressed by the text is *lifestyle.* Both the dinner party at Levi's house and the analogy of the wedding guests suggest that the Kingdom of God is characterized by joy. This joy, transcending social and religious boundaries and overruling the taboos of traditional piety, is the gift of the Holy Spirit, whose coming filled believers as with new wine (Acts 2:13). To say, in effect, "Go to, we must now be joyful" is not helpful. But this text can be used appropriately to defend and uphold those who, in a variety of ways, share the joy of their salvation with all sorts and conditions of people and whose piety, though perhaps unorthodox, glows with the sense of the Lord's presence. While the text warns against mistaking gloom for godliness, it gives no warrant for confusing jollity with Jesus. The joy of this bridegroom and his guests, the disciples, is of sterner stuff than can be organized through group dynamics or programmed in a liturgy. Paradoxically, joy may even be nurtured by fasting which is done not out of external constraint but from a deep inward hunger.

Institutional forms are a third area in which the text is still significant. The passage depicts a group so preoccupied with certain religious forms that they were unable to recognize the substance these forms were designed to preserve. This quality, characteristic of Jesus' opponents then, all too often marks the churches that bear his name today. Jesus' teaching about the incompatibility of old and new shows a strong bias toward the new. The text suggests the desirability of a "sunset law" for customs, groups, and institutions within the church as well as in the realm of civil law.

At the same time, the text's paradoxical counterthrust about future fasting and about preserving the old garment warns against the easy assumption that everything old must be

71

bad and anything new must be good. The church as New Israel has from the beginning clothed herself in rejuvenated forms drawn from Judaism. The use of the psalms in corporate and private worship is one example, and fasting is another. Where unshrunk cloth tears bigger holes, a patch from the old fabric sometimes serves best to preserve a well-worn garment. Often the old garment fits better; and if it has not been used in a long time, it may even be perceived as new.

Observing Lent as a forty-day period of fasting and repentance could be a reusable old form. The lectionary, which sets Mark 2:15–20 as the Gospel lesson for Ash Wednesday, points to an even earlier piece about fasting in Isa. 58:3–12. Verses 6–7 and 9 would revolutionize Lent!

A final issue to be considered is mission. While emphasis in the preceding notes has fallen on social dimensions of the text's demands, the basic evangelical thrust should not be overlooked. When Jesus' opponents chide him for eating with "tax collectors and sinners," he replies: "I came to call . . . sinners." The church, like her Lord, is sent to persons alienated from God (sinners) in order to call them, like Levi, to follow Jesus.

Mark 2:23—3:6
The Question About the Sabbath and the Man with the Withered Hand

Jesus' teaching about the Sabbath in the Gospel of Mark is contained in two stories (2:23–28 and 3:1–6), that conclude the first Marcan controversy section (see Introduction, pp. 2–3). According to Mark, argument about the Sabbath played a critical role in the life of Jesus; it was one of the factors that led to his death. Sabbath observance was a burning question at the time the Gospel was written, when the Christian movement was still separating from the synagogue. In our own time, however, we seem to have learned so thoroughly Jesus' teaching against the strict sabbatarianism of his day that the few sabbatarians left have little if any impact on society. Is it therefore superfluous to take up this text? Or is there here a word of the Lord about *shabbat* which might still breathe *shalom* on those who will hear it?

72

TEXT

The Question About the Sabbath (2:23–28)

This unit is a controversial pronouncement story, fairly typical of those vignettes in which a brief setting that poses some point of conflict between Jesus and his adversaries is followed by an authoritative saying of Jesus that resolves the issue and establishes a Christian position on the question (see Introduction, p. 6).

In the setting (2:23–24), the place is a grain field of some kind. The Greek words used to describe the field and the heads of cereal grain are no more explicit about what the crop was than is "corn" in British usage (e.g., AV, JB, NEB), which can mean wheat or oats or some other cereal, but ordinarily not maize.

The time is the Sabbath, and on this detail the action turns. On any other day, the disciples would have attracted no attention by pushing their way through the standing grain of a field and picking from the stalks a few heads to eat as they walked along. Luke adds that they rubbed the heads in their hands, thereby offering a ground for the Pharisees' accusation that they were doing something unlawful. Deut. 5:12–15 (the O.T. lesson accompanying this pericope in the lectionary) and Exod. 34:21 as interpreted by the Mishnaic tractate *Shabbat* 7:2 made "reaping . . . threshing . . ." along with thirty-seven other classes of work unlawful on the Sabbath.

Although only the disciples break the law, it is Jesus to whom the Pharisees address their accusatory question. They assume that he is responsible for his disciples' behavior (as in 2:18 and 7:5), and he does not object. The master-disciple relationship carries with it a mutual responsibility, the other side of which appears in verse 16, where opponents question the disciples about what Jesus does. With the question of the Pharisees, the issue comes clearly into focus: Why do Christians not keep the Jewish Sabbath laws?

Jesus' answer consists of three sayings. The first, like much rabbinic argument, is in the form of a counter-question. It refers to an incident recorded in I Sam. 21:1–6 as precedent for the priority of human need (in this case, hunger) over law. Matthew and Luke, perhaps noticing that the name "Abiathar" (2:26) is incorrect, omitted it. The presence of this lapse of memory or slip of the tongue in Mark may be some consolation to preachers and teachers embarrassed by their own occasional inexactitudes. The point of the argument is quite clear: Scripture itself admits of exceptions to the law.

Two further sayings are added in the form of positive principles applicable to Sabbath observance. First, "the sabbath was made for man, not man for the sabbath." This word grounds Sabbath law in the welfare of humankind, making explicit the essentially humanitarian argument of the preceding counterquestion. It challenges every legalism which makes of the Sabbath a burden to bear rather than renewal for the road. Second, "the Son of man is lord even of the sabbath." This word not only affirms the authority of Jesus, the Son of man, to reinterpret Sabbath law, but asserts also that the Sabbath remains God's day. Designed for the welfare of men and women, the proper use of the Sabbath is determined by the Son of man. As a human figure, he best knows human needs; as a divine figure, he has the authority to say how the Lord's day should be used.

The Healing of the Man with a Withered Hand (3:1–6)

The second unit in this pair is a miracle story. It presents a problem (v. 1), a solution and evidence of cure (v. 5b and c). However, like 2:1–12, it includes a controversy which occupies the central place in the story. This segment of the text, set apart by the repeated expression, "and (he) said to the man" (vv. 3, 5b), features an authoritative word of Jesus: "Is it lawful on the sabbath to do good or to do harm, to save life or to kill?" (v. 4).

The unit differs from the usual miracle story in another way: The response of the onlookers, instead of being amazement, is cold hostility. The conspiracy between religious and political leaders to kill Jesus (v. 6) represents the first explicit reference in Mark to Jesus' death. It is the climax and conclusion of this first controversy section (2:1—3:6), and it foreshadows the climax of the entire Gospel in the passion narrative. The Sabbath, designed to enhance life, becomes an occasion for malicious hostility that produces death, even to the lord of the Sabbath.

Jesus' opponents do not speak in this scene. Their hostility is depicted by their "watching in order to accuse him" (v. 2),

74

language that conjures up the image of figures lurking at a discreet distance, observing closely. Jesus flushes out their represssed hostility and confronts it boldly. His word to the disabled man, "Stand up out in the middle!" (JB) shatters the illusory peace of Sabbath worship in the synagogue. His question to the congregation, and to the Pharisees in particular (v. 4), confronts them squarely with the issue of the intention of the Sabbath law and therefore of what constitutes proper Sabbath observance. Their silence is poisonous, for it says they care more about their custom than they do about their brother; they are more eager to bring Jesus down than to restore the man's useless hand.

Jesus' response to this attitude is explicit in the text. He "looks around at them," confronting their surreptitious surveillance by the sweeping gaze which Mark depicts as characteristic of him *(periblepomai:* 3:5, 34; 5:32; 9:8; 10:23; 11:11; elsewhere only in Luke's parallel to the present passage). He is angry, a strong word used only here and perhaps in 1:41. "Grieved," which further describes his anger (3:5), may mean either "aggrieved by their attitude" or "he felt sorry for them" (TEV). He views their attitude as "hardness of heart." Various translations catch the nuances present in this vivid semitic idiom: "Obstinate stupidity" (NEB; similarly JB), "they were so stubborn and wrong" (TEV; similarly NIV), and "they had closed their minds" (NAB). The expression is used in the Old Testament to describe various persons who resisted the Lord (Exod. 7—9, *passim;* Ps. 95:8; Josh. 11:20; II Chron. 36:13; Prov. 28:14). In Mark "hardness of heart" elsewhere refers to human resistance to the divine will for marriage (10:5) and to the denseness of the disciples (6:52). The vivid language used (3:5) to describe Jesus' attitude toward defenders of the Sabbath law is unambiguous: to place religious scrupulosity above concern for human need is not pleasing to God.

SIGNIFICANCE

The move from meaning then to meaning now is facilitated by careful reflection on three of the authoritative words of Jesus preserved in these stories.

First, "the sabbath was made for man, not man for the sabbath." This principle, applicable to individuals and communities alike, though explicitly Christian is not exclusively so. Jews, Muslims, and humanists in general assent to its fundamental premise: The human body and psyche need regular times of rest. Religions that observe a day of rest understand the Sabbath law as a divine provision to meet that human need. By stating first the principle that human need takes precedence over rit-

75

ual law, Jesus challenges every form of legalism that reduces religion to the keeping of rules. Sabbath rules are not vital for most Christians today, but our need for security through clear structures and attainable goals is such that we continually create customs and rules that function for us as the Sabbath law did for the Pharisees. They separate "insiders" from "outsiders"; they make us feel good about God while protecting us from the demands of neighbors in need. For instance, many of us feel good if we attend church once on Sunday, though our use of the rest of the day may leave us exhausted and our neighbors ignored. Jesus' Sabbath principle helps us keep our priorities straight.

Second, "the Son of man is lord even of the sabbath." This principle is a necessary corollary to the first if the Sabbath is to retain its transcendent dimension. Without it, the first principle can be misunderstood. If "the sabbath was made for man," then whatever day of rest is observed in my religious community can be viewed as *my* day, to do with as I please. Such reasoning has led even religious persons to adopt rather easily the secular Sunday of Western culture, so that there is no longer any day to which one can point as "God's day." Jesus' claim to be lord of the Sabbath challenges two conflicting ideas: Since all days are ours, none belong to God; or since all days belong equally to God, the Sabbath is simply abolished in Christ. By adopting Sunday as the "Lord's day" (I Cor. 16:2; Rev. 1:10) the early church intended to preserve the substance of Jesus' principle while sitting loose to its forms. In our own time we risk preservation of the forms without the substance, or loss of substance and forms as well. Over against the easy license of our time into which our tolerance so easily degenerates, Jesus challenges Christians to ask, "How can I (we) so keep Sabbath as to honor God and acknowledge the lordship of the Son of man?"

The third principle, a counter-question of Jesus, helps us to answer our question: "Is it lawful on the sabbath to do good or to do harm, to save life or to kill?" To do nothing is not enough, says Jesus. Rightly to observe the Sabbath is not only to rest and worship but also to do good, to *save* life; that is, to make life whole, both our own and that of our neighbor. The principle suggests to Christians that Sundays be spent not in self-indulgence nor in self-denial, but in renewal and in service. Undertaken out of genuine reverence for God and love for neighbor, acts of kindness on a Sunday can be restorative not only of the persons healed by those acts, but for the healer too.

In the controversies over plucking grain and healing on the Sabbath, Jesus points opponents and disciples beyond picky rules to concern for human need and beyond them both to the wholeness of life under his own lordship.

Mark 3:7–12
Transition: Healings by the Sea

Are crowds a good measure of the progress of the gospel? Are public professions of faith in Jesus Christ an appropriate indication of commitment to him? If these questions evoke an ambivalent response, part of the reason may lie in surprising features of the present text.

TEXT

The passage serves as the transition between two parts of Jesus' Galilean ministry (see Introduction, p. 3). Two elements summarize the preceding material: Growing opposition from religious leaders leads Jesus and his disciples to withdraw from danger (3:6), and the crowd that follows them to the sea attests his growing popularity with the masses (1:28, 32–33, 37, 45; 2:2, 13). One element points ahead: The list of places from which the crowd comes includes the south (Judea, Jerusalem, Idumea), the east (beyond the Jordan) and the north (around Tyre and Sidon), foreshadowing the wider mission which the naming of the Twelve will inaugurate. The transition is a sort of "state of the ministry" report. Jesus' healings have attracted large and enthusiastic but unperceptive crowds from an increasingly wide area. The only ones who perceive Jesus' true identity and significance are the unclean spirits, but these Jesus silences.

The crowd (multitude), mentioned three times, figures prominently in the passage. Their motivation is evident: They have come to touch the healer and be made well (v. 10). They are attracted to Jesus but have no real understanding of him.

Jesus does not rebuke their self-interest. He accepts the throng of people without approval or disapproval, and he meets the needs they bring. He does ask his disciples to have a boat

77

ready so he can distance himself from the mob if necessary to avoid being crushed. The crowd's attitude is ambiguous, that of Jesus somewhat reserved.

The demons that apparently afflict some of the sufferers in the crowd play an important role in the scene. Theirs is the only voice we hear directly. As soon as they see Jesus, they cry out, "You are the Son of God." The theme is important in Mark (see Introduction, pp. 10–11). Their confession is correct, but hostile. It is not a confession of faith, but of fear.

Jesus' response to the unclean spirits is surprising. He had set out to preach the Kingdom of God throughout Galilee and he had called five men to follow him and share his mission of fishing for people (1:16–20; 2:14). Now he and his disciples, surrounded by an expectant throng, are in a situation that seems ideal. If getting large numbers of men and women to confess that Jesus is the Son of God were the goal of the Galilean ministry, Jesus would surely welcome this assistance from an unexpected source. Why, then, does he command the unclean spirits, who confess that he is the Son of God, not to make him known? And if readers are being led through this Gospel to understand that he is the Christ, the Son of God, why does Jesus not acknowledge here the verbal accuracy, at least, of the demons' confession?

The problem has been called that of "the messianic secret" (see Introduction, pp. 12–13). It is better resolved on literary grounds than by any historical hypothesis. The fact that the only ones on earth who recognize Jesus are the demons who are implacably opposed to his kingdom is a basic example of Marcan irony. Mark's two-level communication (see Introduction, pp. 7–8) appears in the fact that the reader hears "Son of God" as a correct assessment of Jesus, while the actors in the story dismiss it as demonic babbling and continue to grope for understanding. In the development of the narrative in Mark, it is not yet time for a full and appropriate understanding of who Jesus is, since the traditional titles can be rightly understood only in light of Jesus' passion, death, and resurrection.

SIGNIFICANCE

78

Two dimensions of the text's abiding significance may be seen in Jesus' attitude toward the crowd and in his silencing the demons.

Jesus accepts without complaint the large numbers of people that come to him, but he sees in those numbers no cause for gratification. Instead, he shows a measure of reserve toward them. The parable of the sower in the following chapter will underscore the deceptive nature of enthusiasm that springs up quickly but fades equally fast. Yet this summary of Jesus' ministry presents the crowd positively, as evidence of a popular response to Jesus' authoritative words and deeds. Crowds, then, are not to be sought as ends in themselves or used as measures of success; but neither are they to be despised. Mark 3:7–12 suggests to leaders in the community of faith today that Christian words and deeds may have in them the ring of authority which attracts a crowd; yet if attracting a crowd is the goal, the word or deed is not authentically Christian. To the degree that we are like our Lord, we will respond to human needs as they are presented and at the same time maintain a kind of psychic distance from the crowd. Such distance frees us for genuine service by delivering us from false standards of success.

Jesus' silencing of voices that clamored, "You are the Son of God!" teaches us that no matter how orthodox may be our christological confessions, Jesus Christ remains unknown to us until we follow in his way. The text pushes us beyond concern for numbers of professions of faith and beyond debates about creedal formulations to the more basic issue of trust in and commitment to Jesus Christ. The Lord who silenced ill-timed and hostile confessions of demons, even though they were formally correct, seeks in us, his disciples, something more than numbers and something other than exactitude. We need to know him rightly before we try to make him known.

PART TWO

From the Naming
of the Twelve
to Rejection
by His Own People

Mark 3:13 — 6:6

Mark 3:13–19*a*
The Naming of the Twelve

The naming of the Twelve begins the second major section of Jesus' Galilean ministry. One natural reaction to the list of names in this paragraph is to attempt to discover biographical information about each of these men who will come to be known as apostles, an attempt which in the early years of the church produced a rash of apocryphal writings but no hard data. Viewed as gospel, the passage invites reflection on the meaning of being set apart for special responsibility within the community of faith.

TEXT

The passage unfolds in three parts. The setting (v. 13) shows Jesus leaving the sea to go up on a mountain. Earlier editions of the RSV used the more poetic expression "into the hills" here. The same expression appears (6:46) where Jesus goes "up on the mountain to pray" before walking on the sea. Luke 6:12 characteristically adds "to pray" in the parallel account of the naming of the twelve as well. The Marcan text, however, simply indicates Jesus' withdrawal in order to call and set apart certain chosen disciples. The mountain setting may carry with it certain nuances of revelation and authority (as at 9:2 and 13:3).

The second part of the passage (vv. 14–15) is a three-fold

80

commission: to be with him, to preach, and to cast out demons. Their ministry, like that of Jesus himself, will be to announce and in a sense to embody the presence of the Kingdom of God. They are to be with him and to share his mission. Being with him comes first. Preaching and healing (in this text, specifically exorcism; the variant "and to heal" does not recognize that in Mark healing and exorcizing are functionally synonymous) are to go hand in hand for the twelve as they do in Jesus' own ministry.

The operative verb governing the entire commission is literally "made," variously translated as "ordained" (AV), "appointed" (RSV, NIV, JB, NEB), "named" (NAB) and "chose" (TEV). The object of this verb is simply "twelve." A variant reading adds "whom also he named apostles," but the word "apostle" is never used in this technical sense elsewhere in Mark (see 6:30 for the only other use) and its presence in verse 14 is readily explained as a harmonizing gloss from Luke 6:13 or Matt. 10:2. Although the TEV and NIV include the phrase in the text, it probably represents an institutional understanding of the Twelve which developed after the writing of Mark but before Matthew and Luke. Jesus is here appointing twelve chosen disciples for a special function. Only later will his action be understood as ordination to the ecclesiastical office of apostleship. Though the persons named are both disciples and apostles, "the twelve" in Mark means something more than "the disciples," but something less than "the apostles."

The list of the Twelve (vv. 16–19) constitutes the final part of the passage. Four of the Twelve are further identified by relative clauses. To the inner circle of three, Jesus gives surnames. Simon is here for the first time named Peter. Peter will appear frequently and prominently throughout Mark, but only once (in Gethsemane, 14:37) will he again be called Simon. James and John are called "sons of thunder," a surname which scarcely fits our image of the beloved disciple of the fourth Gospel with whom John is traditionally identified, but which accords quite well with the brashness of John (9:38) and of both brothers (10:35–41). Judas is identified as the one "who betrayed him," just as the betrayer will be identified as "one of the twelve" (14:10, 20, 43), underscoring the weight of his perfidy. Andrew, though given no surname and separated from his brother Peter in order to leave the inner group of three intact (see 5:37; 9:2; 14:33), is named as a fourth in the list (see 1:16–20;

81

1:29; 13:3). Simon the Cananaean is identified by Luke as a Zealot, and a variant in Mark calls Matthew a tax collector, thus accommodating the traditional identification of this apostle with the Levi whose call is reported at 2:14. Such remarks move beyond the original text of Mark, however. Most of the names in the list remain just that. They are not distinguished either by outstanding personal characteristics or by meritorious subsequent performance. Their only significance lies in the fact that Jesus called them to be with him, to preach and to cast out demons.

SIGNIFICANCE

The passage is of significance in the community of faith whenever certain of its members are set apart for particular tasks. This situation occurs whenever men and women are to be ordained. It also occurs when teachers are to be installed in the church school or when persons are inducted into any office in the church.

Just as for the Twelve the most important aspect of the call was to be with Jesus, so with any church members the most important part of being set aside for a particular task is also to be with him. From their close companionship with Jesus came the power to preach and to cast out demons; so today from our prayer life, Bible study, and Christian fellowship comes the power to serve in his name.

On occasions of installation or ordination it is appropriate to interpret the present text in terms relevant to the situation, recalling and applying the purposes for which Jesus commissioned the Twelve. There may be some value in pointing to the setting on the mountain, or in mentioning the diverse (and, on the whole, undistinguished) kinds of persons named. But the supremely significant elements embrace the setting and the commission: "He called . . . they came . . . and he *made* them."

Mark 3:19*b*–35

82 *Jesus' True Kinship*

The Jesus who presents himself in Mark's Gospel, unlike the one we meet in the creeds of the church, makes few, if any, explicit claims for himself. He submits himself to the judgment of the crowds, the religious leaders, the disciples, and his own family. Through the text of Mark, he submits himself to our judgment as well. The evidence he presents consists of deeds and words of power and authority, but his stance of awaiting our response is, paradoxically, one of lowliness. He subjects himself to the possibility of being misunderstood. The present text reports two erroneous judgments about Jesus and thereby points us toward a correct one. At the very end of the passage, however, Jesus expresses once more his inherent authority by making a promise that shifts the question from who Jesus is to that of who we may become.

TEXT

The unit is defined first by a common setting announced in verse 19b (some recent translations include "then he went home" in v. 20) which does not change until 4:1. All of the action between these points occurs "in a house" and is rightly translated as an idiomatic expression for "home," perhaps referring to the Capernaum home of Simon and Andrew (1:29). Although Jesus withdraws to a house, the crowd and two particular groups respond to him by pursuing him there.

In this passage the two groups who should have recognized Jesus first, his own family and the teachers of the law, are both blind to his true identity. Jesus' relatives respond out of concern for him and perhaps for the reputation of the family. The scribes from Jerusalem respond out of hostility, rejecting Jesus and his message. Here the two are bound closely together by the familiar Marcan device of bracketing, or sandwiching, one account within two parts of another.

The close connection of verse 21 with verses 31–35 turns on identifying "those around him" (v. 21) with "his mother and brothers" (vv. 31–33). The AV and the first edition of the RSV obscure that identity by using "his friends" (v. 21), more aptly rendered by "his family" or "his relations" in most contemporary translations. Jesus' blood relatives "set out to take charge of him" (v. 21, TEV); then they arrive and send a message in to him from outside the house trying to persuade him to come with them (v. 31). They think he is insane. The verb used with Jesus (v. 21) means literally "to stand outside of," an image reflected by the idiom "to be beside oneself" or "to be eccentric" but rightly rendered by "he is out of his mind" or "he's

83

gone mad!" (TEV). Verses 20–21 appear only in Mark and constitute the opening bracket of the entire unit.

Between the two parts of this misunderstanding by Jesus' family, Mark presents (vv. 22–30) a response of rejection on the part of the scribes who explain Jesus' deeds of power by accusing him of collusion with Satan. "Beelzebul" is a Canaanite divine name applied here to the prince of demons. The variant "Beelzebub" (AV, NIV, NEB) refers to the Philistine idol of II Kings 1:2 ("Baalzebub," RSV), meaning "the lord of the flies." The number of other New Testament references establishing some link between Jesus and Satan (e.g., Matt. 9:34; 10:25; 12: 24, 27; John 7:20; 8:48, 52) suggests not only that the accusation was in fact made against Jesus during his lifetime, but also that it probably figured in arguments between the church and the synagogue.

Jesus' confrontation with the scribes takes the form of a pronouncement story (see Introduction, p. 6) in which verse 22, the scribes' accusation, constitutes the setting.

Jesus' answer consists of a series of sayings which the text calls "parables," an example of the broad usage of this term in the first century. The general principle that Satan cannot cast out Satan, announced in the form of a rhetorical question in verse 23b, is followed by a cluster of three proverb-like sayings in "if . . . then" form (vv. 24–26). The point of these is that any entity divided against itself cannot stand, whether a kingdom (country), a house (household or family), or Satan. Verse 27 then interprets the exorcisms (reported in 1:23–28, 34, 39 and 3:11–12) as the binding of Satan ("a strong man") and the plundering of his house by Jesus. Jesus enjoys no kinship with Satan, but is his deadly enemy.

Whereas all the sayings in verses 24–27 presuppose a setting in the life of Jesus, the saying about the unpardonable sin of blasphemy against the Holy Spirit suggests rather strongly the life-setting of the early church. Introduced by "Truly, I say to you," it is one of the "Amen-sayings" of Jesus. It functions as a "sentence of holy law"; that is, a rule for the life of the early Christian community in the form of a saying of Jesus with an eschatological sanction.

84

The question of an unpardonable sin is treated variously in the New Testament (see I John 5:16; Heb. 6:4–6; 10:26). Here the point is that the spirit at work in Jesus Christ, by which he casts out demons, is the Holy Spirit of God. To confuse that Holy

Spirit with an unclean or demonic spirit, reversing good and evil and attributing the saving acts of God to the destructive power of Satan, is to place oneself outside the realm of God's forgiveness. This point is made by verse 30, which concludes the encounter with the scribes by pointing back to the setting of the bracketed pronouncement story in verse 22.

The closing element (vv. 31–35) in this composite passage again has the form of a pronouncement story which could stand on its own, witness its appearance in a different context in Luke. Part of the setting (vv. 31–32) concludes the theme of the blindness of Jesus' own family. By Jesus' question (v. 33), and his characteristic sweeping gaze (v. 34a; see 3:5; 10:23), the focal point of the passage is shifted from Jesus to the crowd and thereby to the reader. The saying of the Lord (vv. 34b–35) addresses us directly:

> "Here are my mother and my brothers! Whoever does the will of God is my brother, and sister, and mother."

This principle, so difficult for Jews (including Jewish Christians) to understand, was important for the early church to remember as the basis for its Gentile mission. It came to the earliest church, and it still comes to the community of faith today, as a marching order, an invitation, and a promise. Whoever will hear *and do* this word may become the true relative of Jesus.

SIGNIFICANCE

Of the many ways one might take up this text for preaching and teaching, two will be suggested here.

The first would focus on the distraught response of Jesus' family who said, "He is beside himself." Calling upon a current expression of the same idea, one could develop the ways in which Jesus appeared to be eccentric. His family had ample reason to think Jesus was eccentric, or "beside himself," because his life revolved around another center than that of his immediate relatives or of humankind in general. For Jesus, that center comes to expression in verse 35. It is doing the will of God. For most of us most of the time, life consists of the struggle to do our own will. The difference between us and Jesus in this regard is striking. Someone is in fact off center, "beside himself." Either Jesus is or we are. The issue is what it means to be truly human and how the self is most fully actualized. Jesus was and is fully human. The gospel, with all its promise and demand,

85

is that whoever does the will of God is not only the brother, sister, and mother of Jesus, but by that very fact, is also his or her own true and deepest self. The promise is real selfhood in kinship with Jesus. The demand is that we do the will of God. We, with Paul (II Cor. 5:13) and like Jesus, could do worse than to be "beside ourselves" for God. (The author is indebted for this interpretation to a sermon preached by Dr. W. Taliaferro Thompson in the late 1940s.)

A second handle by which to take up the text is the question of the unpardonable sin. It is a question which most readers of the Bible ask at one time or another, and some sensitive souls become troubled by the fear that they have committed a sin that cannot be forgiven.

The intention of the text is not primarily to define the unpardonable sin and even less is it to equip us to decide who has committed it. Jesus himself does not state that his adversaries had done so, according to Mark, though he warns them in the most serious terms. Mark 3:30 (not found in the parallels) does, however, offer a particular understanding of the unpardonable sin. The sin is to recognize a supernatural power at work in Jesus and yet to call that power unclean or evil. The sin is unforgivable because it rejects the very agent of God's healing and forgiveness (see 2:17 and 10:45). The imperfect tense of the verb in verse 30 is significant: ". . . because they *were saying*, 'He has an unclean spirit.' " This indication of repeated or habitual action, unfortunately obscured in the RSV, suggests a fixed position, a firm decision, and not simply skepticism. The doubt of honest inquirers is always honored in Mark. What places one in mortal danger is considered, deliberate rejection of the God at work in and through Jesus. The text continues to function as a warning to all readers of the seriousness of our response to the One who confronts us here.

Those readers who not only define the unpardonable sin, but believe that they have committed it, should observe, first, that the very fact of their concern means they are not guilty of the deliberate, obstinate rejection of God's Holy Spirit which alone is unforgivable. Only those who set themselves against forgiveness are excluded from it. But, secondly, preoccupation with the warning (v. 29) must not be allowed to obscure the good news (v. 28): "Truly, I say to you, all sins will be forgiven the sons of men, and whatever blasphemies they utter." The whole word of Jesus is not light or easy, but there is gospel in it.

86

Mark 4:1–34
Jesus Teaches in Parables

Is the effort to follow Jesus, to live in and to proclaim the Kingdom of God worthwhile? Why does the preaching and teaching of the gospel not bear more fruit? What difference, if any, does hearing the gospel make? What do hearing, seeing, and understanding mean in this passage and in life? Do the parables in this chapter each have a single meaning? If so, what is it? If not, what limits, if any, does the text impose on meanings we find in the parables? How do parables work, anyway? How are we to receive them?

These are some of the questions Mark 4:1–34 answers . . . and raises. Attractively simple on the surface, the parabolic discourse of Jesus in Mark invites an ever-deepening dialogue through which we begin to perceive the promise of the kingdom and in which we encounter Jesus' repeated call to hear.

THE LARGER UNIT

The unity of this passage is established by the introduction (4:1–2) and conclusion (4:33–34) about teaching in parables. Although the setting by the sea (v. 1*a*) does not shift formally until 4:35, it no longer controls the passage after the break at verse 10 (". . . and when he was alone . . ."). The unity of the passage is not historical. The discussion in verses 10–12, however, and the parabolic nature of the material in verses 13–32 identify the passage as a collection of parables.

The composite nature of the collection is important for interpretation in several ways. This editorial unit represents the first explicit elaboration in Mark of the message of the Kingdom of God which Jesus announced (1:14–15). The teaching of 4:1–34 and the preaching of 1:14–15 may therefore be used appropriately to interpret each other (see Introduction, pp. 23–24). Further, the successive settings in which these parables functioned (the life of Jesus, the experience of the early church, the evangelist's use of the tradition) may all be expected to shape the text and to be reflected in its interpretation. In addition, almost all of this material except the parable of the seed

87

growing of itself is found also in Matthew and Luke. Their particular situations bring to a total of five the historical settings which may influence the form and interpretation of these parables. It should not be surprising, then, if various elements in the passage seem to suggest differing interpretations.

Any reconstruction of the five historical settings is necessarily hypothetical. Therefore, the notes that follow are not based primarily upon these settings but upon literary clues in the text itself, especially on the analysis of its surface structure. The meanings of these parables in Matthew and Luke will be excluded except as they may illumine, by contrast or by reinforcement, the Marcan form of the text. The canonical text in Mark will function as criterion and guide for deciding among differing possible interpretations.

The passage contains three parables about seeds (the sower, the seed growing of itself, and the mustard seed) with an explanation of the first. To these are added a word of Jesus about parables in general and a cluster of sayings about light and hearing. These elements are arranged as follows:

Parables by the sea	4:1–34
Introduction: subject and setting	1–2
Parable of the sown seed (the sower)	3–9
Explanation to the disciples	10–20
About parables	10–12
Interpretation of the sown seed (the soils)	13–20
Sayings about light and hearing	21–25
Parable of the seed growing of itself	26–29
Parable of the mustard seed	30–32
Conclusion: Jesus' parabolic teaching	33–34

Two dominant motifs occur throughout this discourse: encouragement and exhortation. Encouragement is evident in the repeated contrast between small or discouraging beginnings and great or gratifying endings. Exhortation takes the form of repeated calls to hear and warnings about failure to hear rightly.

THE SMALLER UNITS

88

The following notes, combining remarks about text and significance, will show how attention to the recurrent themes of encouragement and exhortation can help to resolve substantive problems of interpretation in the smaller units that comprise Mark 4:1–34.

Introduction: Parables by the Sea (4:1–2)

Jesus teaches a very large crowd by the sea. The great emphasis on Jesus as teacher in Mark (see Introduction, p. 23) comes to a focus in the following discourse, the first and longest single collection of the teachings of Jesus in this Gospel. At the narrative level, the crowd is continuing evidence of Jesus' growing popularity. The crowd also signals to the reader that the teaching which will follow (through v. 9) is for everybody. As a "fisher of men" (1:17), Jesus casts his net broadly. Although the sea may sometimes function in Mark as the delineation between Jewish and Gentile territory (e.g., 5:1), here (as at 2:13 and 3:7) the sea is the theater for his unhampered proclamation of the Kingdom of God to the crowds.

Jesus teaches in parables. The word *parable* is used in Greek much more broadly than in English. We distinguish between parable (vv. 3–9, 26–29, 30–32), allegory (vv. 13–20), and saying (vv. 21–25); whereas "parable" in the New Testament (like *mashal* in the Old) is used to refer to all these sorts of comparisons and others, too, including proverbs and riddles. (See also p. 213.) Interpreters of Mark 4 should, therefore, handle with care the modern categories which restrict the meaning of parable in a way the New Testament does not. Modern distinctions can be useful, but they can be misleading if allowed to imply that Jesus can have told only one sort of story and that such a story can have only one meaning.

As a metaphorical mode of communication, parables are open to multiple meanings. Even when a parable specifies its referent (e.g., "the kingdom of God," vv. 26, 30), the relationship between the story and the object it is set beside (*parabolē*, "thrown alongside") remains open-ended, inviting reflection rather than definition on the part of the hearer. Often the referent is not mentioned, and the reader or hearer must supply it. What is supplied is usually determined by the setting of the hearer. It is normal, then, that the parables we are about to read in Mark will be interpreted somewhat differently in Matthew and in Luke and that all three Gospels may offer interpretations different from that (those) communicated at the time (times) Jesus uttered or earlier Christians repeated a given parable. The art of the interpreter is to follow the lead of Scripture by taking up these stories in ever-new situations, allowing them the freedom to speak with fresh nuances while assuring continuity with their meaning in the canonical context.

89

Parable of the Sown Seed (the Sower) (4:3-9)

Commonly called the parable of the sower, this story appears in all three Synoptic Gospels (Matt. 13:1-9; Luke 8:4-8) and as saying nine in the Gnostic Gospel of Thomas. In Mark and Matthew it is presented as the prime example of Jesus' parabolic teaching. Interpreters are largely agreed on its importance but differ widely on its meaning. A major reason for diverse interpretations is that the text specifies no referent for this parable. Such open-endedness allows literary critics to view the sower as a parable about parables (see John Dominic Crossan, *The Cliffs of Fall: Paradox and Polyvalence in the Parables of Jesus*, pp. 25-64), while recognizing that the context (vv. 11, 26, 30) determines its referent as the Kingdom of God. To follow the lead of Scripture is to interpret the parable of the sown seed as a word-picture ("Listen!" v. 3 [*"Behold . . . ,"* Greek]) of the Kingdom of God addressed alike to outsiders and to members of the community of faith.

The text takes us with a large crowd to the sloping hillside beside the lake where grain fields run down to the water. Fishermen and farmers can watch each other at their work, and scenes from the life of either would be familiar images to the other. All would know that farmers sowing a grain field in Galilee would first broadcast the seed and then plow it into the soil. Clumps of thistles, evident at the time of sowing, would disappear with the plowing, just as a wide shelf of rock would be revealed only when a plow scratched the thin surface above it. Once distracting agricultural images drawn from Western culture are set aside, the picture is crystal clear: Golden seed, rich with life, is broadcast from a pouch by a steady, rhythmic swing of the sower's arm, covering the whole area from which the sower already anticipates a crop. The seeds encounter various fates: Birds eat those that fall on the path which is not ploughed; rock leaves little room for roots in some parts of the field; thistle seeds, turned under here and there with those sown, spring up and choke the grain; and where the soil is good, the yield varies from stalk to stalk. Though the seeds meet different fates, the overall destiny of the scattered seed is fulfilled when the sower's vision becomes reality.

90 "He who has ears to hear, let him hear," says the storyteller. The scene is vivid, unforgettable; surely we hear! We hear many things, for this parable is patient of many interpretations and applications. How shall we sort them out?

A key question is whether the parable is intended to function as encouragement about the future of the kingdom or exhortation about how rightly to hear the teaching of Jesus. The beginning and the end of the unit are in fact hortatory (characterized by exhortation): "Listen!" (v. 3a, imperative), and "He who has ears to hear, let him hear" (v. 9, hortatory subjunctive). These elements, coupled with the explanation about the kinds of soils in verses 13–20, push the interpreter toward exhortation.

Other elements in the text, however, point in the direction of encouragement: the three kinds of wasted seed followed by three degrees of increasingly abundant yield, the contrast between disappointing beginnings and great results, and the confident initiative of the sower despite the waste inherent in the act of sowing. What the listener is exhorted to hear is good news. Sown seed is rich with promise, and so is the Kingdom (rule, reign) of God.

The substance of these verses, with their vivid imagery and semitic style, doubtless comes from Jesus. He may have told the story to encourage his hearers to see in him and hear in his words the presence of the Kingdom of God in their midst, a kingdom whose abundant fruitfulness only the future would reveal. In any case, the hortatory elements which now bracket the parable are subsidiary to the encouragement which is its central thrust and the initial guide to its interpretation.

The parable of the sown seed is significant in various situations of discouragement. Its promise addresses in an immediate way Christian preachers and teachers, professional or lay persons who are in any way engaged in proclaiming the gospel. When their work seems fruitless, this parable announces good news. The future promises an abundant yield, despite apparent reverses. Its applicability to those who spread the word may explain why this parable has been called "the sower" in Matthew and in subsequent tradition, even though the sower is not mentioned after verse 4a.

The parable speaks in both individual and corporate settings. It addresses the lives of persons who have heard the gospel but in whom it has not yet taken root; committed Christians who are for the moment spiritually dry; congregations, church boards, and whole Christian communions which are disheartened by periods of sterility. It speaks of a power whose life-giving potential is irrepressible.

91

The principle of small beginnings and great endings is not

limited to ecclesiastical or specifically Christian settings. In whatever setting, however, the controlling factor for the interpretation of this parable should be its canonical context which points to the reign of God as the subject under discussion (v. 11) and to the future of the disseminated word as the central issue (v. 14). The promise of the parable of the sown seed echoes that of Isa. 55:11:

> . . . so shall my word be . . . ;
> . . : it shall accomplish that which I purpose,
> and prosper in the thing for which I sent it.

Explanation to the Disciples (4:10-20)

In Mark, private instruction to an inner circle commonly signals an interpretation of the teaching of Jesus adapted to the particular needs of the early church. Verses 10-20 present two such interpretations of the parable of the sown seed, each introduced by "and he said to them."

About Parables (4:10-12)

The first of these explanations is preceded by a somewhat vague setting (v. 10). "When he was alone" interrupts the scene by the sea, to which the text returns only at 4:35. "Those who were about him with the twelve" points to interpretation for the church, just as does "the disciples" elsewhere. In answer to their general question "concerning the parables," Jesus speaks of how parables function. They serve as revelation to disciples and concealment from the crowd ("those outside"), a theme also found in two independent sayings not reported in Mark (Matt. 11:25; Luke 10:21 and Matt. 13:16–17; Luke 10:23–24).

For insiders, members of the believing community, parables have a revelatory function: "To you has been given the secret *(mystērion)* of the kingdom of God." The term *secret* (literally "mystery," AV, NAV) appears in the Gospels only in this verse and its Synoptic parallels (Matt. 13:11; Luke 8:10). In Matthew and Luke the term is plural, which implies that Jesus gives his disciples secrets about the Kingdom of God. Not so in Mark. Here Jesus communicates no privileged information about the kingdom. Rather, in the authentic speaking and hearing of the parables, Jesus gives the kingdom itself as a mystery (genitive of apposition: the secret is the kingdom). The Kingdom of God is at hand in the fruitful word of Jesus Christ. To hear the word of and about Jesus, to believe it and act on it, this

92

is the secret of the reign or rule of God in individuals, in the church, and in the world.

Alternatively, we may understand "the secret of the kingdom of God" to be Jesus himself, present among those to whom he speaks. Either interpretation is possible, and for readers today they come to virtually the same thing. Jesus is present to us in his word, a word in which the Kingdom of God is given in veiled and parabolic form.

The word about the function of parables for "those outside" includes a quotation of Isa. 6:9–10 (the prophet's commission at the time of his call) which poses a serious theological problem. Does God deliberately harden the hearts of some people so that they will not repent and be forgiven? Does Jesus tell parables in order to hide the truth from some people? The text contains two purpose clauses, *"so that* they may . . . not perceive, and may . . . not understand; *lest* they . . . be forgiven."

In Matthew the problem is resolved by shifting the idea of purpose to the disciples' question, "Why do you speak to them in parables?" (13:10) and softening the answer into a statement of result, "because . . . they do not see" (13:13). In Mark, however, while the question is not framed explicitly in terms of purpose, the second part of the answer is. The question is very general, "concerning parables." The two-part answer speaks of the contrasting effects of the parables and, by extension, of Christian preaching in the lives of the hearers. But why do some fail to see and hear rightly? The text reflects the common tendency of its time to attribute all inexplicable phenomena to the will of God. The honest interpreter will acknowledge here a "hardening theory" of parables.

Even in Mark, however, the harshness of this teaching is qualified by further interpretation (vv. 21–23). The hardening is temporary. "There is nothing hid except to be made manifest." As the songs of salvation in Isa. 40—55 supercede, reinterpret, and transcend the oracles of judgment in Isa. 1—39, so Mark 4:21–23 reinterprets and transcends the negative judgment of 4:11*b*–12. (See notes on 4:21–25 below.)

This explanation about parables was encouraging to the early readers of Mark in several ways. First, to the community of faith the Kingdom of God is given in parables. Second, Christian preachers need be neither surprised nor discouraged if not all hearers receive their message; the outcome is in the hand of God. Third, though the initial effect of parables (and of Chris-

93

tian preaching and teaching) may be to veil the truth and harden hearts, their ultimate purpose is to reveal, to illumine, and to save.

Interpretation of the Sown Seed (the Soils) (4:13–20)

The second explanation to the disciples is no longer about parables in general (cf. Matt. 13:10) but about this particular parable, the sown seed (cf. Luke 8:9). Jesus' double question introducing the interpretation shows that the parable is as unclear to the Twelve and other insiders as it is to the outsiders. The questions are phrased as a rebuke: The disciples should understand but they do not.

The thrust of this explanation is not encouragement but exhortation. The reader is led to ask, "What kind of soil am I?" Consequently, the entire parable (4:1–20) is sometimes called "the four kinds of soils."

Unlike the open-ended parable (vv. 3–9), the interpretation (vv. 13–20) specifies referents for six details; the seed (the word), the birds (Satan), and the four kinds of soil. The allegory is not carried through consistently. The sower is not identified; the soil can be either the hearers or the difficulties hearers face; and hearers are likened to the soil, which is receptive in various degrees, and to the plants, which spring up to wither or to bear fruit. The teaching, however, is clear. The language used in this allegorizing interpretation and the problems to which it points reflect the life of the early church. (For fuller discussion, see Joachim Jeremias, *The Parables of Jesus*, 1963, rev. ed., pp. 77–79.) In this explanation the church applies Jesus' parable of the scattered seed to her own experiences in preaching and hearing the gospel ("the word").

Certain of those experiences are reflected also in the discourse about last things in Mark 13. The "tribulation or persecution" of 4:17 is specified in 13:9–13 as being "delivered up" and "brought to trial" before religious and civil authorities, being betrayed by one's own family, and being hated by all for the sake of Jesus' name. The Book of Acts portrays many such scenes in the life of the early church. The epistles not only reflect similar experiences of believers, but also echo several of the key terms in Mark 4:13–20: *tribulation* (literally, "pressure"), *persecution* (literally, "the chase"), *cares* (anxiety, worry), *riches, desire* (longing, lust). These were the special problems of the early Christian community which first read the

94

Gospel of Mark. Preachers and teachers will recognize their analogues in the experiences of believers today.

The one term that is constant throughout all four vignettes in the allegorical interpretation is *hear.* The story is about four kinds of hearers: those who hear but immediately reject the message; those who hear gladly but not persistently; those who hear many conflicting voices along with the gospel; and those who hear, receive, and act appropriately upon the gospel. At base, then, the explanation (4:13–20) takes up and elaborates the call to hear which brackets the parable itself (vv. 3, 9) and which will be recapitulated in saying form (4:23–25).

The central thrust of these three portions of Mark 4:1–34 is the exhortation to listen. Verses 13–20 focus on how we are to hear the gospel. When the word of Jesus Christ confronts us in any form, we are challenged to be receptive, persistent, single-minded, and responsive.

When a parent gives a command to a child and adds, "Do you hear me?" the child's obedience will attest that the message has been heard. Really to hear the gospel is to act upon it.

In a secular age which sometimes seems impervious to the message of Jesus Christ, in a culture in which social and political pressures make persistence in the Christian life difficult and in which mass media bombard the public with incentives to get, to spend, and to consume, this passage retains its original significance: "those . . . sown upon the good soil are the ones who hear the word and accept it and bear fruit. . . ."

Sayings About Light and Hearing (4:21–25)

The following paragraph, a cluster of five sayings of Jesus, consists of a double arrangement of two with one in the middle:

And he said to them, "Is a lamp brought in . . ."	21
"For there is nothing hid . . ."	22
"If any man has ears to hear, let him hear."	23
And he said to them, "Take heed what you hear; . . ."	24
"For to him who has . . ."	25

All these sayings appear in various contexts in Matthew and in Luke, but the particular arrangement of two sayings, plus "hear," plus two sayings is found only in Mark. The first pair of sayings follows up the theme of encouragement found in the parable of the scattered seed (vv. 3–9) and in the first explanation of it (vv. 10–12). The second pair of sayings summarizes and concludes the hortatory thrust announced in verses 3 and 9 and elaborated in the second explanation of the parable (vv. 13–20). The pivotal call to hear (v. 23), echoing that of verse 9, serves to conclude the word of encouragement found in the sayings about light and to introduce the word of exhortation found in the sayings about hearing.

The RSV obscures a significant peculiarity in the saying about the lamp (v. 21). In Greek the verse reads "A lamp does not come in order to be put under a measuring-bowl (i.e., to be snuffed out) or under a bed (i.e., to be hid), does it?" The awkward construction suggests that the saying may refer to Jesus who "came into Galilee preaching the gospel of God" (1:14). Readers familiar with Johannine thought would almost surely have heard in the lamp saying an allusion to Jesus' coming as a light into the world. In the present context, however, the lamp refers primarily to the parabolic teaching of Jesus. Jesus' parables are meant to be understood just as surely as a lamp is meant to give light (see notes on 4:10–12 above).

The word about things hidden or secret which will surely be made manifest or come to light is the definitive reinterpretation of the "secret of the kingdom of God" saying (v. 11a) and the enigmatic word for outsiders (vv. 11b–12). For believers, the parables convey the Kingdom of God as a secret; but the true nature of God's rule will become evident to them in the death and resurrection of Jesus. Mark 4:22 therefore belongs to the so-called "messianic secret" pattern in Mark (see Introduction, pp. 12–13). For outsiders, the verse stands as a mitigation of the harshness of 4:11b–12. All may be in riddles now, but a riddle is told only to be answered or revealed eventually. Insiders and outsiders, therefore, are encouraged to keep on listening. What is obscure at the beginning will be clear at the end.

"Take heed what you hear" (v. 24a) can mean either "select the right things to listen to" or "pay attention to what you hear." In today's culture, whose mass media convey lush embodiments of the thorns (thistles) (vv. 18–19), the former understanding invites persons whose eyes and ears are assailed by trash to exercise their prerogative of selectivity. Luke, however, expresses the latter meaning: "Take heed then *how* you hear; . . ." (Luke 8:18). Most modern translations of 4:24a agree with Luke's interpretation: for instance, *"Take notice of what you are hearing"* (JB); *"Pay attention to what you hear!"* (TEV). This understanding is in line with the explanation of the para-

96

ble (vv. 13–20) and with the sayings that follow (vv. 24*b*–25).

The sayings about the measure one gives and gets are applied in Mark to hearing. (The TEV erroneously interprets v. 24*b* to be about judging, a usage made of it in Matt. 7:2 but not in Mark.) In context, the first saying affirms that the more carefully we give attention to the word, the more we shall hear. Mark alone adds, ". . . and still more will be given you," a transition to the next saying which applies the use-or-lose principle to hearing the gospel. Fruitful hearers of the gospel are given to hear even more; fruitless hearers will, after a time, hear nothing at all.

These sayings are significant for those who read this commentary as well as for those who will hear what the interpreter is preparing. The way we hear the gospel each time it is presented makes a difference in our capacity to hear it next time. These sayings address an exhortation to all hearers. The final word, "and from him who has not . . ." is a warning to lazy or indifferent listeners. Yet even in this word of exhortation the note of encouragement is present. At the heart of the final pair of sayings lies a great promise to those who hear, receive, and respond: ". . . still more will be given you. For to him who has will more be given."

Parable of the Seed Growing of Itself (4:26–29)

While the first of the three seed parables was developed extensively (4:1–25) as characteristic of all the parables, the last two are presented as brief similitudes. Each is introduced by "and he said"; each states the referent explicitly (the Kingdom of God); each is offered without explanation and belongs to Jesus' teaching to the crowd, like the original parable (vv. 3–9). Like all three of the seed parables, that about the seed growing of itself contrasts beginnings and endings. The language about putting in the sickle because the harvest has come (v. 29) is taken from Joel 3:13 which refers to the day of the Lord and the last judgment. Harvest time is when the abundant effects of the preaching and hearing of the word will at last be revealed.

These verses (27, 28) call attention respectively to the mysterious growth of the seed and to the astonishing fertility of the earth. The point is that the Kingdom of God grows in a hidden, mysterious way, independently of human effort. Though the parable speaks of growth, its meaning is not that the Kingdom of God develops naturally in history thanks to human efforts;

97

nor is the function of the parable hortatory. Rather, growth is spoken of as the miraculous work of God and harvest as an outcome that is both gift and miracle.

The parable is significant whenever and wherever we Christians take ourselves and our efforts too seriously, seeking by our plans and programs to "bring in the kingdom of God." Against such arrogant self-importance stands "of itself " *(automatē)*, a subtle allusion to God's hidden presence and power.

More basic than the warning, however, is the encouragement. Whether on the stage of world history or in the individual human heart, the reign or rule of God is like seed growing of itself: pregnant, mysterious, fruitful. As a man scattering seed on the ground, we work at preaching and teaching, at supporting each other, at serving those in need, and at creating a more just social order. Our efforts sometimes seem to be in vain, but in the end we shall marvel, as a sower at harvest. Growth and change occur while we sleep, we know not how. "I the LORD have spoken, and I will do it" (Ezek. 17:24).

Parable of the Mustard Seed (4:30–32)

The parable of the cedar in Ezek. 17:22–24 is the Old Testament lectionary lesson accompanying the two seed parables and summary in Mark 4:26–34. The choice is apt, not only because of the eschatological promise which each text announces, but also because of the continuity and contrast between the cedar and the mustard plant when they are set side by side. Reference to the birds which "can make nests in its shade" (4:32) ties the parable of the mustard seed to that of the cedar, in the shade of whose branches "birds of every sort will nest" (Ezek. 17:23; see also Ezek. 31:6 and Dan. 4:21).

Both parables are about hope in the Kingdom of God. Both affirm that God will accomplish great results from small beginnings. Through the image of the birds, both affirm the inclusive nature of the Kingdom of God in the end. It is probably the allusion to the eschatological cedar of Ezek. 17:22–24 that accounts for the surprising affirmation in Luke 13:19 that the mustard seed "grew and became a *tree.*" In Mark, "it grows up and becomes the greatest of all *shrubs*" (4:32), and Matthew characteristically conflates the two: "when it has grown it is the greatest of shrubs and becomes a tree" (Matt. 13:32).

The Marcan insistence that a mustard plant is at best a

shrub, and not a tree, preserves botanical verisimilitude and establishes a contrast between the mustard plant and the cedar. The prior contrast between smallest seed and greatest shrub (4:31–32) proclaims hope in the future of God's kingdom. The further contrast between cedar and mustard shrub suggests that the hope proclaimed by Jesus is of a different quality than that of Israel's prophets and of the usual human vision of greatness.

The parable of the cedar announces a restoration of the Davidic kingdom among the kingdoms of the earth. Other kingdoms will dry up, while that of David will flourish and outlast them.

The parable of the mustard seed speaks of a kingdom which, for all its miraculous extension, remains lowly. Mustard is an annual plant; its perpetuation depends on renewed sowing, and its perennial promise depends on the life of the seed. It is an image which corresponds closely to the picture of the Kingdom of God in Mark: a mystery whose realization will come as a surprise; a reality whose weakness is its power. (For further development of this interpretation in an allusive mode, see Robert W. Funk, "The Looking-Glass Tree Is for the Birds," *Interpretation* 27:3–9 [Jan. 1973].) The function of the story is encouragement, the issue is hope, and the mode of teaching is metaphor. Interpretation, therefore, should point to meaning but should not pontificate; it should suggest significance but should not define it, to the end that the weary may be sustained by the word.

Conclusion: Jesus' Parabolic Teaching (4:33–34)

In these two verses the evangelist speaks, summarizing and concluding the preceding selection of parables typical of Jesus' message. The expression "he spoke the word to them," translated earlier by "preaching" (2:2), here echoes "teaching" (4:1–2; see Introduction, pp. 23–24). Jesus' parabolic teaching is characteristic of his announcement of the advent, nature, and promise of the Kingdom of God.

The conclusion preserves the distinction between public proclamation and private instruction, as well as the tension between the revelatory intention of parables (". . . as they were able to hear it," v. 33) and the effect of concealment from outsiders and revelation to insiders (v. 34). Parables reveal the

Kingdom of God, but reveal it as a mystery. They do this by drawing attention to the mystery and miracle in commonplace activities and events.

The significance for interpreters is evident. We are called not to explain the mysteries of God in prosaic language that makes them commonplace nor in esoteric language that stifles understanding. Rather, the teaching of Jesus invites us to see and to hear God in the familiar rounds of daily life and in familiar texts like this one . . . to sit still and contemplate quietly until the commonplace wakes our minds and hearts to wonder.

The significance of Mark 4:1–34 for all persons lies in the repeated invitation, "Whoever has ears to hear, let him hear." To such is given the secret of the Kingdom of God.

Mark 4:35–41
The Stilling of the Storm

How can we hear afresh so familiar a story as that of Jesus stilling the storm? What elements in the text can help us to identify with the original participants in the scene? How did the text address its first readers, and how does it move forward to encounter us today?

TEXT

The vivid details of a dramatic story help us to feel our way into the text. It is evening, after a full and exhausting day of teaching (vv. 33–34). Jesus' decision to cross to the other side is the only way he and his disciples can leave the crowd. "In the boat, just as he was" means to draw attention not to Jesus' appearance but to the boat, first held in readiness (3:9), then used as a pulpit from which to teach (4:1–34), and now about to figure importantly in the action. All the fishermen among Jesus' most intimate disciples know from experience the danger of sudden storms on the Sea of Galilee. As the wind and the waves fill the boat with water, the disciples become fearful (v. 40a). They are sinking, and they really might drown (v. 38)! In terror they turn to Jesus who, calmly asleep on a cushion in the stern of the boat, is apparently unaware of their plight. They waken him with words we often address to God: "Do you not care?"

100

In the original text, Jesus speaks only two words at this point, both in the imperative: "Be quiet! . . . Be still!" (TEV). The simplicity and brevity of his command to wind and waves express the assurance of one who is in control. The response of the natural elements to his command is evidence of his authority. The disciples' question to each other eloquently expresses their awe at depths in Jesus they do not understand: "Who then is this?"

The text takes the form of a miracle story: a setting which ties the story into its present context (vv. 35–36), a problem (vv. 37–38), a solution (v. 39a), evidence that the miracle has occurred (v. 39b), and a response of wonder (v. 41). The one element that expands upon the usual form is Jesus' reproach in verse 40, "Why are you afraid? Have you no faith?" The expansion draws attention to a major function of the narrative. This is an appeal to the reader to have faith in—that is, to trust—Jesus. The concluding and climactic question of the disciples, "Who then is this, that even wind and sea obey him?" shifts the focus back to Jesus and to the question of his identity. By its structure, the text addresses two questions to the reader. Who is Jesus? Will you trust him?

The stilling of the storm, like the other Marcan miracles that are not healings (6:30–44, 45–52; 8:1–10; 11:12–13, 20–23) affirms that Jesus Christ is the "ruler of all nature." This may have been the main function of the story as it first circulated among the miracle-seeking common folk who flocked to see, hear, and touch Jesus, as well as when the earliest Christian missionaries used it to testify that Jesus Christ is Lord.

In its present setting in the Gospel of Mark, however, the story addresses a community of believers in Jesus Christ who, in the guise of the disciples, are challenged to trust Jesus more. They may also be challenged to "cross over" to the Gentile mission, despite the turmoil this movement stirred up in the early church, for this unit lies between Jesus' ministry on the west bank of the Sea of Galilee and his first mighty work in pagan territory.

Certain words in the text merit particular attention. *Lai-laps*, the word for "storm" (v. 37), is also the word for "whirlwind" in Job 38:1 (the Old Testament reading accompanying Mark 4:35–41 in the common lectionary). It carries overtones of demonic power (see "rebuke" and "be silent" in 1:25, two of the same verbs used in 4:39). Just as God had authority over the

101

primeval chaos at the creation (Job 38:8–11; Ps. 74:13–14), so Jesus has authority over the demonic forces of nature.

Jesus' abrupt command (v. 39) means literally "Be silent! Be muzzled!" The familiar "Peace! Be still!" may have powerful associations for many people, but contemporary translations help to recover the force and shock of the original; for example, "Quiet now! Be calm!" (NEB).

"Have you no faith?" (v. 40) fails to catch the temporal significance of the more likely of two readings found in the Greek text. "Are you still without faith?" (TEV; similarly NEB and NIV) is a preferable translation. Faith in Mark means in part a recognition that Jesus is Christ and Son of God (1:1; 5:7), but in this unit faith means primarily the trust which the disciples lacked when they feared for their lives and cried out in panic. An appropriate paraphrase of Jesus' questions in verse 40 is therefore: "Why are you afraid? Do you not yet trust God, whose rule is present in me?"

All the foregoing elements—the vivid details of the story, its form, its literary and historical setting, its particular language—help us to step back into the text. First repeated to generate enthusaism for a wonder-worker and to bring pagans to belief in Jesus as Lord, this story is incorporated in the Gospel of Mark to nurture trust in Jesus Christ in the midst of stress and persecution.

SIGNIFICANCE

The text becomes interesting as we move back into its world; it becomes significant as it moves forward to address us in ours.

The corporate dimension of this text's significance is embodied in an early Christian symbol adopted by the World Council of Churches at its formation during the dark days of World War II. The church universal is depicted as a storm-tossed boat with a cross for a mast. The stilling of the storm continues to reassure the church in every time of persecution and distress that Jesus Christ is Lord, that he is ruler of nature *and* history, and that he is present with his disciples in their anxiety.

102

The text is also significant for individual Christians. In times of tumult and grave danger, a natural human reaction is to wonder whether or not there is a God, and if so, whether God is even aware of *my* problem. We cry out to God in the midst of our storms, "Don't you care?" We try to wake God up to take care of us. At such times the text speaks to our condition. It pictures Jesus in the boat with his disciples, present with us and concerned for us even when we do not perceive his care.

The perennial relevance of this image of Christ stilling the storm is reflected in hymns (e.g., "Eternal Father, Strong to Save," "Jesus Savior, Pilot Me," and inner stanzas of "The King of Glory Standeth" and "O Sing a Song of Bethlehem") and in art (e.g., Rembrandt, "The Calming of the Sea"). These testimonies are fruitful resources for interpretation. They may stimulate or reinforce the experience of a sensitive reader sitting quietly before the text who suddenly finds that Jesus, speaking to the storm outside, also addresses the storms within when he says, "Peace! Be still!" Over the heads of his first disciples he says to us as well, "Why are you afraid? Can you not yet trust the God you see in me?" The word to the storm becomes for us a voice from the whirlwind.

Who then is this?

Mark 5:1–20
The Gerasene Demoniac

This story appears at first to be about one tormented individual but turns out to involve a large number of demons. So also its interpretation appears at first to be simple and straightforward, but the careful reader is soon confronted with a host of possible interpretations. The story moves from unity to complexity to resolution in clear responses to the miracle. Similarly, the following comments will show how the interpreter may approach the story as a unified whole, may address any one of several elements in it, or may seek to incorporate unity and diversity in one coherent interpretation.

Essential Unity

One way to approach the interpretation of this message is to treat it as a unified whole with a single point: the amazing power of Jesus.

The narrative is obviously a unit. The longest and most detailed of Mark's exorcisms (see Introduction, pp. 19–20), this

103

story tells how Jesus healed a demon-possessed man in the country of the Gerasenes. His authority extends over the realm of unclean, hostile spirits; and he brings healing to troubled persons.

The first voice heard in the story is that of the unclean spirit, speaking through the man and addressing Jesus as "Son of the Most High God." The recognition formula is thereby given prominence, even at the cost of upsetting the flow of the narrative (see v. 8). The demon's confession embodies the text's main message: Jesus can heal because he is the Son of God.

Jesus seems to bargain with the demoniac and his demons (vv. 10–13a). The man begs Jesus not to send the demons out of the country; the demons beg him to send them into the swine. Jesus accedes to both requests, but in doing so he effectively sends the demons back to their place: the primeval abyss, the depths of the sea. (Compare Luke 8:31, which makes this point more explicitly.) Jesus accepts their proposal but defeats their purpose. His authority prevails.

With this narrative an important new element is introduced into the Gospel of Mark: This healing is in Gentile country. The story is set in the territory of one of the Hellenistic towns of the Decapolis (v. 20) on the southeastern shore of Lake Tiberius (the Sea of Galilee). The incident is preceded by a crossing of the sea (4:35–41) and followed by a notice of the return crossing (5:21). Textual variants muddy the name of the town (v. 1) in all three Synoptic accounts. The uncertainty of the text does not permit us to satisfy our geographical curiosity but pushes us to see the interest of the text in the fact that this is Gentile country, "opposite Galilee," as Luke 8:26 specifies. Nothing about it is kosher; everything is unclean: the spirit(s), the tombs, the pigs, the territory. In this alien place, Jesus' authority and healing power is just as great as in a synagogue and even more amazing.

The significance for secularized lives is striking. There is no human disorder, anywhere, anytime, that Jesus cannot heal. This affirmation immediately raises a question: If Jesus can heal all disorders anywhere, why does he not heal all the persons for whom we pray? One point relevant to this problem emerges clearly from the exegesis of Mark 5:1–20. Whereas Jesus' power to heal and to cleanse knows no bounds, his exercise of it belongs absolutely to his own decision. In the present text no one asks Jesus to heal the demon-possessed man. On the contrary, the man and the onlookers want to be left alone. Jesus takes the initiative. As Son of the Most High God, he exercises his authority and healing power in sovereign freedom. This implies that we can neither control what he will do nor ever fully know what to expect of him. We can, however, be assured that whatever he does—or does not do—is consonant with the Kingdom of God. He acts in accordance with the divine rule whose presence he embodies and whose coming he announces (see Introduction, p. 24, and, notes on 1:40–45, pp. 61–62).

Various Options

Interpreters can and often do focus on one or another of the elements in the story and discover various meanings. One such element is found in the contrast between plurality and integration, between chaos and disorder.

The tormented individual says, "My name is Legion" (5:9). The word *legion* is borrowed from Latin and refers to an army unit of four to six thousand men. Jesus does not confront just one unclean spirit but a whole body of Satan's troops. He meets them in single combat and puts them to rout.

The expression "their name is legion" has passed into pious vernacular to refer to any large group or class of which a given individual is representative. The idiom affirms that the one who is seen represents many who are unseen.

The expression in the vernacular carries no pejorative connotation, but in the text the shift from singular ("an unclean spirit," "do not torment me," "my name is Legion . . .") to plural (". . . for we are many," "*he* begged him not to send *them* . . ." "and they begged him . . .") is ominous and filled with evil portent. Though they seem at first to be but one, and though as an army they concentrate their attack on one unfortunate individual, the demonic forces are as numerous and chaotic as a mob (see TEV). Their plurality is revealed only in answer to Jesus' question, "What is your name?" To know the name is to discover the inner character and thereby to exercise power over someone. The essential nature of this demonic power is multiplicity, disorder, violence. Of such is the kingdom of Satan . . . and much of life in the world. "The crowd—that is the lie!" (Kierkegaard).

105

This element in the text parallels an insight of contemporary medicine and psychology: The causes of emotional disorder are often complex. Under any single diagnosis may lurk multiple causes, physical and psychic. Furthermore, the effects of illness are often chaotic and self-destructive.

A second element upon which the interpretation may focus is the avarice of the crowd which valued their pigs more highly than their neighbor. When they learned what had happened to the demoniac and to the swine, "they began to beg Jesus to depart from their neighborhood" (5:17). The reaction places the crowd in the same situation the man was in before his demons were exorcised. He wanted nothing to do with Jesus and found his very presence painful (5:7); he loved his demons and did not want to be separated from them (5:10). We may find it difficult to identify with the man, who is obviously insane, but in a variety of ways this madman reveals a basic truth about us all. The crowd's desire to be rid of Jesus, their discomfort in his presence, demonstrates that they, too, are in fact demon-possessed, subjected to a power or powers hostile to the Kingdom of God.

Was it really the loss of the pigs which prompted this reaction? The point is not made explicitly in the text, and to limit the interpretation to a condemnation of greed narrows the focus of the text. Yet the text does allow this interpretation; its persistence in our time reflects the fact that our love of material possessions is one of the demons that plague us.

The connection between verses 17 and 18a is significant in this regard. When the crowd begged Jesus to depart, he got into the boat to leave. For all his power, Jesus does not force himself on those who fear the cost of his healing more than they love the cure . . . or the healer.

A third element to which the interpreter may point is the commission, "Go home to your friends, and tell them how much the Lord has done for you, and how he has had mercy on you" (5:19). This, with the man's obedience to Jesus' command, forms the climax of the account. The note that everyone marveled is linked more directly to the man's proclamation than to the healing itself. Perhaps his obedience in witnessing to his own neighbors, who demonstrably wanted nothing to do with Jesus, is the clearest proof that a miracle had occurred.

If this element is chosen as a focus for interpretation, then Jesus' commission to the healed demoniac can be fruitfully compared to the call of the first disciples (1:16–20). Obedient discipleship may mean different tasks for different persons, and for one person obedience may set a variety of tasks within a single lifetime. For the four, the call to follow Jesus meant leaving boats and nets, father and servants, to go into regions as yet unknown to them. For the demoniac, who wanted to get into the boat and follow Jesus, the Lord's command was "Go home to your friends. . . ." With "friends" like his, this man received the more arduous assignment and an equally important one. His call is the first example of the Gentile mission in Mark. It grounds that mission in the demonstrated authority of Jesus Christ on Gentile turf, and it suggests a pattern for personal witness that is not limited to any time or place. The significance of the text for domestic, home, or national mission is evident.

A Complex Whole

If the initial unity of the story lies in its witness to Jesus' authority over demons even in Gentile territory, the resolution of its complexities may be seen in the pattern of responses to that authority. A final, unified approach to the text would focus attention on the response of the crowds and of the cured man (vv. 14–20), as well as that of the possessed man and his demons (vv. 7, 10). The demons recognize Jesus and oppose him. The crowds fear and reject Jesus without ever having really recognized him. The healed man, perhaps without fully recognizing who Jesus is, yearns to be with him, but in obedience foregoes that privilege and loyally goes to tell his friends what Jesus has done for him. The last is a paradigm for discipleship, all the more powerful because Mark does not identify it as such. The repetition of terms in a pattern of command and obedience (vv. 19, 20) makes the point.

One subtle change in the wording of a repeated term is significant for preachers, not so much when they interpret the text for others as when they listen to it for themselves. "Proclaim" *(kēryssō)* in verse 20 is substituted for "tell" *(apaggellō)* in verse 19. The distinction between "tell" and "proclaim" or "preach" discloses two nuances in the text. Verse 19 underscores the intimate, personal nature of the witness the man was asked to bear while verse 20 points to its broad public dissemination. But the two are synonymous. Surely the simple telling of "how much the Lord has done for you, and how he has had mercy on you" is a powerful proclamation of the gospel. And surely the most effective preaching is done by those who can, and from time to time do, simply tell how much Jesus has done for them.

107

The contrast between the man possessed and the man cured is sharp. Freed of his demons, the man sits quietly, clothed, and in his right mind (5:15). In the midst of a disorderly world alienated from God, Jesus brings order, individuality, integration, and peace to a tormented personality.

Mark 5:21–43
Jairus' Daughter and the Woman with a Hemorrhage

Jesus can handle storms in nature (4:35–41) and demons (5:1–20), but does he care about our more common human woes? What does faith in Jesus mean, and how does it bring wholeness? These and related questions are addressed in the interwoven stories of the raising of Jairus' daughter and the healing of a woman with a hemorrhage. The setting is Jewish ("the other side" from the Decapolis, the synagogue ruler, two mentions of the number twelve in vv. 25, 42). Jesus demonstrates his authority over presumably incurable illness and even over death. His Lordship knows no bounds.

TEXT

The structure of this passage is noteworthy as an example of the technique of insertion, so characteristic of Mark. The story of Jairus' daughter is begun in verses 21–24*a*, interrupted by the story of the woman with a hemorrhage in 24*b*–34, then concluded by the raising of the daughter in 35–43. (For other examples, see 6:7–13, 14–29, 30–32; 11:12–14, 15–19, 20–25; 14:1–2, 3–9, 10–11; 14:53–54, 55–65, 66–72.)

The interruption serves a dramatic purpose by heightening the suspense (Will Jesus get there in time?) and by intensifying the severity of the problem from terminal illness to death itself. It serves an interpretive purpose by elaborating in the story of the woman the meaning of the faith called for in the story of Jairus. Each juxtaposed story illumines the meaning of the other. The significance of Jesus' ministry to a ritually unclean woman is heightened by the fact that he allows it to interrupt his service to a synagogue leader. Conversely, the significance

108

of the raising of Jairus' daughter is deepened by the fact that the girl dies while Jesus is speaking with the woman and must, therefore, be raised from the dead.

Each of the two incidents has the inner structure of a miracle story, but in each case the typical pattern is broken in a significant way. In the story of the woman with a hemorrhage, the healing is complete at verse 29. The problem has been set forth with full attention to the severity of the illness (past all human help), the solution has been reported (her touching Jesus' garment and the cessation of her bleeding), and evidence is given that the cure has occurred ("she felt in her body that she was healed of her disease"). Yet the account is only half done. Thus far the story has read like superstition and magic, for the cure has occurred at the woman's initiative and by touching an object ("If I touch even his garments . . .") she believed to have supernatural power. While not denying the possibility of such a cure, the text will not leave it at that. Jesus insists on personal contact with the healed woman. He stops and looks around to see who has touched his clothing. The woman, who could have slipped away in the crowd, shows integrity and courage. Ostracized as unclean, she comes to him in fear and trembling, falls down before him, and tells him the whole truth. Though Jesus does not rebuke her initial, stealthy approach, it is only after her second, personal encounter that he pronounces the saving word which includes not only health but *shalom*. The most significant part of the story, then, occurs in its uncharacteristic expansion (vv. 30–34).

Similarly, the account of the raising of Jairus' daughter differs from the usual miracle story form in two significant ways. First, the description of the severity of the problem (vv. 23–40) is vastly expanded: The interruption on the road is functionally part of this building tension. The point is that Jesus here confronts death itself. His words (v. 39) are not to be taken in such a way as to suppose that the girl only appeared to be dead. The text intends to affirm that in the presence of Jesus and under his authority death itself, real death, is but a sleep. After reporting the wonder-working word, the narrative ends with concise evidence that the miracle has occurred (v. 42*a*), a note of the amazement of the onlookers (v. 42*b*), and another of Jesus' commands to silence (v. 43*a*; see Introduction, p. 13). Here the story should normally end. Jesus' command "to give her something to eat" is a second departure from the usual miracle story

109

form. It may be considered simply as evidence of the restoration of the girl's life, since ghosts do not eat. That it is detached and placed last, however, suggests a warm and human Jesus for whom this twelve-year-old was not just a "case," but a little girl.

In addition to the structural elements that unite these stories, they are bound together by certain key terms: *faith/ believe* and *save/make well*.

Faith appears at the climax of the healing of the woman with a hemorrhage (v. 34). *Believe* appears at a critical moment in the raising of Jairus' daughter when the father, having just learned of the girl's death, is expected to abandon hope (v. 36). Both stories link the effectiveness of Jesus' power to the faith of persons involved, whether on one's own behalf (the woman) or on behalf of someone else (Jairus' daughter). Each is desperate, but desperation joined to hope and action is not despised.

The Greek verb *(sōzō)* translated "make well" in this passage (vv. 23, 28, 34) is usually translated "save" in the New Testament. In the present passage it retains a nuance of more than physical wholeness, for it stands over against a more common word for physical healing with its cognate term for a healer (vv. 26, 29). Adopting the stronger, literal translation of *sōzō*, we read that Jairus begs Jesus to "come and lay your hands on her, so that she may be saved, and live" (v. 23). The woman's ardent hope is that "If I touch even his garments, I shall be saved" (v. 28). In both cases, the use of "saved" may indicate the person's belief that the illness is past cure except by some miraculous intervention. But "saved" also carries theological overtones in this passage. When the woman's bleeding stops in response to her surreptitious touch, the text says not that she was "saved," but that she was "healed of her disease." Only after she had come in fear and trembling to Jesus, prostrated herself before him, and told him the whole truth, does he say, "Daughter, your faith has saved you." Jesus' further blessing, "Go in peace," speaks of the *shalom* which in the Old Testament is the equivalent of wholeness or salvation, to which he adds, "and be healed (the Greek word for "health" is introduced) of your disease." No longer ritually unclean, she is freed of her fear and reintegrated into the life of the community. Similarly, the "saving" Jairus asked for as a sparing of life (v. 23) turns out to be restoration to life after death (vv. 41–43).

110

SIGNIFICANCE

The raising of Jairus' daughter speaks to persons confronted by death, whether in reflection on our common mortality or because, as in the text, a particular death is expected imminently or has recently occurred. The Old Testament readings which accompany this pericope vary in different lectionaries, but all are related to the theme of death and resurrection. Gen. 4:3–10 portrays in Cain's murder of Abel the sin and death which Christ overcomes by bringing wholeness and life. Wisdom 1 and 2 teach that death comes from the devil, but God wills life.

Lam. 3:22–33 speaks positively of the steadfast love of the Lord which never ceases, of mercies new every morning, "great is thy faithfulness." There may yet be hope, this Old Testament text goes on, because though the Lord may cause grief, he will have compassion, "for he does not willingly afflict or grieve the sons of men." "There may yet be hope" is a fit companion text to Jesus' "Do not fear, only believe" addressed to the distraught father just when it seemed too late for hope. It is never too late for Jesus. His "Fear not," so characteristic of appearances of God in the Old Testament (e.g., the theophanies in Gen. 15:1; 21:17; 26:24; 46:3), represents here as well the divine intervention to save and to give life. Not even after death is it too late to hope.

The command to silence at the end could have little meaning for participants in the event then. How could the crowd of scoffing mourners just outside the door fail to know what Jesus had done? But these words to chosen witnesses are repeated (9:9) to the same three disciples. They are to tell no one what they have seen "until the Son of man should have risen from the dead." Readers today are to understand the raising of Jairus' daughter in the light of Jesus' own resurrection. Beside an open casket or at the moment of our own death we are invited to respond to the words *Talitha, cumi* not with a historical question about a past event but with a thrill of anticipation.

The healing of the woman with a hemorrhage is significant whenever one asks "What does faith mean?" Her words and deeds offer to the interpreter a useful case study of the growth of faith. Interpretation could move in two stages, focusing first on the mixture of desperation and hope, fear and expectation that moved the woman to action and physical healing (vv. 25–

111

29), then on the awe and honesty of her encounter with Jesus himself (vv. 32–34) that culminates in full restoration.

The contemporary significance of this incident is well expressed in one stanza of the hymn, "Immortal Love, Forever Full:"

The healing of his seamless dress
Is by our beds of pain;
We touch him in life's throng and press,
And we are whole again.
    (from John Greenleaf Whittier's poem, "Our Master").

If, with certain of the lectionaries, the interpreter chooses to work with the entire passage, then the lesson or sermon might explore the relationship of faith, healing, salvation, and life. Such a treatment would develop the key terms *faith, make well, save,* and *life,* showing both in the text and out of current experience how these are inextricably interwoven. Such an interpretation is difficult because it treats several abstract themes but useful because it encompasses a wide spectrum of values in this rich text. The text itself avoids abstraction by telling of specific people and their problems. It pulls together the several concepts by its clear focus on Jesus, his warm humanity and his sovereign authority.

A further dimension of this text's significance lies in the way Jesus deals with interruptions. We can imagine the desperate impatience of the father when Jesus stopped to see who had touched him. A little girl is dying, yet Jesus stops to ask a question which even his disciples thought was absurd. Jesus, sensitive to the father's anguish, might have pressed on. He might have been content with the knowledge that the woman was healed, but he took time out for the personal touch. The interruption offers food for thought to busy people in the twentieth century: to physicians pressured by specialization and overwork, to parents harried by the demands of neighborhood children or their own, to professors distracted by students with problems, to preachers interrupted in the middle of sermon preparation. A teacher once remarked, "You know . . . my whole life I have been complaining that my work was constantly interrupted, until I discovered that my interruptions were my work" (Henri J. M. Nouwen, *Reaching Out,* p. 36).

112

Jesus is interrupted repeatedly in Mark: by Peter when he is at prayer (1:35–39), by a leper when he is preaching in the synagogue (1:40–45), by a paralytic when he is "speaking the word" (2:2), and by a sick woman while on his way to heal a dying girl in the present text. The crowd rebukes an importunate blind beggar whose cry for help interrupts Jesus on his way up to Jerusalem on a mission that is literally crucial (10:48). The preacher or teacher could bring these incidents together, focusing on the present one in which the interruption, though secondary as a motif, plays a significant role in the structure of the text. Jesus' divine authority is placed at the service of desperately importunate people. His sensitivity can make us patient, just as his powerful care, working through our faith, can make us whole.

Mark 6:1–6
Rejection by His Own People

Rejection by one's own is a human experience which evokes sharp emotions: anger, outrage, self-pity, hurt. The consistent witness of the New Testament is that Jesus was rejected by his own people. New Testament texts register this fact differently. John 1:11, "He came to his own home, and his own people received him not," carries a note of pathos but serves as a dark background against which to affirm the bright good news that all who believe in him may become children of God. In chapters 9 through 11 of Romans, Paul wrestles with the rejection of Jesus Christ by his own people, the Jews, as a serious theological problem. In Mark 6:1–6 the theme is the same but the treatment is distinct. Jesus' own people in this passage are not the Jews as a whole but friends and relatives in his home town, and the dominant emotion on his part and theirs is astonishment. This particular treatment of the theme is of direct relevance to the church which, in her own eyes and in the eyes of the world, constitutes the family of Jesus Christ.

TEXT

The passage serves as conclusion to part two of the Gospel (3:13—6:6a). Having begun with the attempt of his family to take him home as a deranged person, the section concludes with this account of Jesus' rejection by friends and relatives

113

when finally he did come home. The astonished questions of many who heard him teach in the synagogue at Nazareth ("his own country" or "home town," see 1:9) reflect the contents of the preceding section. "Where did this man get all this? What is the wisdom given to him?" refers not only to his teaching on that particular occasion but also reminds the reader of the great block of teaching in 3:23—4:34. Similarly, "What mighty works are wrought by his hands!" calls to mind the entire preceding series of miracles in 4:35—5:43.

The astonishment of Jesus' home-town audience represents a potentially positive response to these striking demonstrations of authority. When they reflect on who he is, however, in categories familiar to them (the carpenter, son of Mary, brother to the neighbors named), their astonishment turns to rejection. They take offense at him. Literally, "they stumbled" or "were scandalized"; more picturesquely, "they fell foul of him" (NEB) or "found him too much for them" (NAB); more plainly, "they rejected him" (TEV). If the passage begins with the astonishment of his friends and relatives, it ends with the amazement of Jesus: ". . . he marveled because of their unbelief."

Though bracketed by these expressions of amazement, the passage is not a miracle story. Its basic form is that of a biographical story about Jesus in which a memorable saying of the Lord is placed in a brief setting. The usual form is altered here, however, in that the saying (v. 4) is found in the middle of the story rather than at the end. This alteration serves to underscore the shocking contrast between the remarkable words and deeds of Jesus and the unbelief of Jesus' own people. The final, clinching word is, in fact, "unbelief." Because of this unbelief, the narrative is in effect an un-miracle story.

Jesus' saying in 6:4, "A prophet is not without honor, except in his own country, and among his own kin, and in his own house," has direct parallels in Matt. 13:57 and Luke 4:24 and an indirect one at John 4:44. The latter two mention only the prophet's *patris* (country, village); Matthew includes both place and people ("in his own country and in his own house"); only Mark includes a double reference to the prophet's own people ("among his own kin, and in his own house"). The Marcan text underscores, then, the scandal of Jesus' rejection by his own kin, echoing the misunderstanding by his family earlier (3:21, 31–35).

114

A fuller form of this proverb is attributed to Jesus in the Gospel according to Thomas, saying 31:

> Jesus said: "No prophet is acceptable in his village;
>   no physician works cures on those who know him."

This form of the saying incorporates two major thrusts of the Marcan passage: the rejection of a prophet by his own people, the hindrance of overfamiliarity to healing.

The first of these themes, common in prophetic literature, appears in Ezek. 2:1–7, the Old Testament reading which accompanies Mark 6:1–6 in several forms of the lectionary. In this portion of the call narrative of Ezekiel, the prophet is commissioned to go to a rebellious people and to speak the word of God to them, whether they hear or refuse to hear.

The second theme appears in Mark not in the saying of Jesus, but in the concluding report that "he could do no mighty work there, except that he laid his hands upon a few sick people and healed them; and he marveled because of their unbelief" (vv. 5–6). The point is not that Jesus is impotent without our faith, for he did sometimes work wonders without reference to faith (see Introduction, pp. 22–23). On the other hand, the point is that the unbelief of Jesus' own people had a restrictive, dampening effect on his work in their midst. It also marked the end of his work there. Rather than stay to argue with his own people, or to try to convince them by further mighty works, Jesus moved on (see 6:11 below).

"And he went about among the villages teaching" (v. 6b) marks the transition between part two and part three of the Galilean ministry. Brief as it is, it corresponds structurally to 3:7–12 which marks the transition between parts one and two. This brief, transitional note includes bad news and good news. Bad news, in that Jesus' accepts his own family's verdict of rejection and leaves. Good news, in that their rejection neither discourages him nor puts a stop to his work. He continues his ministry of teaching, continuing to offer the gospel of God to whoever has ears to hear.

SIGNIFICANCE

Jesus' rejection by his own people addresses the community of faith today as a warning and a challenge. In the context of the narrative, "his own people" refers to those he grew up

115

with in Nazareth: friends, relatives, and even those members of his nuclear family whose names are listed in the text, for they, too, responded by unbelief (3:21, 31; cf. John 7:5). In the context of the earliest readers, "his own people" was extended to include the Jews whose rejection of their own Messiah was so shocking. In our context today, "his own people" is best understood as the group that formally claims Jesus as its own, claims to be his, and feels some proprietary rights toward him; namely, the church. Does not 3:35 redefine the family of Jesus as those who are his disciples? The text invites reflection on various dimensions of the church's unbelief. In the course of that reflection, it is useful to juxtapose the present text with 3:31–35, on the basis of which we Christians identify ourselves as brothers and sisters of Jesus Christ in the family of God. There, the promise is not to those who take the name of Jesus but to those who do the will of God. Here, the warning is to those who in name are the family of Jesus but who in fact misunderstand and reject him.

The lectionary appoints this text for the seventh Sunday after Pentecost, but it would be appropriate for any time when the community is considering the meaning of church membership, and especially when new members are received. The message for new members is weighty since, in Mark, Jesus' own family consistently fails to believe and follow him (15:40 would be an exception if, as is unlikely, it referred to the mother of Jesus). In the broader context of the canon, however, certain members of the family of Jesus play prominent roles in the church after the resurrection (Acts 1:14; 12:2 with 17; 15:13; 21:18; Gal. 1:19; 2:11–12; cf. James 1:1; Jude 1). It is possible even for Jesus' own unbelieving family to come to faith.

In addressing unbelief in the church, this passage speaks a nuanced word regarding the relationship between faith and wonderful events. On the one hand, because of their unbelief, Jesus could do no mighty work among his own people except to lay his hands on a few sick people and heal them (!). The clear implication is that if they had believed in him Jesus could have done a great deal more. The spiritual climate of a congregation, its sense of expectancy, its openness to the power of God at work through Jesus Christ, will in fact have a great deal to do with how much God's power can accomplish in that particular community. Our unbelief does not render God impotent, but when it is dominant in a congregation its dampening effect on

116

the mighty acts of God in that time and place is evident and sad.

On the other hand, the reason his own people did not believe in Jesus was that they thought they knew him so well. "Is not this the carpenter, and are not his (relatives) here with us?" (v. 3). It was inconceivable to them that God could be at work in the commonplace. To persons who, echoing the Pharisees' demand for signs (8:11), seek God only in the exotic and the marvelous, the text suggests that the one we meet in these Bible stories is one we know well in the familiar patterns of corporate worship, in the common disciplines of the Christian life, and in the lives of ordinary people around us. Yet this "common" one is the Holy One in whom the Kingdom of God draws near.

PART THREE

From the Sending of the Twelve to Misunderstanding by His Disciples

Mark 6:7 — 8:21

Mark 6:7–13
The Sending of the Twelve

Mark delineates the major stages of Jesus' ministry in Galilee by his dealings with an intimate group of disciples: the calling of the first four (1:16–20), the naming of twelve (3:13–19), and now the sending of the Twelve to extend Jesus' own work (see Introduction, pp. 2–4). These whom he has first called, then set apart, have not yet really understood him (4:10, 13, 41). Even less do they share his way of obedience to the will of God (8:32; 9:34; 10:32, 37). They are always on the way to understanding, but up to the end of the Gospel (16:8) they never fully understand. Always they are vowing and trying to follow him, but their repeated failures are more spectacular than their achievements. Yet Jesus does not await full understanding or admirable discipleship on their part before associating them with himself and his mission. Flawed as they are, he sends them out. How does he dare to send them? How do they dare to go? And why does anything good come of so problematical an operation? Their situation is that of the church in every age. What word does the Lord address to us through the sending of the Twelve?

TEXT

This is the Marcan version of the missionary discourse, expanded to a full chapter in Matt. 10 and split into the mission of the Twelve and of the seventy in Luke (9:1–6; 10:1–16). In Mark the foundation of the Christian mission in Jesus' earthly ministry is linked, by the familiar Marcan device of bracketing, with the fate of John the Baptist (see following passage). Christian missionaries are here set in the singular company of John the Baptist and of Jesus himself, extending the line whose mission and destiny they are to share.

In Mark it is not the institutional church that extends the line of apostleship. The one time the word "apostle" appears in Mark is in 6:30 which concludes the sending of the Twelve and links it with its succeeding context. In this case the designation of the Twelve as "the apostles" (sent ones) grows directly out of Jesus' sending them on a particular mission (6:7). Paul insists on his own authority as an apostle, but speaks more of a function than an office and includes in the term far more than the Twelve. In Luke-Acts, the apostles are identified with the Twelve, and apt texts may be found there by those interested in preaching or teaching about mission in the context of ecclesiastical continuity. Here in Mark the emphasis lies on the direct authorization and empowerment of the messengers by Jesus himself: He "gave them authority."

The mission is, however, a communal one. No single charismatic personality is mentioned. They go two by two, to assure the validity of their witness (Deut. 17:6) and to exemplify their participation in a community of faith (see early church practice, e.g., Acts 8:14; 15:36–40). They incarnate the community; but they are agents of Jesus Christ who sends them out, just as he himself has come out, to announce the gospel of God (1:14–15).

He charges them to travel light (6:8–9) in view of the urgency of their mission and as a sign of their reliance on God alone to accomplish it. Their only resource will be the authority they have received from Jesus.

He charges them to accept whatever hospitality is offered them when they enter a village and not to go shopping about for better accommodations. This is a discipline which will keep their minds and energies focused on the accomplishment of their appointed task. 119

He tells them how to respond when people refuse to receive or to hear their message. They are to "shake off the dust that is on (their) feet for a testimony against (or: warning to) them." The gesture was used by pious Jews of that time when they returned to Israel from a Gentile land to symbolize separation from any clinging remnant of ritual defilement. It was a formal disavowal of fellowship which at the same time warned the unreceptive village of the danger they incurred in rejecting these messengers. As Jesus acknowledged with disappointed wonder his rejection by his own people and moved on to other villages (6:6), so his emissaries on this mission are enjoined not to tarry, seeking to persuade those who refuse the message, but to move on.

If their simple dress and penury indicates lowliness like that of Jesus who, without pretention, came "not to be served, but to serve," so their formal warning to those who would not receive them expresses the authority of Jesus himself and the seriousness of rejecting those whom he has empowered and sent.

The passage closes by recording the obedient response of the Twelve ("so they went out"), specifying what they did and noting the positive results. Their program corresponds to the teaching ministry of Jesus (see verse 30: "all that they had done and taught"). It includes preaching (v. 12), exorcizing, and healing (v. 13). The content of their message, "that men should repent," parallels that of John the Baptist. This message and their anointing the sick with oil, like a number of other details in the passage, reflect the practice of the early church.

SIGNIFICANCE

The entire unit doubtless functioned as a missionary manifesto for the Marcan community which expected the early coming of Jesus in glory as the Son of man. In the urgency of the interim, they announced "the gospel of Jesus Christ, the Son of God" by preaching, teaching, exorcizing, and healing in his name, relying on no resource except the authority of Jesus Christ whose power was now known to them through his resurrection from the dead.

What significance, if any, has the text for an institutional church in an affluent culture living two millenia after those first missionaries who anticipated the Lord's return during their generation? Just as the sayings of Jesus incorporated in this text are here shaped and colored by the situation of the evangelist and the community of original readers, so the historical and cultural context of our time will shape our understanding of the Lord's charge and promise, while preserving their basic content and thrust.

The charge to travel light and to accept whatever accommodations are offered is an abiding call to Christians to simplify our lives and to trust God completely. Interpretation could well raise the question of what baggage encumbers the church in her mission, of how concern for physical comfort and dependence on material resources spoils the credibility of missionaries in other lands and in their own country. The text coincides with the demand for a simpler life style imposed on us in our time by growing populations and expectations, coupled with shrinking planetary resources; but the text moves on other grounds. It invites us to a simplicity born not of panic or necessity, but of trust in and obedience to one who for our sake became poor, so that by his poverty we might become rich (II Cor. 8:9). We are invited to choose the authority Christ gives, and, in the security born of that real wealth, gladly to strip ourselves of the clutter of things which would rob us of authority. In this regard, we of the twentieth-century American church need first to repent in order effectively to proclaim repentance to others.

The command to shake the dust off our feet against those who will not receive us or our message is a reminder that we are responsible for our obedience in mission, but not for the response of others or for results. We are not to force ourselves on other people or to assume responsibility for their decision. At the same time, we are to understand, and to try to help them understand, the seriousness of their decision and response. Changing circumstances may dictate the timing of our moving on, of our accepting the fact of a negative response. The principle, however, does not change: It is God's mission, and it is their decision.

The promise of the passage is also permanent. When those first, flawed Twelve went out in obedience, the authority Christ gave them became operative and effective. They preached repentance, they cast out demons, and they healed many that were sick. The power of God became evident through their weakness (II Cor. 12:9–10), for those earthen vessels contained real treasure (II Cor. 4:7). Paul's experience of the truth of this text is paradigmatic for all who will take it seriously. Our re-

121

sources do not accomplish the work of God, nor, finally, does the quality of our own lives. What counts is the power of God conferred on us by Jesus Christ. That is why he dares to send us, why we dare to go, and why remarkable good still comes through the obedience of inadequate messengers.

Mark 6:14–29
The Death of John the Baptist

The account of John the Baptizer's death, with its flashback to a birthday feast in Herod's palace, has all the marks of a good story: anecdotal style, vivid and dramatic details, an adulterous king, a scheming woman, a dancing girl, a violent death. No wonder its historicity is suspect. The generative power of legend is seen when the dancing girl, unnamed in the Gospel accounts, is identified as Salome, known from Josephus' *Antiquities*. The performance is later elaborated into a dance of seven veils and the theme repeated with endless variations, including an opera by Richard Strauss and a Hollywood Western film tied loosely to the frontier town of Salome, Arizona, entitled "Salome, Where She Danced."

TEXT

What is such a story doing in the Gospel of Mark? Its central figure, John, is overshadowed by the flamboyant characters surrounding his death. And even his death is not obviously related to the unfolding story of Jesus into which it is inserted. This final episode concerning John the Baptist would seem to belong better with the account of John's preaching before the ministry of Jesus begins; and that is where Luke 3:19–20 puts it, reduced to a simple notice.

In Mark the story is intentionally linked with the mission of the Twelve. This is evident from the bracketing effect of the report of the apostles' return (6:30) after the story of John's death. (Other examples of bracketing appear in 5:21–43; 11: 12–25; 14:53–72.) Also, verses 14–16 tie Herod's knowledge of Jesus' growing fame to the immediately preceding account of wonders performed by the Twelve on their mission. Here, as at 8:27–29, Mark reports the prevailing judgment that Jesus is a prophet, at the same time indicating the inadequacy of that evaluation.

This point could be made, however, without the elaborate retelling of the story of Herod's birthday party and the death of John the Baptist (used interchangeably with "Baptizer" in Mark; cf. 6:24 and 25). Even the dramatic concern of leaving time for the mission of the Twelve could have been accomplished by a brief note, as in Luke. Why the inclusion of this expansive, secondary account in an otherwise single-minded, fast-moving narrative about Jesus?

The importance of the text lies in the way it links the initial message of the Twelve to the death of John the Baptist, just as the initial preaching of Jesus was linked to John's arrest (1:14). Furthermore, this passage tells the story of John's condemnation to death by Herod Archelaus (a fact confirmed by Josephus) in a way that parallels Jesus' condemnation to death by Pontius Pilate (Mark 15:1–15). Both rulers are favorably impressed by the Jewish religious figures whose lives they therefore would prefer to spare; both wish to please the crowd by a gesture of magnanimity; both are manipulated to carry out the deadly hostility of a third party; both, though seemingly in charge, become unwilling actors in a drama beyond their control.

By means of these parallels, the Marcan account depicts the death of John the Baptist as foreshadowing that of Jesus. This will emerge only after the reading of Mark 15, of course; but when it does, the figure of John will stand forth as the forerunner par excellence. This relationship of John the Baptist to Jesus is important in Mark because of a pattern which includes the disciples as well:

John the Baptist preaches	1:4–8	
and is delivered up		1:14; 6:17–29
Jesus preaches	1:14–15	
and is delivered up		9:31; 10:33; 14—15
The disciples preach	6:7–13	
and are to be delivered up		13:9–13

Norman Perrin, who discerned this pattern (*The New Testament: An Introduction*, p. 144), understands the Gospel of Mark to be an apocalyptic drama from whose perspective Jesus will come as Son of man during the time that Christians are being delivered up and put to death, but before the death of all in the generation in which the Gospel was written. How can such a

123

message be heard by a church still alive and engaged with history two thousand years later?

SIGNIFICANCE

The gospel pattern in which this text is a key element describes a relationship between the bearers of God's message and the powers that be (in this text, the political powers). The relationship is of permanent relevance to the disciples of Jesus Christ.

Christian witnesses should not be surprised when, despite some signs of a positive inclination or response, they are crushed by political and religious power structures. The Gospels never promise us a rose garden, and least of all does the Gospel of Mark nourish any hopes for easy discipleship. In Mark the court of Herod, like the Sanhedrin and Pilate's court, is viewed with the cold eye of realism. The ruler's good intentions are engulfed by ambition, envy, fear, and compromise. God's faithful witness becomes a victim.

One way to read the passage, then, is in terms of success versus significance. Success, as the world measures it, is seen in the court of Herod. There we find the chief of state and his advisers, the military commanders, the leading people of the country; they are the ones who can afford leisure and pleasure; they can get what they want when they want it. John the Baptist, alone in his cell, doomed and helpless to save his life, appears in shocking contrast to the glitter of the successful people of his time. Our minds are perpetually and perversely fascinated by the wealth, power, and intrigue of Herod's court; yet the significance of the text lies in the death of that starkly simple prophet in Herod's prison. The Gospel here invites us to look closely at success . . . and then to choose significance as we follow Jesus on his way.

Mark 6:30–44
The Feeding of the Five Thousand

The feeding of the five thousand is the only miracle of Jesus reported in all four Gospels; its doublet, the feeding of the four thousand, occurs in two. The early church cherished the memory of Jesus' feeding the hungry multitude and told the story in many contexts. Several levels of meaning may be discerned in the Marcan narrative alone. (These notes are adapted from the author's expository article in *Interpretation*, 30:169–73 [April, 1976].)

TEXT

This passage and the feeding of the four thousand (8:1–10) frame the third part of Jesus' Galilean ministry, introduced by the sending of the Twelve (see Introduction, pp. 3–4). Tied together by this structural relationship, both feeding stories are interpreted by the discussion concerning bread (8:14–21).

The text consists of two parts: an extensive setting (6:30–34) and a miracle story (6:35–44). Verse 30 concludes the sending of the Twelve (6:7–13), so the setting of the present passage actually begins with the formula "and he said to them" in verse 31. The entire setting is transitional, pointing back to the mission of the Twelve by its mention of weariness and ahead to the feeding miracle by moving the action to a lonely place.

The feeding narrative includes the elements characteristic of a miracle story: problem (vv. 35–40), solution (vv. 41–42), and evidence that the miracle has occurred (vv. 43–44). The story, reminiscent of the incident about Elisha in II Kings 4:42–44, was probably told originally to glorify the wonder-worker. In Mark it attests the authority of Jesus and points to his relationship to his disciples and the crowd.

SIGNIFICANCE

Of the several levels of meaning and many dimensions of significance which the text offers, three will be explored here as handles by which the text may be taken up for preaching or teaching.

The Good Shepherd

At a climactic point in the setting of the story stand the words, "and he had compassion on them, because they were like sheep without a shepherd" (v. 34). Since Matthew uses this saying in another context, we can assume that it once circulated independently. Its redactional use in Mark serves as a clue to the meaning of the entire feeding scene.

Jesus' compassion for the Twelve is apparent (vv. 30–32). They are called "apostles" in the transitional verse, echoing the

125

fact that they had been "sent out" (v. 7) to cast out demons and heal the sick. On hearing their report on all they had done and taught, Jesus, tired himself, is keenly sensitive to their great need for rest. Compassion . . . shepherd . . . rest. It is already a picture of the good shepherd who cares for the welfare of his undershepherds.

However, Jesus' plans for a retreat "to a lonely place by themselves" were spoiled (vv. 33–34). The crowd saw them leaving and knew . . . "them" (RSV and others) or "where they were going" (JB). Either translation is possible and true to the intent of the story. People ran ahead, so when Jesus got out of the boat he saw a great crowd in the "lonely place." At this point his compassion for the throng, "like sheep without a shepherd," takes precedence over his concern for his disciples or for himself. Bone tired or not, "he began to teach them many things."

Here the Marcan emphasis on teaching is evident. Only Mark includes this term in the report of the Twelve (v. 30). Now, in response to a crowd probably seeking a miracle, Jesus offers teaching. So intent is he on teaching that his disciples have to remind him of the crowd's physical hunger (vv. 35–36). The suggestion by the disciples that Jesus send the crowds away introduces the feeding scene itself.

"You give them something to eat." The disciples protest this apparently insensitive, impossible demand, saying in effect, "We do not have it in us." "Well, what do you have? Go and see," Jesus retorts. When they bring him what they have, he uses it to feed the whole crowd of five thousand (one loaf per thousand) and there are enough leftovers to assure one whole basket full for each of the twelve disciples.

So, far from being insensitive to those around him, Jesus, as the good shepherd, sits the crowd down "on the green grass" and meets their physical need. Led by compassion to teach them (for man shall not live by bread alone), Jesus in compassion gives bread as well. Furthermore, his seemingly insensitive demand of his disciples reveals his confidence in them as undershepherds; and that confidence is undergirded by his power to provide all they need for the task with plenty left over for themselves.

126

Seen in this light, the text is above all a word for weary disciples who find the demands of ministry overwhelming. It confronts us with the sharp demand, "You give them something to eat"; it supports us with the abundant promise of more than enough.

The way the setting is constructed points the reader to this understanding of the text. So does the lectionary, which limits this gospel pericope to 6:30–34 and links it with a prophetic word against self-serving undershepherds (Jer. 23: 1–6).

Blind Disciples

A second approach to the passage takes as its clue the interpretation of the two feedings (8:14–21), which shows how 6:30–44 functions in the unfolding purpose of Mark's Gospel.

The first half of Mark is dominated by the question, "Who is Jesus?" culminating in Peter's eventual but inadequate recognition that Jesus is the Christ (see Introduction, pp. 2–5). Miracle stories, like the feeding of the five thousand, are one prominent means of disclosing, to those who have eyes to see, who Jesus is. All but the demons are blind to these signs, however, and the disciples are part of the pattern of obtuse misunderstanding. In his discussion with the disciples about bread (8:14–21), Jesus indicates clearly that both feedings were signs which the disciples should have understood but did not (see notes on 8:1–21 below). Had the disciples understood the very act in which they participated, they would not, like the Pharisees (8:11–13), have needed a further sign. They, too, were blind; the epiphany was aborted.

By setting forth the first disciples' blindness, this Gospel invites its readers to see. As a call to faith the text invites us to see that the Jesus who multiplied the loaves long ago stands before us now, in this story, and raises a question about his authority over us. This same Jesus, through the story in Mark, invites both the writer and the reader of this commentary to trust his mighty power and abundant blessing. His gracious power exceeds by far that of the miracles of the Old Testament, and it still emanates from Jesus in the very telling of this story. Interpreters participate in the sharing of a word which is bread indeed, for Jesus is present in his teaching. Failure to perceive that and to respond in faith is what Jesus called "the leaven of the Pharisees and of Herod" (see comment on 8:15, pp. 143–44).

127

Bread in the Wilderness

A third approach to the understanding of the text is suggested by the series of verbs ". . . he looked up . . . , and blessed, and broke . . . and gave" (6:41). The strong echo of sacramental language is evident when one sets this beside Mark 14:22, "he took bread, and blessed, and broke it, and gave it to them. . . ." It is highly probable that this connection was made in the tradition earlier than Mark. Mark retains the sacramental allusion, Matthew seems to heighten it slightly (Matt. 14:19), and in John it is elaborated in a lengthy meditation on bread in the wilderness, on Jesus as the bread of life, and on the body and blood of Christ (John 6:25–59). The sacramental emphasis in the feeding story is minimized in Mark, yet it is there.

In addition to the wording (6:41), the expression "lonely place" repeated three times (6:31, 32, 35) and characteristically Marcan, is a clue to the sacramental theme. The *eremos topos* refers to the desert or wilderness, where a great crowd is gathered around God's representative. The bread and fish here seem to echo the manna and quail (flesh from the sea) in the wilderness. The vivid description *symposia symposia epi tō chlōrō chortō* ("by companies upon the green grass") and *prasiai prasiai kata hekaton kai kata pentēkonta* ("in groups, by hundreds and by fifties") could be the trace of an eyewitness account, but it may also be a conscious allusion to the encampment of Israel in the wilderness and to the eschatological change of the wilderness into the land of fertility and rest ("green grass"). The feeding of the five thousand, then, points back to Moses and the manna in the wilderness and forward to the messianic feast at the end-time, while the words describing Jesus' prayer and breaking of bread tie the scene contemporaneously to the Lord's Supper.

Seen in this light, the story becomes a suggested sacrament. It serves to mediate the meaning of the Eucharist for each communicant. It sets us in the presence of Jesus himself ("surely one greater than Moses is here!") as we draw apart to a "lonely place" and yet find ourselves part of a great throng there. That crowd not only includes contemporaries who, like us, seek bread, but also hosts of folk both past and present who constitute the people of God and who anticipate God's future. By mediating this meaning, the story becomes part of the sacrament, its words become living bread that satisfies our deepest hunger and gives us strength to make it home.

128

Choosing a Handle

How should one choose among possible approaches? Here the audience and the occasion become determinative. For a group of ministers or church professionals, the good shepherd theme would be most appropriate. If one is preaching through the lectionary and this text falls on a communion Sunday, the sacramental approach might be best—though if one is freely choosing a text for communion, it might be better to opt for the Johannine treatment of the feeding where the sacramental theme is central. Finally, if one is preaching a series on Mark, or following the lectionary, the blindness of the disciples may be taken up as a theme appropriate for most occasions and central to the intention of this particular Gospel.

Mark 6:45–56
Walking on Water and Healings at Gennesaret

Nowhere is the distinction between reading Mark as history and as gospel more important than here (see Introduction, pp. 17–18). Read as history, this passage has produced through the centuries a kind of good-humored or sometimes cynical disbelief. "Walking on the water" has entered common usage as a metaphor for something utterly incredible. Read as gospel, however, the passage offers strong comfort to fearful disciples.

TEXT

The text includes two distinct units: Jesus walking on the water and the report of many healings at Gennesaret. Both tell of miracles, yet in each case other elements are significant for interpretation.

Walking on Water (6:45–52)

The editorial transition and setting (vv. 45–46) indicates that the destination of the sea-crossing story which will follow is Bethsaida on the northeast shore of Lake Tiberias (the Sea of Galilee or Gennesaret, all synonymous). The actual landing occurs at Gennesaret on the northwestern shore of the lake, about

129

half way between Capernaum and Magdala; not until chapter 8 will we read of the arrival in Bethsaida, where Jesus heals a blind man (v. 22). Though it is possible to explain this anomaly on historical grounds (the storm blew the boat off course?), on literary grounds it appears likely that at an earlier stage in the tradition the healing of the blind man may have followed immediately the present passage but has been moved to its present location to serve as the opening bracket for the discipleship section (8:22—10:52).

The expression "made his disciples get into the boat" (6:45) indicates a firm intention on the part of Jesus to be alone and pray (v. 46; cf. 1:35). This reveals the source of Jesus' authority and power. The order to depart suggests that then and now the Lord sends his disciples into situations of danger where their faith will be tested. It is clear that, as the story opens, the disciples are in trouble and do not know that Jesus is aware of it, while Jesus, though absent and in communion with God, knows their distress and moves to their support.

Seen in this light, 6:46–51 is a fairly typical miracle story, though it is a nature miracle rather than a healing. Several significant elements of these verses, however, belong to another literary type: the setting in the lonely three hours at the end of the night (the fourth watch, 3:00 A.M. to 6:00 A.M.); the miraculous appearance of Jesus, unrecognized, walking on the water; the terror of the disciples confronted by this apparition; the words "It is I" and "have no fear"; and, finally, the verb "pass by." All of these elements are characteristic of the general category "epiphany," that is, a story of the appearance or manifestation of a divine figure.

Hellenistic miracle stories depicted gods and heroes walking on the sea, but this text is tied more specifically to Old Testament pictures of God who "trampled the waves of the sea . . . (who) passes by me, and I see him not . . ." (Job 9:8, 11; cf. Ps. 77:19; Isa. 43:16). It is reminiscent of Old Testament manifestations of God ("theophanies," e.g., Gen. 3; 15; 17; 18; 28; Exod. 3; 19; Josh. 5; I Sam. 3; Isa. 6) in which the divine presence is sometimes at first unrecognized and often inspires awesome fear. The words "It is I" (Greek, *egō eimi*, Mark 6:50) represent the basic revelation of God in the theophany at the burning bush (Exod. 3:14) and in the Johannine discourses of Jesus (John 8:24, 28, 58; 13:19; 18:4–6). "Fear not" is a characteristic reassurance in theophanies (Gen. 15:1) and in divine revelation through angels ("angelophanies," Judg. 6:23; Dan. 10:12; Luke 1:13; 2:10) when the message is a word of promise or salvation. The salvation oracles of Deutero-Isaiah are characterized by the divine *egō eimi* ("It is I," "I am He," Isa. 41:4; 43:10–13) and sometimes by both together (Isa. 41:13).

The note that Jesus "meant to pass by them" (6:48), which is puzzling if this is a miracle story about a rescue from the storm, makes perfectly good sense if this is the story of a divine manifestation (a "christophany," since it is Jesus Christ whose presence is here manifested). In Exodus 33:19 and 22, "pass by" is used to describe God's revelation of his gracious presence when Moses was fearful of going ahead alone with Israel. In an echo of this theophany, when Elijah at Horeb felt utterly alone and feared for his life, God commanded him to come out of his cave and stand on the mount, "and behold the Lord passed by" (I Kings 19:11). So also, when the disciples were struggling against a stormy sea, Jesus meant (literally, "wanted") to pass by to show a divine, saving presence.

The disciples do not perceive this intervention to be gracious at all. They cry out, "It's a ghost." Jesus not only reassures them by words indicating a divine presence, but he also shows his full humanity by getting into the boat with them. The text reports that the wind ceased, but there is no word about the disciples' fears being calmed. Their astonishment is noted as an indication that they still do not understand who Jesus is, neither by virtue of his multiplication of the loaves in the preceding passage nor by the present christophany. This failure to understand is the "hardness of heart" which grieved and angered Jesus when he saw it in the Pharisees in the synagogue (3:5).

Healings at Gennesaret (6:53–56)

In striking contrast to the disciples who, seeing Jesus, did not understand who he was, the people on the shore recognized him immediately and "began to bring sick people on their pallets to any place where they heard he was." To be sure, the crowd recognized him only as a healer; and their desire to touch even the border of his cloak reflects what is now ordinarily called superstition. The text, however, passes no judgment on their action and reports that as many as touched it (or him; both translations are possible) were healed. The final word is *sōzō*, but it can hardly convey here any of its pregnant meaning: "to save."

131

INTERPRETATION

This passage summarizes in very general terms the healings of Jesus in the region of Gennesaret and the continued manifestation of his extraordinary power and authority. The superficial but ready acceptance of Jesus by the crowd (6:53–56) is contrasted with the misunderstanding of the disciples (6:45–52) and with the hostility of the Pharisees and scribes (7:1–23).

SIGNIFICANCE

The passage speaks to fearful disciples in every age. Its message is effective corporately, with the church viewed as the storm-tossed ship on a hostile sea, and individually, with each disciple understanding the buffeting in terms of his or her own experience. It is significant that the element in their situation which struck terror to the hearts of the disciples on the sea was a manifestation of the presence of God.They thought it was a phantom; it was, in fact, their Lord, mighty to save. They did not recognize him; and even after he got into the boat with them, they did not understand. Each group of hearers will know best which manifestations of God's presence among us is most frightening to them. Is it the liberation of the oppressed? Is it some unforeseen development in one's own life that throws the future into question? The Lord "passes by" in various ways.

Jesus goes his way in the world unrecognized and misunderstood in a variety of ways. The self-interested enthusiasm of the crowds in Mark is not unknown in the church today, nor is the hostility of those who reject out of hand Jesus' most compelling claims. But the attitude most specifically addressed by Jesus' walking on the water is fear. The good news is that Jesus sees and knows our troubles and that, like the eternal Father himself, Jesus is strong to save. Disciples who are gripped by fear are those who do not understand his epiphanies. His presence with us is elusive, and we know him sometimes most profoundly as "a great wind of light blowing, and sore pain" (Samuel Terrien, *The Elusive Presence*, p. 95).

The interpreter who wishes to develop the link between the theophany to Elijah at Horeb and the appearance of Jesus to his disciples on the sea may note that the two are brought together in the common lectionary for the twelfth Sunday after Pentecost, year A, based on the parallel passage in Matt. 14: 22–33.

132

Mark 7:1–23
Controversy About Tradition

This passage, in which Jesus dismisses all Jewish dietary regulations, constitutes a major block of controversy with the religious leaders of his time (see also 2:1—3:6 and 11:27—12:34). Jesus' adversaries did not agree with his teaching about what is clean and unclean in the sight of God, nor have the strictest forms of Judaism to this day. Even Jesus' own disciples did not understand his teaching (v. 17), and that remains true of some parts of the church today.

TEXT

This is Jesus' final encounter with his Jewish adversaries in Galilee. Their opposition and the misunderstanding of the disciples stand in contrast to the first glimmers of faith in a Gentile woman (7:24–30) and the further spread of the good news of Jesus in the Gentile territory of the Decapolis (7:31–37). In the life of the early church, a more liberal view of the law (expressed in 7:1–23) characterized the Gentile mission (foreshadowed in 7:24–37).

The inner structure of the text, determined by introductory expressions (vv. 1, 9, 14, 17), can be represented by the following outline. Verse 16, a scribal gloss, is omitted from consideration.

Word of God versus Human Tradition	7:1–23
Controversy with Pharisees and scribes	1–13
Opponents' question: unwashed hands	1–8
Jesus' counter-attack: Word of God versus human tradition	9–13
Jesus' teaching on defilement	14–23
Public teaching: ritual versus real defilement	14–15
Private explanation to disciples	17–23

The text includes two foci: defilement (7:15) and tradition (7:9, 13). The question the Pharisees and scribes asked about the disciples' behavior includes both concerns (7:5). Jesus' answer

133

draws attention to the relationship of Scripture and tradition as the underlying issue. The question of defilement, a specific example of this issue, is addressed by reference to two cases: handwashing and kosher laws. Both involve taboos related to eating.

The practices which Mark (and Mark only) details (7:3–4) were intended to serve as a "fence around the law" to preserve its function by protecting the law from careless or inadvertent violations. The present passage distinguishes carefully between the law and the fence around it.

The terms *tradition of the elders, tradition of men,* and *your tradition,* like *precepts of men* in the Isaiah quotation (7:7), are all used synonymously to refer to the body of case law built up to show how the Torah was to be put into practice. By the time of Jesus the interpretive tradition, designed to protect the law, had become a heavy burden (cf. Matt. 23:4). Jesus opposes this "tradition of the elders."

On the other hand, Jesus makes positive use of the terms *commandment of God* and *word of God,* referring to the laws in the Hebrew Bible. As a specific example, Jesus cites the law on honoring father and mother, quoting Exod. 20:12 and 21:17 (or parallels). Far from attacking the law, in this passage Jesus affirms the word of God which comes to expression in the law and attacks the would-be defenders of the law for subverting it.

In upholding the "commandment of God" over against "your (our?) tradition," Jesus does not abolish the concept of "defilement" or the "clean/unclean" distinction. He does, however, reinterpret the latter in a way that picks up the prophetic and ethical understanding of uncleanness and rejects the ritual and Pharisaic understanding of it. Jesus is depicted as simply sweeping away Jewish dietary laws (7:15), while he affirms ethical values (7:21–22). The criterion is fidelity to the intent of God's commandment mediated through Scripture.

Mark 7:1–23 is properly viewed in the wider perspective of the early church's struggle with Jewish law. In that struggle, Matthew's picture of Jesus as the authoritative interpreter of the law (e.g., Matt. 5:17–48) and James's ethics grounded in "the perfect law, the law of liberty" (James 1:25, part of the epistle lesson accompanying Mark 7:1–23 in the lectionary) stand to the far right. Paul's repudiation of law as a basis for either salvation or ethics (e.g., Gal. 3—5) stands to the far left. In between stands Mark's picture of Jesus, who upholds the law in its fundamental intention and in its Scriptural expression, while denouncing the "fence" around it in the form of secondary regulations and traditions. Acts 10—11 (the Cornelius episode) takes the same position as the Marcan Jesus, while Acts 15 (the Jerusalem council) represents a compromise on kosher law.

In the spectrum of New Testament positions relative to the law, Mark 7:1–23 presents an understanding of the teaching of Jesus which can bring clarity to our confusion and offer guidance to a church which often, like its surrounding culture, is morally adrift.

SIGNIFICANCE

The significance of this text, in which Jesus opposes the traditions of the elders and upholds the commandment of God, may be seen differently according to the situation and needs of the particular community gathered around it.

Where lifestyle is an issue, the text may be entered through the question of Jesus' opponents, "Why do your disciples not live (literally, walk) according to the tradition of the elders?" Their question is about lifestyle, a characteristic way of living. While Jesus views as unimportant the elements they were concerned about, he attaches great importance to one's style of life. We are called to examine our lifestyle lest through it we "leave the commandment of God" (v. 8) and make "void the word of God" (v. 13).

Where responsibility for aging parents is a problem, interpretation might focus on the example Jesus uses for a commandment of God that is nullified by human tradition (vv. 9–13). Religious obligation is seldom the excuse used for neglect of parents in our time, but our cultural traditions provide other means of avoidance. Jesus' controversy with his opponents can provide an apt context within which contemporary disciples seek to understand the implications of "honor" and of "parents."

The formalism attacked in the text may be a live issue in many churches. Wherever people are greatly concerned about outward forms, Jesus' word to his disciples (v. 18) still stings: "Are you also without understanding?" The examples of formalism in the text are handwashing and kosher laws. Analogous forms assiduously observed among Christians today may include patterns of language (e.g., a particular prayer book), social custom (e.g., what to wear to church), or ritual acts (e.g., a mode

135

of baptism). Jesus' two-part answer to his opponents levels two charges against formalism: It majors in minors (vv. 6–8) and it masks avoidance of the word of God (vv. 9–13).

In other situations asceticism may be the appropriate focus of interpretation. When he says there is nothing outside us which by going into us can defile us (v. 15), Jesus challenges whatever taboos we observe in order to make ourselves fit for God. This interpretation would concentrate on verses 14–23, emphasizing the priority of what comes from within.

Some congregations struggle with tensions between traditionalists and innovators. This text is hard on traditionalists (the Pharisees and scribes), but it does not promote innovation. Calvin rightly warned that innovation can be the source of many stultifying traditions. He wrote of the Catholic Church of his time, "They are always inventing new forms of worship" (*Harmony* II, 156). Yet the traditionalism of Calvin's heirs is at least as sterile as the formalism he attacked and as capable of producing innovations that quickly become empty traditions.

If innovation is not always good, neither is tradition always bad. Tradition *(paradosis)* is used elsewhere in the New Testament to refer to the basic teachings of the gospel (e.g., I Cor. 11:2; 15:3; II Thess. 2:15; 3:6). All interpreters of Scripture are guardians and passers-on of tradition. Jesus' attack in the present text is against *"your* tradition which you hand on" (7:13, TEV). The problem addressed is tradition alienated from the word of God. By emphasizing the secondary place of human traditions and the primary place of the commandment of God, this text calls us beyond arguments over what is old and what is new to a concern for what is vital.

Finally, in the very first verse of the passage, we read that Jesus' adversaries "had come from Jerusalem." Here Jerusalem, the center of opposition to Jesus, symbolizes the defense of customary ways of doing things, concern for appearances, and censorious inquiry into peccadilloes, combined with indifference to—even complicity in—substantive sins. This is not a particularly Jewish syndrome. In every religious community there are some who "come from Jerusalem." This syndrome is not limited to certain persons, either. "Jerusalem" tendencies lurk in each of us. Mark 7:1–23 invites every reader to ask if there are times when he or she is "coming from Jerusalem."

Mark 7:24–37
The Syrophoenician Woman and the Deaf-mute of the Decapolis

If in the preceding passage Jesus "declared all foods clean" (7:19), in these stories he declares all persons clean, whether a Gentile woman in a pagan city or a man of indeterminate race in the unclean territory of the Decapolis. The stories are two examples of the same principle: Both advance Jesus' repudiation of traditional taboos.

TEXT

This text includes two units. The first (7:24–30) is set in the region of Tyre and is about a Gentile woman and her demon-possessed daughter; the second (7:31–37) is set in the Gentile territory of the Decapolis and is about a deaf man with a speech impediment. Since the interpreter may choose to address only one of the two incidents, it will be appropriate to note certain particularities of each and then see how they are linked.

The Syrophoenician Woman (7:24–30)

In the story of the Syrophoenician woman, the accent falls on the question of a mission to the Gentiles. Several observations bear out this judgment:

1. The woman who shares the stage with Jesus was "a Greek, a Syrophoenician by birth" (v. 26); that is, a Gentile. It is really superfluous to give this information, since the story is set in Tyre, a large Phoenician port city of Syria. The detail could conceivably reflect a primitive setting in Galilee, where this lineage would be noteworthy. However that may be, its persistence in the present text, like the textual variant "and Sidon" in some manuscripts (v. 24), underscores the fact that Jesus here encounters a Gentile.

2. The structure of this miracle story, an exorcism, has been considerably expanded in its first movement (presentation of the problem) to include a conversation about the propriety of Jesus' healing a Gentile (vv. 26–28), while the effective word of

137

Jesus has been reduced to a simple announcement of the cure. The response of amazement, frequent in Mark, is omitted altogether. The focus is not on the exorcism as such but on the Gentile question.

3. Jesus' initial rebuff of the woman, an aphorism (v. 27) for which no clear precedent can be found in Jewish sources, affirms the priority of the Jews in Jesus' mission. The woman's response (v. 28) allows that priority to stand but persistently asks for attention to Gentiles also. Jesus' granting of her request (v. 29) approves the woman's attitude and provides for the early church a warrant for its mission to the Gentiles by grounding that mission in the earthly ministry of Jesus himself.

The Deaf-mute of the Decapolis (7:31–37)

In the story of the deaf-mute of the Decapolis, the accent falls on the eschatological significance of Jesus. This unit is the last of a sequence of miracle stories concerned with the question of Jesus' identity. It leads up to the christological affirmation of Peter (8:29), subsequently corrected in 8:33 and in the remainder of the Gospel. Again, several observations may be cited to support this judgment:

1. This miracle story is expanded precisely where the preceding one is most brief. The circumstantial description of Jesus' healing gestures (thrusting fingers into ears, touching tongue with saliva, casting eyes heavenward and sighing) and the mysterious healing word (*ephphatha,* in Aramaic) all heighten the sense of the miraculous. The crowd's expression of astonishment (v. 37) points to an appreciation of Jesus himself as the appropriate response to this miracle.

2. The word used to describe the man's infirmity (v. 32), *mogilalon,* appears only twice in the entire Greek Bible: here and at Isa. 35:6, a verse to which verse 37 may also point. (Incidentally, the word means that the man spoke indistinctly, not that he could not speak at all. "Deaf-*mute*" is therefore a convenient but not altogether accurate description of the man.) Significantly, the reference in Isa. 35 is to the glorious fulfillment of God's saving purpose in the end-time. "He has done all things well," followed by a reference to Isa. 35:5–6a, is therefore far more than a character reference for a good man. The Marcan text will suggest to sensitive readers and hearers that in Jesus the eschatological reign of God is present.

3. This perception is not yet meant to be public knowledge.

138

The charge to tell no one (v. 36), so characteristic of Mark's Gospel, qualifies this as a hidden revelation. The reader is meant to understand more than do the participants in the story. Both reader and participants, however, will need the further unfolding of the Gospel story to understand the full import of the veiled christological affirmation in verse 37.

Passage as a Whole

The stories of the Syrophoenician woman and of the deaf-mute of the Decapolis, though quite distinct, may nevertheless appropriately be treated together. The text links them in at least three ways.

First, both follow upon the controversy about clean and unclean (7:1–23) in such a way as to illustrate and exemplify the teaching of Jesus.

Second, the pair of stories is bracketed by references to the so-called "messianic secret" (see Introduction, pp. 12–13). The second verse from the beginning points out that Jesus tried not to let his presence in Tyre be known, but "he could not be hid." The second verse from the end reports that although he urged the crowd to keep silent about the healing of the deaf-mute, "the more he charged them, the more zealously they proclaimed (literally, 'preached') it." Both stories affirm that there is no hiding the revelation of Jesus, though it can be perceived only by faith.

Third, the concluding accolade, "He has done all things well . . . ," though it refers primarily to the healing of the deaf-mute, serves also as a conclusion to both stories and may indeed have been the "punch line" for an earlier, larger collection of miracle stories. We are to understand all the miracles of Jesus as witness to the extraordinary power at work in him and as evidence that in him the Kingdom of God is at hand. Both the inclusion of the Gentiles and fulfillment of eschatological promises are signs of the presence of this kingdom.

SIGNIFICANCE

The interpreter who chooses to take up only the first of these two units may focus upon the attitude of the Syrophoenician woman as a model of faith, even though the word "faith" is not used in the text. Her combination of submission, persistence, and expectant trust exemplifies dimensions of faith which are apt for the instruction and nurture of a community under-

139

going a faith crisis. Such an approach should be used with caution, since it easily slips into moralizing on the side of the hearers, while on the side of the text it makes a point which, though explicit in Matt. 15:28, is only implicit and secondary in Mark.

A focus on mission would be more clearly in line with the thrust of the Marcan text. The first story urges the validity of mission to foreigners, the second to areas near at hand but disdained. Both point to the universal scope of God's gracious action in Christ. Both are examples of elements within the gospel which defy any limitation of it, pushing Christians of every age to faithful proclamation and compassionate service in every place and to all people, regardless of results. The text does not state that either of these persons followed Jesus; but the fact that Jesus met their needs and so revealed his own glory is absolutely clear.

Finally, both stories are about Jesus. They tell of the irrepressability of the reign and power of God in him. The lectionaries which link Mark 7:31–37 with Isa. 35:1–6 on the sixteenth Sunday after Pentecost point the interpreter toward this significance. Contemplating nature, a Christian poet wrote:

> The world is charged with the grandeur of God.
>   It will flame out, like shining from shook foil;
>   It gathers to a greatness, like the ooze of oil
> Crushed. . . .

What Gerard Manley Hopkins' sonnet, *God's Grandeur*, affirms of God's splendor in the world, Mark 7:24–37 affirms of God's power in Jesus. It is the sign of God's ultimate, glorious purpose for this world. It flames out in the most unlikely places. It gathers to a greatness in the experience of this Syrophoenician woman, that deaf-mute man of the Decapolis, and who knows what other hearers in the presence of this word.

Mark 8:1–21
The Feeding of the Four Thousand: "Do You Not Yet Understand?"

140

The above question, which refers to the confusion of Jesus' original disciples, may also apply to the consternation of the reader confronted by this text. Why does the Gospel report this second feeding story when the first one (6:35–44) was more impressive? Why is the incident about the Pharisees seeking a sign inserted here when the story would read more smoothly if verses 11–13 and 15 were left out? And why does the text have Jesus raise a question for the disciples that remains a riddle for the reader? Firm answers are elusive, but certain clues to understanding will be observed in the text, and several options will be offered for interpreting its significance.

TEXT

The structure and setting of this composite block of material are the first clues to its understanding. As paragraph divisions in the RSV indicate, the passage includes three smaller units as follows:

The feeding of the four thousand (bread)	1–10
On seeking a sign ("leaven of the Pharisees," 15)	11–13
The discussion about bread	14–21

Each of the above sub-units occurs in different contexts in the other Gospels, with different persons involved. The three are held together in Mark, however, by the question in verse 20 about the feeding story (vv. 1–10), by the close linkage of "the leaven of the Pharisees" (v. 15) to the Pharisees' demand for a sign (vv. 11–13), and by the common theme of bread-leaven-bread in a pattern of insertion characteristic of Mark.

This entire unit serves as the conclusion to Part Three of the Gospel (from the sending of the Twelve to misunderstanding by his disciples) and to the Galilean ministry as a whole (1:14 —8:21). It depicts another spectacular display of Jesus' power and records two inappropriate responses to him, that of the Pharisees and that of his own disciples.

The Feeding of the Four Thousand (8:1–10)

This narrative, like the feeding of the five thousand (6: 35–44), is a classical example of the literary type *miracle story*. The form of the text argues against any interpretation which would seek to minimize the miraculous element. The miracle calls not for explanation but for response.

141

"How can one feed these men with bread here in the desert?" (v. 4) is a remarkable question from those who had recently participated in the miraculous feeding of five thousand people in another desert place. Some commentators find such dullness incredible and explain that these are varying accounts of the same incident. The Gospel narrative, however, presupposes that these are different, successive incidents, for the disciples will be asked to remember each of them in detail (8:18*b* –21). The incredible dullness of the disciples is precisely the point the feeding of the four thousand intends to make in its present context.

Although the one explicit geographical reference, Dalmanutha (v. 10), is textually uncertain and historically unknown, placement of the narrative immediately after incidents in the region of Tyre and Sidon and in the Decapolis points to a Gentile setting for the present feeding. This arrangement may suggest that by the feeding of the four thousand in Gentile territory Jesus himself authenticated the Gentile mission in which the Marcan community was engaged.

The eucharistic element observed in the feeding of the five thousand (see notes on 6:30–44 above) is heightened in the present text by the use of "having given thanks" (*eucharistēsas,* v. 6) before the distribution of the bread. The same term appears in Paul's account of the eucharistic tradition (I Cor. 11:24). Christians from the first century onward have understood feedings and Eucharist alike as acted parables of the way Jesus sustains his people (see also John 6:52–59).

On Seeking a Sign (8:11–13)

The Pharisees who ask Jesus for a sign may not have observed the feeding of the four thousand, since the scene has shifted (v. 10). However, the Pharisees have repeatedly been confronted by his mighty works (2:1—3:6), and yet they ask for a sign.

Nowhere else in this Gospel are "sign" (*sēmeion*) and "mighty work" (*dynamis*) brought together. The only other uses of "sign" in Mark (exclusive of the ones in the long ending, 16:17, 20) refer to the end-time (13:4, 22). The "sign from heaven" demanded here by the Pharisees probably refers to some incontrovertible proof that Jesus is the Messianic figure who will usher in the end-time. Jesus' authoritative words and deeds (his "mighty works") are not "signs" in the sense of incontrovertible proof; yet, for those who have eyes to see and ears to hear, they are sufficient evidence that he is God's anointed one.

142

The Pharisees come "to argue with him" and "to test him." They seek a sign not for enlightenment but because they think they already know what God must do. They want to measure Jesus against their preconceived criteria.

Instead of giving a sign, Jesus responds with a sigh (v. 12), a non-verbal way of saying, "If only . . . ," an expression of weary sadness and frustration. Jesus' verbal response is a categorical refusal of their request, reinforced by a formula of solemn assertion: "Truly, I say to you. . . ." This refusal is expressed in the form of a semitic oath. Translated literally, the oath reads, "If a sign shall be given to this generation. . . ." Its form is like Ruth's oath to Naomi: "May the LORD do so to me and more also if even death parts me from you." Its function, however, may be to express an anger like that in Mark 3:5 (also 1:41, NEB). In sadness, and in anger at their stubborn blindness, Jesus refuses their demand and leaves them (v. 13).

The Discussion About Bread (8:14–21)

These verses, with which the public manifestation of Jesus in Galilee is brought to a close, have two major emphases: the leaven of the Pharisees and the misunderstanding of the disciples. The first points back to verses 11–13 and the second to verses 1–10. The word about leaven (v. 15) seems to be an independent saying (see Luke 12:1) incorporated into the discussion about bread in order to interpret the Pharisees' demand for a sign (vv. 11–13) and to relate it by means of verse 16 to the theme of misunderstanding (vv. 17*b*–21).

The text does not specify what "the leaven of the Pharisees and the leaven of Herod" is. This ambiguity is resolved in the Synoptic parallels, each of which interprets Mark differently. Matt. 16:12 explains that "he did not tell them to beware of the leaven of bread, but of the teaching of the Pharisees and Sadducees." Luke 12:1 reads, "Beware of the leaven of the Pharisees which is hypocrisy." In the Marcan context, however, the meaning is related neither to false teaching nor hypocrisy, but to misunderstanding.

By failing to explain "the leaven of the Pharisees and the leaven of Herod" in specific terms, Mark involves readers in a search of the text and of their own souls. "Leaven" here has its usual Jewish sense of something evil (see Lev. 2:11; I Cor. 5:6–8; Gal. 5:9). The reader is invited to ponder what that evil might be and to take seriously Jesus' warning against it.

143

In light of the immediately preceding demand for a sign, "the leaven of the Pharisees" appears to mean the Pharisees' failure to respond in repentance and faith to the message of Jesus (1:14–15). Similarly, "the leaven of Herod" refers to Herod's failure to respond in repentance and faith to the message of John the Baptist (6:14–29). This failure had led the Pharisees and the Herodians to active hostility against Jesus (3:6), a hostility which underlies their demand for a sign (8:11–13). Theirs is the blindness of willful misunderstanding.

The misunderstanding of the disciples is underscored by Jesus' repeated question, "Do you not yet understand?" (vv. 17b, 21), which brackets the final part of the passage.

The introductory rhetorical question, "Why do you discuss the fact that you have no bread?" (v. 17b), could perhaps be Jesus' rebuke of the disciples' not-so-subtle demand for a sign ("We have no bread," v. 16) or perhaps his rebuke of their trivial concern for physical bread when they had the bread of life in the boat with them. However, a more obvious interpretation is probably intended: The disciples have taken Jesus' warning about the leaven of the Pharisees literally but not seriously. Like the Pharisees, they fail to discern who Jesus is and what he is about. Their dullness, like the Pharisees' rejection, is a form of blindness. "Having eyes do you not see?" (Jer. 5:21; see also Introduction, pp. 4, 14–16, and notes on Mark 8:22–26 below.) Their blindness is not that of willful rejection (like the Pharisees), but of insensitivity.

The meaning of the numbers in verses 18b–21 continues to perplex interpreters: "Remember? Five loaves . . . five thousand . . . twelve baskets *(kophinous)* left over; seven loaves . . . four thousand . . . seven baskets *(spuridōn)* left over." The disciples' memory corresponds to the written text of the preceding accounts in Mark, even to preserving the distinctive word for "basket" in each text. But the disciples have not understood what they remember. What is the reader expected to understand that the disciples did not?

Patristic commentators such as Augustine and Bede interpreted the numbers allegorically so that the first feeding represented the Old Testament (five loaves and five thousand symbolizing the five books of Moses) and the second represented the New (seven loaves for seven graces of the Holy Spirit, four thousand for the church founded on four Gospels). In the twentieth century commentators have referred the num-

144

bers to Jews (twelve baskets for twelve tribes) and Gentiles (seven baskets for completion of all humankind, or seventy Gentile nations).

On the other hand, one literary critic (Frank Kermode, *The Genesis of Secrecy*, pp. 24, 46) has suggested that these enigmatic numbers are deliberately introduced to set the mind wrestling with a riddle whose answer lies in quite another direction. He uses as a reverse analogy the riddle that asks how you fit five elephants into a Volkswagen. The riddle hints at a problem of size, while the answer has only to do with number: two in the front and three in the back. Mark 8:17*b*–21 hints at a problem of number, while its meaning(s) may lie elsewhere.

Most contemporary critics, rejecting both alleogrization and mystification, think the numbers intend to show Jesus' power to meet abundantly every need, a truth so evident to the reader that the disciples' misunderstanding of who Jesus is and what he can do stands out in bold relief. One can hold this view and at the same time see the numbers as an enigma forcing readers to recognize that we, like the first disciples, do not fully understand.

SIGNIFICANCE

Several meanings noted in the foregoing exposition of the text are significant for the community of faith today. The feeding of the four thousand, with its explicit use of the verb *eucharistein* ("give thanks," v. 6), lends itself to a communion meditation which might also explore the possible symbolic significance of "one loaf with them in the boat" (v. 14).

Alternatively, interpretation could focus on clues that 6:35–44 is a Jewish feeding story while 8:1–10 is a Gentile feeding story. The significance of this Gentile Eucharist is that the gospel (and the church) is for all kinds of people. Jesus nurtures and sustains all who come to him, not just in spite of but because of the long way from which some of them have come.

The discussion about bread (v. 16) challenges significantly our tendency to trivialize discipleship by preoccupation with the material trappings of church life rather than the inner essence of faith, with the equipment in the church kitchen more than the relation of church officers and members to Jesus Christ, with the literal meaning of Scripture more than with response to its intention.

While all these meanings are present in the text and may

145

be significant in a given situation, the text itself draws attention to the misunderstanding of the disciples and of the Pharisees and Herod. "Do you not yet understand" (vv. 17, 21) is the last and climactic word not only of this unit but of the entire first half of Mark (the Galilean ministry). Two kinds of misunderstanding are challenged. The Pharisees respond to Jesus with judgmental hostility. Jesus, denying their demand for a sign, in anger and in sorrow leaves them. The disciples respond with friendly dullness. Jesus does not give up on them, but his series of questions to them shows dismay at their misunderstanding and his desire to lead them to understanding.

The interpreter, taking seriously the implication that the disciples should have understood far more than they did on the basis of what they had seen and heard, could evoke reflection on evidences of Jesus' presence and power in our own lives, to which we are insensitive or unresponsive. The point of verses 18–21 would turn not on some meaning hidden in numbers but on the failure of the disciples to draw any conclusions about Jesus from what they had plainly seen and could accurately remember. Further, Jesus' warning his disciples against the "leaven of the Pharisees" suggests that unperceptiveness can easily slip into rejection,for both are kinds of blindness.

If, on the one hand, the disciples should have understood more than they did on the basis of their previous experience, on the other hand they cannot really understand who Jesus is till they have followed him from Caesarea Philippi (8:27) to Jerusalem (11:11), the cross (15:33–39), and an empty tomb (16:1–8). A certain open-endedness in our understanding of who Jesus is and what it means to follow him is therefore appropriate. For if, in one sense, Jesus' final question functions as a statement reproaching the disciples' present incomprehension, in a deeper sense it retains the interrogative force of an invitation. "Do you not yet understand?" is an invitation to read on in the Gospel, and in our lives to stay with Jesus till we do understand.

PART FOUR

PART FOUR

Discipleship: The Way of Jesus

Mark 8:22 – 10:52

Mark 8:22–26
The Blind Man of Bethsaida

For once, in Mark, Jesus' attempt to heal someone seems not to be immediately successful. The need for a second touch may explain why Matthew and Luke leave this story out. Yet this two-stage movement is the very point of the story in Mark, tying it closely to its context and pointing most clearly to its significance for disciples today.

TEXT

The text is brief. In only five verses it presents a miracle story typical in every way except that the cure and the evidence of it are doubled. In the initial healing gesture, Jesus uses saliva (common both as a home remedy and in Hellenistic miracle stories) by spitting on the man's eyes and laying his hands upon him—doubtless on his eyes, in light of the "again" in verse 25. Instead of a healing command, Jesus asks a question which gives the man occasion to attest a partial cure, thereby preparing for the second stage of the healing. Jesus lays his hands on the man's eyes again. The man "looked intently," or "saw properly" (either translation is possible for *dieblepsen;* the AV "made him look up" is based on a secondary reading in the Greek text); then the text gives evidence of a complete cure. The account closes with Jesus' "Do not even enter the village," which certain manuscripts, followed by the AV and NEB, correctly interpret as a command to silence. There is no expression of amazement. All the emphasis is on the repeated touch of Jesus and on the man's seeing.

"Seeing" in this passage moves at two levels of meaning. At the first level, seeing refers to physical vision. The passage demonstrates that Jesus has power to heal the blind. His authoritative gesture restoring sight to this blind man is reminiscent of salvation oracles in Isaiah (29:18; 35:5; 61:1 Grk.) which specify the opening of blind eyes as one of the features of the coming time of deliverance. This subtle clue to the meaning of Jesus' ministry is made more explicit in Luke 4:18, when Jesus in the Nazareth synagogue announces the fulfillment of Isa. 61:1, and in Luke 7:22, where the restoring of sight to the blind is the very first evidence by which John the Baptist should recognize who Jesus is.

At a second, symbolic level, seeing refers to inner perception or understanding. This level of meaning becomes evident when the text is considered in its context. In verses 14–21, when the disciples discuss the fact that they have no bread, Jesus rebukes them by asking, "Do you not yet perceive or understand? . . . Having eyes do you not see . . . ?" And at the very end of that passage he adds, "Do you not yet understand?" This passage introduces the section on discipleship, which is closed by another restoration of sight story (10:46–52). (See Introduction, pp. 4–5, and notes on 6:52, p. 131.)

If the immediately preceding context is the blindness of the disciples, the context immediately following depicts Peter who finally sees, but sees imperfectly. He will need a second, harsh touch from Jesus to rectify his hazy view of who Christ is and what he, and therefore his disciples, must do. Jesus' teaching about discipleship in connection with the three passion predictions throughout this section (8:22—10:52) represent his "laying his hands on (his disciples) again," as does his actual passion, death, and resurrection in chapters 14—16. The positioning of this story in the Gospel suggests that what the reader has been led to see of Jesus up to this point, namely his wonder-working power, his authority even to forgive sins, and his enormous popularity with the crowds, represents only a partial vision of who he is. The reader, too, is invited to look again and more intently as the story of Jesus unfolds from this point forward.

148

SIGNIFICANCE

This narrative can speak with power to persons who are unsighted or whose vision is seriously impaired. While it should not be construed to suggest that Jesus will heal every such person who is brought to him, it does affirm Jesus' special concern for the blind. Furthermore, there is a certain analogy between the experience of this blind man in Bethsaida and that of persons in our own time, who, under any circumstances, have their eyesight restored. The healing sometimes occurs by stages. At Bethsaida Jesus first restored the man's sight and then enabled him to see clearly; that is, to understand what was seen. By identifying with him, we can experience the recovery of physical sight as a miracle of grace.

At the deeper level of inner understanding the interpretive move from then to now may touch a larger number of disciples. The interpreter can show how, thanks to some contact with Jesus, we see him, other persons, and the world around us in a new way. The interpretation could encompass the context as well as the narrative itself, considering how we may be more like Peter, who thought he saw clearly, than like the blind man who knew he did not.

Inclusion of the context is especially important if the interpreter is led to speak of "the second touch." This expression is, in our time, associated with spiritual blessings and warm inner experiences. The entire section in Mark to which this passage provides a transition and introduction (8:22—10:52) shows Jesus confronting his disciples with a Christ who must be rejected, suffer, and die, and only then will be raised. He speaks of discipleship which consists not of power and glory but of lowly service and loss of life. Jesus' way leads to a cross at Skull Place, not to chief seats by the throne. The goal of "the second touch" is really to see these things and therefore to see *all* things clearly: God, ourselves, other persons, and the tragic dimension of life. The interpreter may wish to reflect on how painful such a second touch may be for comfortable disciples in a complacent church and an affluent society. It is as though Christ spits in our eyes. Yet to see clearly is one effect of Jesus' healing touch, and this text dares to affirm that he is powerful enough to make us see. The interpreter's task is that of the anonymous ones who brought the blind man to Jesus and begged for his touch.

149

Mark 8:27—9:1
Caesarea Philippi: First Passion Prediction

What does it mean to believe that Jesus is the Christ? What difference does or should it make to be a Christian? Can I be identified as a follower of the Son of man? The fundamental nature of these questions, treated in the present passage, suggests the importance of the place this text occupies in the Gospel of Mark and in the Christian life.

TEXT

The place of the text in the Gospel may be viewed in two ways. First, it is the geographical and theological fulcrum at the mid-point of Mark (see Introduction, p. 4). The public ministry in Galilee is essentially finished; from this point onward the action is directed toward Jerusalem. The question of Jesus' identity is here answered by Peter's confession that he is the Christ (v. 29), and immediately the theological focus shifts to what it means for Jesus to be Christ (v. 31) and for his followers to be Christians (v. 34), themes which will dominate the remainder of the Gospel. Second, this is the opening, thematic passage in the body of Mark's section on discipleship (see Introduction, p. 14) in which the way of Jesus is set forth as the way of the Christian.

Because Jesus' way defines the way of his followers, the place of this text in the Christian life is clear. Mark 8:27—9:1 is the heart of the matter.

The passage is a close-knit whole whose structure and flow may be represented as follows:

Setting	27a
Peter's Confession	27b–30
First passion prediction unit	31–9:1
Prediction	31–32a
Conflict with Peter	32b–33
Instructions on discipleship	34—9:1

150

The sequence of passion prediction, misunderstanding by one or more disciples, and corrective teaching about discipleship (8:31—9:1) is the first of three similar units that establish the contours of this discipleship section in which Jesus moves from Galilee to Jerusalem (see Introduction, p. 5). The linkage between the passion prediction and Peter's confession (vv. 27–30) is crucial for the meaning of the whole. Precisely those who profess faith in Jesus as the Christ are the ones who misunderstand his mission and who must now be asked again if they really want to follow him. (For this idea and several others in this unit, the author is indebted to James L. Mays, "An Exposition of Mark 8:27—9:1," *Interpretation* 30:174–77 [April, 1976].) Who Jesus is and what he does are intimately related to who his disciples are and what will be required of them.

The contrast between "he charged them to tell no one" at the end of Peter's confession (v. 30) and "He said this plainly" at the end of the first passion prediction (v. 32*a*) is also significant. Jesus commands silence about the christological confession, but concerning the way of rejection, suffering, death, and resurrection he speaks "quite openly" (JB). Integrity in confessing the name of Jesus Christ is measured by consistency in following him on his way.

Peter's Confession (8:27–30)

Jesus and his disciples are on the way to the villages around Caesarea Philippi. The geography fits the function of the text. From this location in the foothills of Mount Hermon (now in the Golan Heights a few kilometers from the Lebanese border) the view to the south stretches across Galilee toward Jerusalem. In the text, Jesus invites his disciples to look back across the Galilean ministry and reflect on who he is, then to look ahead and understand that they are "on the way" not only to Caesarea Philippi, but also to Jerusalem, to suffering, to death, and to resurrection. The invitation is not to be understood as past history, but as present call to the reader.

These verses constitute a little catechism:

The identity of Jesus	27*b*–28
Others: a prophet	27*b*–28
Disciples: the Christ	29

Removed from Galilee and Jerusalem, yet with both in view, Caesarea Philippi is well suited for objective reflection ("Who do men say that I am?") and for personal confrontation ("Who do you say that I am?"). In this moment of withdrawal, Peter, speaking for all the disciples, articulates what the reader

151

has known from the beginning: "You are the Christ." (See Introduction, pp. 9–10.)

The disciples, like the demons earlier, are commanded not to talk about this discovery, for their understanding of Messiah is flawed. Like the blind man whom Jesus asked "Do you see anything?" (8:23), the disciples see indistinctly. They think that by naming Jesus they have defined him and secured for themselves a special relationship to him (v. 32b). Jesus knows they do not yet see clearly. He must lay his hands upon them again. He does so in the remainder of this unit, throughout the discipleship section, throughout the Gospel, and beyond. His first move is to turn their answer into another question: What does being Christ mean?

First Passion Prediction (8:31–32a)

The introductory formula, "and he began to teach them," appears only in Mark's account of this incident. Use of "begin" with the infinitive is characteristic of Mark, but in this case it is more than a stylistic touch. Jesus' teaching about his passion signals a new beginning in the narrative. Until now the accent has been on Jesus' authority and power. From now on his rejection and death will be emphasized. The christological motif shifts from the fact of Jesus' messiahship to its meaning. In addition, the discipleship theme, introduced in a major key (1:16–20), now swells to a crescendo, but in a minor mode.

This change is marked by the substitution of "Son of man" for "Christ" (v. 31). In Mark "Son of man" is the only title Jesus uses for himself, and with one possible exception (9:9), he alone uses it. By using this title Jesus declares his sovereign freedom to define himself. He does so by speaking of himself as the Son of man who has authority (2:10, 28), who will suffer, die, and rise again (8:31; 9:12, 31; 10:33; 14:21, 41), and who will come in glory to judge and to reign (8:38; 13:26; 14:62). Jesus redefines "Christ" in terms of the Son of man (see Introduction, p. 12).

His freedom, however, is subject to the will of God: "the Son of man must suffer . . . be rejected . . . be killed . . . and rise again." The sequence of verbs outlines the narrative of chapters fourteen through sixteen. The scenario is inevitable: "The Son of man must (dei) suffer." The necessity of Jesus' passion ("had to, " NEB; "was destined to, " JB) lies in the divine ordering of history (see also 9:11; 13:7, 10). More precisely, Jesus must suffer because his understanding of the will of God runs counter to that of the religious authorities: members of the governing council, officiants in the community's liturgical life, and authorized interpreters of Scripture. Obedient to God, Jesus is on a collision course with God's human surrogates. Members of the Jewish religious establishment are not the only ones who find Jesus' teaching unpalatable. So does Peter, and again he speaks for all of Jesus' disciples.

Conflict with Peter (8:32b–33)

Peter's prior understanding of the Messiah (Christ) doubtless hindered his acceptance of Jesus' passion prediction. Attention in the text, however, is drawn to Peter's relationship to Jesus rather than to his understanding of christological terms. Peter "took him" and "began to rebuke him." Both verbs express superiority and authority. "Take him" implies taking aside to instruct (Acts 18:26) or taking over to care for, as a child or an invalid. "Rebuke" is used of Jesus' word of command to demons (1:25; 9:25), to the storm (4:39), and to his disciples (10:13); translated "ordered" or "charged," it is also used of his commands to silence (3:12; 8:30). "Rebuke" structures the present confrontation between Peter and Jesus:

Peter rebukes Jesus   32b
Jesus rebukes Peter   33

The issue is, who is in charge. To say "Christ" to someone is to give up the right to define what "Christ" means; it is to acknowledge the other's authority to define the term and with it the meaning of the confession. Peter tries to behave like a patron, not a disciple.

Jesus will not be patronized. His sharp "Get behind me, Satan" cuts in two ways. First, the use of "Satan" recalls the temptation of Jesus in 1:12–13. While Matthew and Luke spell out at that point a threefold temptation, in Mark the temptation of Jesus is defined here. Jesus is tempted (and so are we) to think that God's anointed can avoid suffering, rejection, and death; that God's rule means power without pain, glory without humiliation. This is Peter's human way of thinking; and Jesus, overcoming this tempting suggestion, identifies it as a devil of an idea. Second, Jesus' rebuke reminds Peter where disciples belong. "Behind me" (v. 33) and "after me" (v. 34) are identical in Greek. Disciples are not to guide, protect, or possess Jesus; they are to follow him.

153

The flow of the text has moved from "Who is Jesus?" (vv. 27–30) through "What does being Christ mean?" (vv. 31–33) and turns now to "What does being a disciple mean?"

Instruction on Discipleship (8:34—9:1)

A schematic representation of the structure of this final climactic part of the passage reveals its artistry:

Introduction: who is addressed	34*a*
Basic principle: deny self, take cross, follow	34*b*
Elaboration	35–38
For . . .	35
For . . .	36
For . . .	37
For . . .	38
Conclusion: urgency of response	9:1

The invitation to follow, first extended to Peter and three others beside a sunny sea (1:16–20), is now redefined in the shadow of a cross. Peter and all the others must be asked again if they really want to follow Jesus. At the same time, the invitation is graciously extended to whoever in the multitude will hear. In this Marcan analogue to the "great invitation" of Matthew 11:28, Jesus invites all who will to come, but to come *after him.*

The Matthean invitation promises rest, but the Markan one (also found in Matt. 16:24) holds out a different prospect. The threefold condition of discipleship—deny self, take up one's cross, and follow Jesus—is a single condition, for the first two terms define and specify the third.

The call is not to deny oneself something, but to deny self. Asceticism can hand the victory to the self, for "self can ride as comfortably on a bicycle as in a limousine." Nor is the call to reject oneself. Self-hatred is not the way of Jesus, but a denial of the grasping self to liberate the greater one.

The cross Jesus invites his hearers to take up refers not to the burdens life imposes from without but rather to painful, redemptive action voluntarily undertaken for others.

What does it mean to be a Christian? In answer to this question Paul and John emphasize believing in Jesus Christ. Matthew stresses obedience to the law as authoritatively interpreted by Jesus. Mark is a lion: strong and tough. Here to be a Christian is to follow Jesus on his costly way in an imitation of

Christ that brushes aside the pieties usually associated with that phrase and goes for the jugular of life itself.

The rigor of this demand is spelled out in four independent sayings, each introduced by "for." In the first, the paradoxical reason for the demand is made clear: "Whoever would save his life will lose it." The other side of this warning is promise: "Whoever loses his life for my sake and the gospel's will save it." Both sides of the paradox, and the following sayings as well, attack a fundamental assumption of human existence. A person can never possess his own life.

The next two sayings are rhetorical questions that underscore the value of one's life *(psyche)*. The word means either "life" or "soul" and can appropriately be translated as "self" (NEB). Here is the guarantee against self-hatred, but also a reinforcement of the attack on human autonomy: No one can raise the price that would buy one's life as a secure possession.

The fourth "for" saying is what scholars call a "sentence of holy law," a literary type in which "the fulfillment of some condition on earth was to be followed in the eschatological future by promise or threat, blessing or curse" (Ernst Käsemann, "Sentences of Holy Law in the New Testament," *New Testament Questions of Today*, p. 79). These examples of prophecy functioned in the early church to strengthen Christians exposed to persecution, to admonish those beset by temptation and to remind them of the demands of their calling. This particular saying (v. 38) is intended to motivate the reader to faithful following and bold witnessing. Whoever is ashamed of Jesus now in the common pressures of life will feel the shame of Jesus in the end, when those who wanted to save themselves stand before one who did not.

A final saying, introduced anew by "and he said to them," concludes the instruction on discipleship and with it the entire passage. Paired with the threat of 8:38, this word motivates by a promise: Some standing here will not die till they see the Kingdom of God having arrived (literal trans.) with power.

In its Marcan context this saying points to the coming of the Son of man in clouds, bringing the Kingdom of God with great power and glory (13:26, 30 with 9:1; cf. Matt. 16:28). The transfiguration (9:2–8) confirms but does not complete the Parousia hope. This expectation was not fulfilled in the generation of Jesus' contemporaries. However, some of those standing there did deny self, take up their cross, and follow Jesus; and in doing

155

so they did see the rule of God come with power in their own lives.

This option is open to every reader in any age, and it carries the same urgency it did for the original hearers. No one has more than one lifetime within which to respond to Jesus' invitation to come after him.

SIGNIFICANCE

The significance of this text lies in its paradoxes. I learn who I am by discovering who Jesus is. The way to self-fulfillment is the way of self-denial.

The apostle Paul understood. "I have been crucified with Christ; it is no longer I who live, but Christ who lives in me . . ." (Gal. 2:20).

John Calvin treated self-denial as the summary of the Christian life:

> We are not our own;
>   therefore neither our reason nor our will should predominate in our deliberations and actions.
> We are not on our own;
>   therefore let us not propose it as our end, to seek what may be expedient for us according to the flesh.
> We are not our own;
>   therefore let us, as far as possible, forget ourselves and all things that are ours.
> On the contrary, we are God's;
>   to him, therefore, let us live and die.
> We are God's;
>   therefore let his wisdom and will preside in all our actions.
> We are God's;
>   towards him, therefore, as our only legitimate end, let every part of our lives be directed. (*Institutes* III,7.)

Dietrich Bonhoeffer made proof of the text's significance both in its radical demand and in its deep answer to the question of identity:

> When Jesus calls a man, he bids him come and die
>   (*The Cost of Discipleship*, Part One, Chap. 2).
>
> Who am I? They mock me, these lonely questions of mine.
> Whoever I am, thou knowest, O God, I am thine
>   (*Letters and Papers from Prison*, Chap. 6).

156

Not all who have understood are giants or martyrs. The woman who devotes her life to raising children in need of a home, the man whose faithful devotion to a mentally ill wife is quiet and steady, the youth whose civil disobedience for con-science's sake leads to prison or exile, these are among countless thousands, who through the centuries and in many contexts, have interpreted the text by their lives.

The text has significance for individuals. By leading to a clear understanding of the correct answer to the question, "Who is Jesus?" this text points to a clear understanding of the question, "Who am I?" I am a disciple: a learner who follows Jesus; a follower who learns from him. What I must learn above all is to follow Jesus in his obedience to the will of God, though it means suffering and death to my ego. I must not be ashamed of him or of his lowly way, lest I be shamed by him in his glory.

The text is also significant for groups and movements. To churches that drift and doze in a comfortable piety, the text calls to take up a cross and follow Jesus on his hard way. To any who busy themselves making people want to "get saved," the text offers a stern warning about preoccupation with saving one's life. To liberation movements that incarnate the self-assertion of a group—and to groups whose own self-assertion leads them to oppose liberation movements—the text issues a challenge to self-denial. The call, the warning, and the chal-lenge are significant because they cut clean across the grain of conventional wisdom, popular piety, and natural inclination.

"I've Gotta Be Me," is a song of the raw self in every age. Jesus, too, sings of self-fulfillment; but his song is made of sterner stuff. The world's song is simple and straightforward, but that of Jesus is more robust and true: "Whoever seeks to save his life will lose it; but whoever loses his life for my sake and the gospel's . . ."

Mark 9:2–13
The Transfiguration

The Marcan Jesus, for all his miraculous power, remains intensely human. He feels pity, anger, hunger, and weariness. Even in so epiphanic a scene as walking on water, Jesus takes a very human interest in his disciples' distress in rowing. In the transfiguration, however, Jesus expresses no emotion, takes no action, and on the mountain speaks no word. Rather, he appears

157

in glory, the passive object of a metamorphosis that reveals his inner nature to his innermost circle of disciples. Here is pure transcendence, of a sort found nowhere else in Mark. What is a latter-day disciple to make of this visionary revelation? How are we to apprehend material so different from most of the Gospel?

The structure of the text suggests two channels of communication.

Christophany on the mountain	2–8
Setting	2a
Appearance: Jesus, Elijah, Moses	2b–4
Disciples' confusion	5–6
Voice: "This is my Son"	7
Conclusion	8
Conversation coming down the mountain	9–13
Silence till after resurrection	9–10
Question about Elijah	11–13

The first half of the text recounts an experience of transcendence; the second half reflects on its meaning. The first half is intuitive, experiential communication; the second half is cognitive and rational.

Christophany (9:2–8)

The first paragraph is suffused with numinous elements. The high mountain is the place nearest heaven, the place of revelation. The cloud symbolizes the divine presence (as in Exod. 13:21; 19:9, 16; 33:9; Num. 9:15). The voice from the cloud is that of God (as in Exod. 24:15—25:1). The brightness of Jesus' garments evokes the light of the *Shekinah*, the divine presence perceived as radiance in the pillar of fire, on the mountain, in the sanctuary, and in apocalyptic visions. That radiance was reflected in the face of Moses when he came from talking with God on Sinai (Exod. 34:29). Two different verbs are used to describe what the disciples saw. One (transfigured) is commonly associated with the Hellenistic mysteries, and the other (appeared) is used often in biblical theophanies and vision accounts.

Though "listen to him" (v. 7) seems to echo Deut. 18:15, suggesting that Jesus is the eschatological prophet like Moses,

158

the narrative gives special prominence to Elijah, naming him first (v. 4). Elijah, like Moses, experienced a theophany on Horeb (Sinai). To Elijah, however, God made himself known not through wind, earthquake or fire, but in a still, small voice (I Kings 19:9–12). Elijah was also anticipated as the herald of the "great and terrible day of the Lord" to fulfill Mal. 4:1–6, a passage in which Moses is mentioned in his role of law-giver. Peter's suggestion of building three booths may reflect an association of the Feast of Booths with the promised Sabbath rest of the end-time.

The language of Mark 9:2–8 is primarily that of theophany, but the vision of Jesus in glory is apocalyptic and eschatological. The evangelist and his readers, standing after the resurrection of Jesus, would understand the scene as a glimpse into the future, a revelation of Jesus as Son of God (v. 7) and Son of man (v. 9) whose imminent coming in glory (8:38—9:1) would consummate the end-time he had announced and inaugurated in his ministry.

Whether this text is to be understood as a displaced resurrection appearance (unlikely on formal grounds), a theophany, or an apocalyptic vision, and whether it reports an actual experience of Jesus with the inner three or reflects the collective experience of the community in which this Gospel was born, its affective power is the same. The language of the passage is more allusive than referential, its mode more intuitive than logical. It communicates in visual and auditory terms a fleeting perception of the eternal splendor, an elusive awareness of the divine presence. Any interpretation which strips this text of the numinous and reduces the holy fear of the disciples (9:6) to intellectual confusion is deaf to a major channel of communication and to much of the text's evocative force. (For a theophanic exegesis of the transfiguration, see Samuel Terrien, *The Elusive Presence*, pp. 422–28.)

Conversation (9:9–13)

Confusion about Christology and eschatology is, however, the central thrust of the second paragraph. Through rational reflection on the meaning of the disciples' experience, the reader is led to a clearer understanding of who Jesus is and what it means to follow him.

Two pervasive Marcan themes recur here. The command to silence (v. 9) is the last and climactic case in which a christological confession, whether by demons (3:11), by Peter (8:29), or by God himself (9:7), is to be kept secret. Only here is a time limit set: "until the Son of man (shall) have risen from the dead." This detail offers a fundamental clue for understanding the entire series of commands to silence, or the so-called "messianic secret" theme. There is no way rightly to understand who Jesus is until one has seen him suffer, die, and rise again (see Introduction, pp. 12–13).

Mention of the resurrection gives rise to a second recurring theme: the misunderstanding of the disciples (see Introduction, pp. 14–15). Just six days before, Jesus had begun to teach them "that the Son of man must suffer . . . and be killed and after three days rise again" (8:31; note that resurrection is "after three days," while "after six days" points to the Parousia). Yet when Jesus now alludes to the Son of man's rising from the dead, their questioning among themselves shows that they have understood neither Jesus' initial teaching nor his explanation (8:34—9:1). The exact nature of their misunderstanding is not stated. It seems to turn in part on eschatology and it surely involves continuing confusion about Christology.

The question about scribal teaching that Elijah must come first (i.e., before the day of the LORD, Mal. 4:5), with Jesus' answer to it (9:11–13), doubtless served as guidance for the early church in its arguments with the synagogue about whether or not Jesus was Messiah. Other texts in Mark show that Elijah refers to John the Baptist (1:6; 6:14–29) and the Son of man to Jesus (8:29–31). Jesus can be the Messiah (that is, Son of man) because Elijah has in fact already come, as Scripture had said.

The prior understanding of the disciples about the relation of resurrection to the end-time is corrected by the present text in at least two ways: The Son of man must himself die and rise again before the final consummation, and there will be an interval between the resurrection and the Parousia of the Son of man.

The prior understanding of the disciples regarding Christology is also reinterpreted. They anticipated a political Messiah, a glorious and triumphant figure (8:32b; 10:37). The transfiguration confirmed the glory of Messiah as Son of God, but that glory was to become evident only at the coming of the Son of man. Just as Peter's confession that Jesus is the Christ (8:29) had to be interpreted by the first prediction of the passion, death, and resurrection of the Son of man (8:31), so here

160

the revelation that Jesus is the Son of God (9:7) is interpreted by reference to Scripture predicting that the Son of man "should suffer many things and be treated with contempt" (9:12).

God's "This is my . . . Son" (9:7) follows Peter's "You are the Christ" (8:29) in a way reminiscent of the juxtaposition of titles in Chapter 1 (v. 1), "the gospel of Jesus Christ, the Son of God." In both cases the two titles are to be understood as synonyms. Whatever overtones of deity "Son of God" carried in the Hellenistic world, in Israel it was a title for God's anointed king (Ps. 2:7). Here, as elsewhere in Mark, the traditional understanding of the messianic king is reinterpreted and corrected by Jesus' substitution of the title "Son of man" (9:9, 12; see Introduction, pp. 11–12).

The suffering and death of Jesus, the Son of man, is to parallel that of John the Baptist as Elijah (vv. 12–13). Both are said to be in fulfillment of Scripture. Though the Scripture references intended (perhaps Ps. 22:7; Isa. 53:3 and I Kings 19:2, 10 respectively) are somewhat tenuous, other New Testament texts show that the early church did apply Ps. 22 and Isa. 53 to Jesus. Furthermore, John's death at the hands of a wicked woman (Herodias) and a weak king (Herod) offers a striking parallel to Elijah's persecution by Jezebel and Ahab. Reflection on the fate of John the Baptist should help disciples to understand that the suffering and death of Jesus as Christ, Son of God, and Son of man is in accord with the will of God. Reflection on the transfiguration of Jesus in light of his death and resurrection should enable disciples to accept the path of suffering as the way of true glory for Jesus, and for themselves as well.

SIGNIFICANCE

For us as for the original readers the foci of this text are two: Jesus and the disciples.

The theme of Jesus, the Son of God, could be developed by setting the transfiguration in the center of three Son of God confessions, as Mark does. The first is the voice of God to Jesus himself at the baptism (1:9–11), in which Jesus' identity as Son of God is established. In the second, the transfiguration, that identity is confirmed to an inner circle of three disciples, offering a parallel to Peter's confession of Jesus as Christ, a counterpoint to the first passion prediction, and a foretaste of the Parousia announced in the verses immediately preceding. The

161

last in the series is the crucifixion, a sort of reverse transfiguration, in which the sight of Jesus dying in utter abandonment to
the will of God wrings from the lips of a Roman army officer the
confession, "Truly this man was the Son of God."

The first of these is full of radiant promise, the last a witness
to steadfastness in despair, and the middle one—the present
text—combines glory (vv. 2–8) and suffering (vv. 9–13, esp. 12)
to present the paradox of divine power and weakness, lowliness
and majesty, in the person of Jesus Christ. Israel's Messiah and
Son of God is the suffering and dying Son of man. For those who
have eyes to see, his very suffering in steadfast obedience to the
will of God is a mark of God's own glory; but that glory can only
be understood by resurrection faith, and it will become evident
to all only at the Parousia of the Son of man. In the transfiguration, then, Jesus is revealed as Son of God, the one in whom is
manifested simultaneously the splendor and the lowliness of
God.

The text is linked in several lectionaries with the sacrifice
or binding of Isaac (Gen. 22). The pathos and power of this text
lies in God's command to Abraham, "Take your son, your only
son Isaac, whom you love, and go . . . and offer him . . . upon
one of the mountains of which I shall tell you" (Gen. 22:2). The
phrase "his son," "your son," "my son" runs like a thread
through the narrative, whose climax is the sparing of Isaac
when God knows that Abraham fears him, "seeing you have not
withheld your son, your only son, from me" (Gen. 22:12). To
relate this story to the revelation of the Son of God on the
mountain of transfiguration is apt and instructive. What we see
in Jesus is not only the Son of man who, by his steadfastness in
suffering, manifests a courage that is glorious, but also God's
Son, his only Son, whom God has not withheld from us. His
suffering, death, and resurrection manifest the glory of the divine condescension and love.

The other focus in the text is on the disciples. The discipleship line here runs from Elijah through Jesus and the earliest disciples to us. We can identify with those three on the
mountain in several ways. Like them, we may sometimes be
granted epiphanic experiences which grip our hearts and
minds but whose significance we cannot fully understand. "I
know I have been spared for a purpose, but I don't know what
it is" is but one expression of such an experience. Like Peter,
on those rare occasions when we experience the elusive pres-

162

ence, what we most want is to "build booths" to prolong or commemorate it. In the conversation coming down the mountain Jesus links mystic experience to costly discipleship and exaltation to suffering. He is the Son of God; we need to listen to him. Like the first disciples, we are frightened by transcendence and confused about the call to suffer, die, and rise in following Jesus.

Paul wrote to Corinth and to Rome before the Gospel of Mark was written, but he may well have known the transfiguration tradition. His two uses of the verb "transformed" (identical to "transfigured" in Greek) correspond closely to the two basic thrusts, mystical and ethical, of Mark 9:2–13. "And we all, with unveiled face, beholding the glory of the Lord, are being changed into his likeness from one degree of glory to another" (II Cor. 3:18). "Do not be conformed to this world but be transformed by the renewal of your mind, that you may prove what is the will of God, what is good and acceptable and perfect" (Rom. 12:2).

Mark 9:14–29
The Boy the Disciples Could Not Heal

This narrative, commonly referred to as "an epileptic boy healed," appears in all three Synoptic Gospels (Matt. 17:14–21; Luke 9:37–43*a*). The Marcan account is the longest and most circumstantial of the three. Though it is not in the lectionary, this incident affords solid grist for teaching and preaching. It speaks of powerless disciples and suggests two channels for tapping the power of God through Jesus Christ.

TEXT

In all three Synoptic Gospels, this incident immediately follows the transfiguration of Jesus. The glory of the Master (vv. 3, 7) is contrasted with the impotence and frustration of the disciples (vv. 18, 28). In healing the boy, Jesus rebukes not only the unclean spirit (v. 25) but also the disciples who should have been able to effect a cure, but could not (vv. 19, 28). The command, "Bring him to me," parallels the one in 9:7, "This is my beloved Son; listen to him." Both point to the authority of Jesus.

163

To disciples who will listen, Jesus here offers authoritative instruction on the cause and cure of their powerlessness.

The passage unfolds in three major sections: a Marcan setting (vv. 14–16), a lengthy and complex miracle story (vv. 17–27), and a Marcan conclusion (vv. 28–29).

Only in Mark does controversy with the scribes characterize the setting of this incident. "Discussing" and "arguing" are represented by the same word in Greek. The text does not state the content of the argument, nor is the Greek text in verse 16 clear even about who is arguing with whom (translations differ legitimately). In verse 14, however, it is evident that the scribes are arguing with the disciples, and the argument seems to turn on the inability of Jesus' disciples to heal the stricken boy. The disciples are being made to look very bad indeed in the eyes of the crowd. This element of controversy may well be present in Mark because of a situation in which the evangelist and his community were involved at the time of writing. Parallels to the argument in the text are all too evident today.

The body of the text follows the typical form of a miracle story in which the problem (vv. 17–24) is greatly expanded. The particular kind of miracle is exorcism, for the boy's illness is attributed to a deaf and dumb spirit (vv. 17, 20, and 25). The symptoms described (vv. 18, 20, and 22), however, sound like the seizures we call "epilepsy" (from *epi* and *lambanō, lēmpsia;* literally, "seize upon"), though this word is not used at all in Mark. From the viewpoint of the text, the boy is a victim of a hostile force which proves to be subject to the authority and command of Jesus (v. 25).

The redundancy in the description of the illness, the assembling of a crowd (v. 25), which was already present (v. 14), and the shift of attention from the disciples to the boy's father have prompted the hypothesis that two stories may have been combined here. One (vv. 14–19) contrasts the faithlessness and impotence of the disciples with the faith and power of Jesus; the other (vv. 20–27) shows Jesus' compassionate response even to the paradoxical, unbelieving faith of the father. Whatever may have been the prehistory of this narrative, in its canonical form all of these elements are present. The story proper (vv. 17–27) is about faith and lack of faith.

164

The disciples' lack of faith is unrelieved. Although Jesus' rebuke (v. 19) could be addressed to all parties present (scribes, crowd, father, disciples), his charge of faithlessness is most telling against the disciples. By accusing his disciples of faithlessness, Jesus indicates the cause of their impotence. Their failure is linked to their unbelief.

In contrast, the father's attitude, while imperfect, is amenable to growth. His initial request to Jesus (v. 22) indicates both faith and lack of faith. Jesus identifies the father's doubt by repeating his very words, "If you can," then challenges him to faith by adding "All things are possible to him who believes." (It is possible to see challenge in the initial part of the response also, as the TEV does: "If *you* can.")

Since faith is the main point of verses 17–27, Jesus' general principle, that all things are possible to one who believes, merits close attention. It conveys meaning at several levels. First, "him who believes" includes the faith of Jesus himself. Since Jesus firmly believes in God's power to heal the boy, the healing will be possible and the father is invited to believe that this is so. Second, "him who believes" includes the father's potential faith in Jesus as a channel by which the power and authority of Jesus can become operative in his child's life. Third, since "believe" has no direct object here, the saying includes the general principle that faith itself is effectual in healing, regardless of its object. Jesus does not anywhere in Mark explicitly invite faith in himself, yet the appeal to believe in him is clearly implicit. The general, positive relationship between faith and healing is true; but the reader is intended to understand more than that. The best clue to the text's intention here is the superscription over the whole, "This is the good news about Jesus Christ, the Son of God" (1:1, TEV).

The father's reply gives insight into the nature of faith: "I believe; help my unbelief!" The statement is paradoxical, but not really contradictory. He has shown a measure of faith by bringing his son to Jesus in the first place (v. 17), as well as by his desperate plea for help (v. 22). Yet his motive seems to be desperation (the boy has been sick from childhood), and his "if you can do anything" gives voice to his doubt. He manifests both unbelief and faith. He has come to Jesus not because he trusts him, but because he is willing to try anything. He now cries out for help, both for his tormented son and for his own feeble faith. Jesus answers the prayer by healing the boy, thus 165 confirming the father's faith and granting both kinds of help for which the father has asked.

Significantly, the faith of the boy is not mentioned. In no

case of exorcism in Mark is healing contingent on the faith of the demon-possessed person (see Introduction, pp. 20–21). Indeed, the absence of faith as trust is the very nature of the illness. Demons do believe who Jesus is, but they cannot trust him. Healing in the present case becomes possible through the imperfect faith of someone else who cares deeply for the afflicted boy.

If the body of the story is about faith, its conclusion (vv. 28–29) is about prayer. Withdrawal to a house where Jesus' disciples question him privately, followed by fuller instruction, is a pattern characteristic of Mark's Gospel (7:17; 9:28; 10:10; see also 4:10). This pattern reflects a reinterpretation of Jesus' teaching in the earliest church and alerts the reader to an authoritative teaching for disciples of every time and place. The function of 9:28–29 is to teach the importance—indeed the necessity, in this and other cases—of prayer as a channel of divine power and healing. Prayer in Mark is not pious manipulation of God to get what we want, but communing with God in the wilderness where Satan is confronted and overcome (1:12, 35; 6:46) and wrestling alone in the night to submit one's own will to that of God (14:32–42).

The addition of fasting as a condition for opening the way to healing in certain cases, though present in a large number of manuscripts and in the AV, is almost certainly an addition to the text reflecting a growing emphasis on ascetic practices in the early church. The point of the original Marcan conclusion is that prayerlessness results in powerlessness.

SIGNIFICANCE

The text addresses any disciple or group of disciples frustrated by spiritual impotence. It says that Jesus has authority over demonic forces. Jesus can handle the problems we bring to him. Jesus can heal.

We learn also that disciples should be able to heal, but they lack faith and need prayer. This does not mean that prayer works like magic: Elijah taunted the prophets of Baal with that idea (I Kings 18:27). The point is not that faith makes *us* omnipotent or that faith itself has power. "I have confidence in confidence alone" comes from American civic religion; in the text it is God who heals, through Jesus Christ.

The text does mean that we are always invited to pray, like the boy's father, for more faith (understood as trust in God's

166

beneficent power) so that God in Christ can work his healing will in and through us.

To disciples of every age, the text offers a great promise: "All things are possible to him who believes." Its deepest thrust, however, points beyond the faith or prayer of disciples to the source of healing and wholeness: "Bring him (her) to me."

Mark 9:30–50
Capernaum: Second Passion Prediction

What does it mean to follow Jesus?

This elemental question, first introduced after Peter's confession at Caesarea Philippi (8:27—9:1), is taken up again in a second passion prediction unit enlarged by an early collection of proverbs for disciples. Once again, the teaching of Jesus, in act as well as in word, challenges a fundamental human assumption and cuts across several common patterns of human behavior.

TEXT

For the place of this passage in the discipleship section as a whole, see the Introduction (p. 5).

The limits of this somewhat lengthy and complex unit are determined by geographical notes (9:30 and 10:1); this is the last scene in Galilee according to Mark. Mention of a precise town in Galilee, Capernaum (v. 33), introduces the teaching on discipleship, which is greatly expanded in this case. The common lectionary treats the passage as two pericopes, correctly reflecting the structure of the unit:

Setting	30–31*a*
Second passion prediction unit	31*b*–37
Prediction	31*b*
Misunderstanding	32
Instruction on discipleship	33–37
Proverbs for disciples	
(expanded instruction on discipleship)	38–50
The unauthorized exorcist	38–41
Warnings against causes of sin	42–48
Conclusion: Salty Christians	49–50

167

Verses 30–37 are the basic unit, verses 38–48 are expansions with particular significance for the life of the Christian community, and verses 49–50 are the conclusion of the independent sayings and of the entire passage.

Setting (9:30–31a)

Galilee is a symbol for the place from which Jesus calls persons to follow him (1:16–20), to which he bids them return to watch for his coming (14:28; 16:7), and through which he leads his own disciples (9:30). It is our own home turf, on which we become strangers and pilgrims as Jesus leads us on the way to Jerusalem. When the text speaks of Jesus passing through Galilee with his disciples, it speaks of us.

The text also expresses Jesus' special concern for us when it says, "Jesus did not want anyone to know where he was, because he was teaching his disciples" (TEV, NIV). Here, his care for his own flock takes precedence over his compassion for the crowd. This is a special moment for disciples. Like corporate worship or church school today, it is a moment of withdrawal from the crowd designed to help Jesus' followers understand the journey; but these occasions are not to be confused with the service of which Jesus speaks. In a larger sense the trip itself, culminating in the death he here predicts, is the teaching.

Prediction (9:31b)

This briefest, and perhaps oldest, of the passion predictions is in one sense the most sweeping of the three. In addition to his rejection by Jewish religious leaders (8:31; 10:33), Jesus must suffer at the hands of representatives of the whole human race: "The Son of man will be delivered into the hands of men" (9:31). Ironically, all humankind is implicated in the death of the one who came to die for all (see notes on 10:45, p. 190). "Were you there when they crucified my Lord?" is a question for every person in every time and place.

"Delivered" *(paradidōmi)*, commonly used in Jewish literature to describe the fate of the prophets, is used in Mark to speak of the fate of John the Baptist ("arrested," 1:14), of the crime of Judas Iscariot ("betrayed," 3:19; 14:10–11), and of the suffering and death of Jesus (14:41; 15:1, 10, 15). For the pattern that links John, Jesus, and the disciples in the sequence of preaching and being delivered up, see notes on 6:14–29 (p. 123). Early Christians understood the term *delivered up* not only as an expression of the divine necessity of Jesus' death (Rom. 4:25; 8:32; Gal. 1:4; 2:20; Eph. 5:2, 25; I Tim. 2:6; Tit. 2:14) but also of their own inevitable experience in the service of the gospel (Mark 13:9–13; Acts 8:3; 15:26; 21:11; 28:17; II Cor. 4:11).

Misunderstanding (9:32)

The disciples did not understand Jesus' word about death and resurrection, and they were afraid to ask him to explain it. Later disciples who read the text can identify with their human limitations, though Luke 9:45 excuses them and Matt. 17:23 omits any mention of misunderstanding. For the "misunderstanding" theme in Mark, see the Introduction (pp. 14–15).

Instruction on Discipleship (9:33–37)

In these verses the action builds by two stages to the climactic saying of the unit. "Capernaum" brings Jesus and his disciples back home; "in the house" (found only in Mark's account) alerts the reader to watch for special instruction to disciples. In this first stage of the instruction (vv. 33–34) Jesus, rather than the disciples, asks for an explanation. He probes what they have been discussing as they followed Jesus "on the way." The word for "discuss," different from that in 9:14, implies private remarks or asides not intended to be overheard (see 2:6–8; 8:16–17; 11:31). The disciples are struck dumb with embarrassment, for they recognize the discrepancy between Jesus' denial of self (8:31–34) and their own desire for self-aggrandizement as they argue about who is the greatest. Their misunderstanding is not simply intellectual; it is existential. Their following of Jesus is outward only. He challenges them at a key point: the nature of true greatness.

The second stage in these verses is introduced by a threefold formula. "He sat down" indicates formal teaching. "And called the twelve" focuses the teaching upon leaders among the disciples (compare "the multitude with his disciples" at 8:34). "And he said to them" introduces the climactic saying: "If any one would be first, he must be last of all and servant of all."

This saying about first and last marks a significant advance over the instruction in the first passion prediction unit (8:34—9:1). The reversal of values which it teaches is elaborated in 10:43–44 (par. Matt. 20:26–27). The same idea appears in three other Synoptic texts (Matt. 23:11; Luke 9:48; 22:26). To measure greatness by lowly service is apparently as characteristic

169

of Jesus as it is alien to the world in every age. Jesus does not despise the desire to be first, but his definition of greatness stands the world's ordering of priorities on its head and radically challenges a fundamental human assumption about achievement.

Jesus reinforces his teaching on true greatness by an acted parable, identifying with a child by an eloquent gesture. The Greek text leaves uncertain the age and sex of the child, as well as the nature of Jesus' embrace (putting his arms around or taking the child in his arms). The force of Jesus' action hinges upon recognition of the low esteem in which children were held in the Greco-Roman world (see Hans-Ruedi Weber, *Jesus and the Children*, pp. 5–8) and realization that the word used here for "child" is the same as that used for the suffering servant of the Lord in the Greek version of Isa. 53:2 ("We heralded him as a child"). Original readers of Mark would readily have seen in Jesus' embrace of the child his self-identification as lowliest, least, and servant of all.

One would expect at this point an exhortation to the Twelve to be like children, too (as in 10:15). Precisely this connection is made in Matt. 18:3, but in Mark the direction of the argument shifts at verse 37 from being lowly like a child to receiving a child in the name of Jesus. "Receive" (or welcome), "child" (or "little one"), and "in my name" all function as catchwords by means of which the following series of loosely-connected sayings are attached to the second passion prediction unit. Taken literally, this linking saying pronounces a blessing which will be understood by all who work with and care for children. Symbolically, however, "child" here applies to anyone who has need of help and more specifically to new disciples, as the following verses will make clear.

Proverbs for Disciples: Expanded Instruction on Discipleship

Apart from the brief setting (v. 38), all the remainder of chapter 9 consists of originally independent sayings linked together by catchwords and, roughly, by subject matter. The product of a complex redaction history, the text now consists of two clusters of sayings plus a concluding trio.

170

The Unauthorized Exorcist (9:38–41)

This brief exchange between John and Jesus (vv. 38–39a) with its three related sayings (vv. 39b–41) interrupts the flow of

Jesus' teaching about how disciples should relate to children or little ones (vv. 37, 42). Grant that "child" or "little one" is a symbol for new followers of Jesus, however, and the reason for the insertion of the cluster at this point is evident. Formally, this paragraph is linked to the preceding saying both by continuity and by contrast. In contrast to the fourfold "receive" of verse 37 stands John's "we forbade him" (v. 38), followed by Jesus' "Do not forbid him." "In my (your) name" is the element of continuity appearing in verses 37, 38, 39, and (in substance) 41.

The point at issue is whether or not to welcome a charismatic prophet who calls on the name of Jesus but does not belong to the apostolic group. This situation was fairly common in the early church, and various solutions are given in early Christian literature (see Schweizer, *Mark*, pp. 194f.). The problem as presented here is not that the man was not following Jesus, but that he was not following the Twelve ("us," the established leadership of the church). Jesus' answer is categorical: "Do not forbid him." The first two "for-sayings" (vv. 39b–40) urge graciousness and generosity upon disciples as they form opinions about others who call on the name of Jesus. The third (v. 41), introduced by a solemn "Amen, I say to you," pronounces a blessing on all who give physical aid and comfort, as a cup of water, to a traveling evangelist or any needy person who belongs to Christ. The giving and receiving which characterizes disciples is not to be limited to some in-group, but should be common to all who bear the name of Jesus Christ.

Warnings Against Causes of Sin (9:42–48)

"These little ones who believe in me" (v. 42) corresponds to "one such child" (v. 37) and designates not only the physically young but also—even primarily, in light of verses 38–41—recent believers in Jesus. Such persons are to be welcomed into the Christian fellowship (v. 37), not forbidden from working in the name of Christ (vv. 38–41), and not caused to stumble (*skandalizein*, v. 42).

To this warning about becoming a cause of sin to others is added a warning against causes of sin within oneself. The three parallel sayings about hand, foot, and eye (vv. 43–48) are linked together and to verse 42 by the catchwords "cause to sin" (literally, stumble) and "it is better." The language is figurative and hyperbolic, vivid and harsh. Verses 44 and 46, correctly omitted from modern versions, are textual variants that attest the fasci-

171

nation this picture of hell's worm and fire held for ancient copyists. "Cut it off " is a command to be taken not literally, but seriously. The surpassing value of entering the Kingdom of God makes every other good expendable.

Conclusion (9:49–50)

"For every one will be salted with fire" is a transitional verse whose catchwords tie it to the sayings on both sides. "Fire" links it to verses 43–48 and "salt" to the two sayings in verse 50. A textual variant in this case helps to explain the enigmatic expression "salted with fire." Someone early noted Lev. 2:13 ("with all your offerings you shall offer salt") in the margin of Mark 9:49, and a later copyist inserted it into the text as "and every sacrifice will be salted with salt," a reading still preserved in the AV. The reference to ritual sacrifice would be fairly evident to the first readers of Mark. The argument has a coherence deeper than catchwords: Since undisciplined disciples risk the fire of gehenna at the last judgment (vv. 43–48), the hardships that disciples undergo now are disciplines like the fire of a sacrificial offering that purifies, or like salt which stings and smarts but is preservative in its effect. Jesus on his way to Jerusalem is the supreme example of the sacrificial offerings "salted with fire." His sacrificial death is not to shield disciples from costly obedience, but rather to show them the way: "For every one (meaning every disciple) will be salted with fire."

Disciples whose lives are not characterized by lowly service nor by openness to Christians who are different nor by care for those who are young in the faith nor by rigorous self-discipline are like flavorless salt. They have lost the sharpness which sets them apart from their environment and which constitutes their usefulness. Disciples, therefore, are to be salty Christians, in the sense in which Jesus was salty (vv. 31, 35–37). They will then be at peace with one another, for they will be harder on themselves (vv. 43–48) than on others (vv. 38–41) whom they will welcome and assist in the common journey following Jesus (vv. 37, 42).

Like certain fun songs which, by a circuitous route, lead at the end back to the beginning, this collection of Jesus' sayings, strung together by catchwords, ends where it started. Jesus on his way to Jerusalem is a sacrifice salted with fire (vv. 30–32); therefore, have salt in yourselves, and be at peace with one another (v. 50)—that is, stop squabbling about who is the greatest (vv. 33–37).

SIGNIFICANCE

The preceding notes on the text have at several points alluded to its significance: The symbolic meaning of Galilee, the function of private moments with disciples, the way "into the hands of men" implicates all of us in the death of Jesus. Of the many other meanings in the text which are significant for readers today, two will be mentioned here: one for each of the pericopes into which the lectionaries divide this unit.

Whoever Is Not Against Us . . .

The lectionaries link the story of the strange exorcist (9: 38–41) to that of Eldad and Medad in the wilderness (Num. 11:24–30). The analogy is not exact, since these two elders were "among those registered" (Num. 11:26), and Moses mentions Joshua's motives (Num. 11:29a). Moses' response to Joshua's request to forbid irregular prophesying, however, is parallel to Jesus' attitude toward the unauthorized exorcist: "Do not forbid him" (Mark 9:39). The seventy elders prophesied no more (Num. 11:25), so Moses exclaims concerning Eldad and Medad, "Would that all the Lord's people were prophets, that the Lord would put his spirit upon them!"

The response of Moses and Jesus cuts across the common, parochial attitude of possessiveness toward God and hostility toward any person or group whose patterns of worship are different. Both stories enjoin openness and acceptance.

If the Numbers text reinforces the teaching of Mark 9: 39–40, Matt. 12:30 seems to contradict it: Whoever is not with me is against me. The contradiction is apparent, not real. Whoever is not against *us* (Mark 9:40) echoes the "us" of verse 38 and refers to Jesus with the authorized leadership, the Twelve. Whoever is not with *me* (Matt. 12:30) refers to Jesus alone. Mark 9:39–40 is a precept of tolerance; belonging to an in-group is no fit test of discipleship. Matt. 12:30 is a check against fuzzy abuse of this principle; belonging to Jesus is essential.

The text is a pertinent guide for ecumenical endeavor as well as for disputes over charismatic elements in the church: "Whoever is not against us is for us."

Who Is the Greatest? 173

The question of true greatness lies at the heart of international politics and rivalry (e.g., "the great powers"), of social struggles over pecking order and pay scales, of competitive sports (e.g., "I'm the greatest"), of relationships between and within families, and of tensions among and within churches (e.g., "an influential church," "a prominent church leader"). Interpreters using the lectionary pericope 9:30–37 may appropriately focus on this theme as defined by Jesus' word, "If any one would be first, he must be last of all and servant of all" (v. 35).

Particular areas of significance lifted up for consideration will grow out of the experience of the specific community. Measured against the criterion of Jesus, most human quests for greatness as reflected in national budgets, church programs, and private conversations are aptly described by the Old Testament sage: "a striving after wind" (Eccles. 1:17; 2:11; 4:4; 6:9).

A fundamental human assumption is that greatness is measured by power in the form of physical strength and prowess, military might, money, fame, or anything else that enables us to gratify our own desires and impose our will on others. We call the achievement of one or another of these goals "success." Jesus measures greatness not by success but by service. He identifies with the child who is not powerful but vulnerable.

So immersed are we in the world's values, and so familiar with this word of Jesus, that we seldom feel its sharpness and its bite. Those first disciples felt it so keenly that they were struck dumb. How did Jesus achieve that feat of exposition? He asked a question related to their immediate experience; he stated a principle briefly, paradoxically, and without explanation; he enacted a parable in their presence which required them to make the connection; he lived out his teaching in the larger parable of his own life. They got the point, though they could not yet fully understand or appropriate it, for in him they saw true greatness.

Mark 10:1–16
Teachings About Marriage and About Children

174

The form of this passage is controversy between Jesus and his adversaries, but the entire section (10:1–31) functions as a catechism concerning marriage, children, and wealth. The first two of these topics are treated in 10:1–16. The shift from the Pharisees to the disciples (v. 10) marks the move from polemic to instruction. The shift from then to now will occur whenever a reader begins to listen to this Scripture as the lively word of God.

TEXT

The text consists of three sub-units: the evangelist's transition (v. 1), the question about divorce (vv. 2–12), and the blessing of the children (vv. 13–16). The three are united by setting (changes of place are noted in vv. 1 and 17) and by family-related topics. The paragraphs on marriage and children (10:2–16) constitute a gospel pericope in the common lectionary.

Transition (10:1)

Mark 10:1 follows the second passion prediction unit (9:30–50). The message of this transitional verse is clear, and it is important for understanding the paragraphs which follow it. Jesus is voluntarily on his way to Jerusalem to experience the rejection, death, and resurrection of which he has now spoken twice. Mark depicts him in the midst of crowds, *teaching* "as his custom was." Mark in particular emphasizes Jesus the teacher, continuing the instruction of his disciples which he had begun on a retreat to Caesarea Philippi (8:27). Here the crowd forms a background from which individuals emerge (Pharisees, disciples, persons bringing children) to play their roles in the teaching process. In dialogue with them, Jesus teaches the true meaning of discipleship as he goes up to Jerusalem to die.

About Marriage, Divorce, and Remarriage (10:2–12)

This sub-unit includes two parts, the first and older of which is a typical controversy story. Jesus' opponents here are the Pharisees only. The question about divorce was a burning one among Pharisees just after and perhaps during Jesus' time, for the Talmud reports arguments about legitimate grounds for divorce among various authorities within the Pharisaic movement (Shammai, Hillel, Aqiba: *Gittin* IX, 10). The present text states that the Pharisees put this question to Jesus not to learn from him, but to put him to the test (*peirazo*, 1:13; 8:11; 12:15). Their question is tendentious, and Jesus refuses to deal with it

175

on their terms. Twice they speak about what is "lawful" or "allowed" (vv. 2, 4); Jesus on the other hand speaks twice about what is "commanded" (vv. 3, 5). Jesus is concerned about the will of God; his adversaries, while appearing to share that concern, care only about their own rights and how much they can get by with.

The Pharisees' "test" is an attempt to trap Jesus into taking the position of one religious party, thereby alienating the others. Jesus, as if snapping his finger at their scheme, boldly creates a situation in which he confronts—and makes them confront—a far weightier issue. He gets them to quote the Mosaic law on divorce (Deut. 24:1, 3) then opposes to it two texts from the creation story: one from the Priestly account (Gen. 1:27; par. 5:2), and one from the Jahwistic account (Gen. 2:24). Jesus not only takes the side of Shammai against Hillel, but of one text against another, opposing scripture to scripture. What his adversaries design as a trap, the Marcan Jesus seizes as an occasion to teach the primordial and gracious will of God. This is a further example of Jesus' teaching "as one who has authority, and not as the scribes" (1:22).

To the quotations from Genesis, Jesus adds two interpretive remarks (vv. 8b–9) which take a position on divorce even more stringent than that of the strictest rabbis. The school of Shammai held that "one should be divorced from his wife only if he has found something shameful in her." Jesus says one should not separate what God has joined. Yet Jesus does not here instigate a stricter legalism. Instead he shifts the ground of the discussion from what Moses wrote (vv. 3–4) to what God made and meant (vv. 6–7); from loopholes that may be permitted to the intention of what is commanded; from divorce to marriage. Divorce is grounded in law, but marriage is grounded in creation. Rightly understood, this shift marks a fundamental victory over legalism and moves the discussion into the area of gift and grace, which is more demanding but also more free.

Moses wrote the divorce law, Jesus says, "for your hardness of heart." The expression was used by Moses of Israel in Deut. 10:16 (LXX), where the underlying Hebrew image is "uncircumcision of heart," to refer to the people's stubbornness (RSV). It is also used by Jesus in Mark 3:5 to describe those who watched to see whether or not he would heal the man with a withered hand in a synagogue on the Sabbath (see p. 75 for nuances of the term in that context). In Mark 10:5 it is variously

176

translated by "stubbornness" (NAB), "your minds were closed" (NEB), and "you are so hard to teach" or "unteachable" (TEV, JB). In the present context, the latter nuance is particularly pertinent. Divorce laws are necessary because we will not learn from God or from each other. We are obstinate and stubborn toward one another and unwilling to accept God's will for fidelity in marriage. The law of Moses recognizes this fact, but Jesus will not let us believe that God approves these qualities in us or the rupture of human relationships that they entail. Instead, he points us to the goodness of God's design in creation and to the goal of a man and a woman living together "as heirs of the grace of life" (The Marriage Service, *Presbyterian Book of Common Worship;* I Pet. 3:7).

The second part of the unit about divorce (Mark 10:10–12) recognizes that the divine purpose in marriage is not always achieved. It is introduced as a private explanation to the disciples "in the house," a signal in Mark of "in-house" instruction from the Lord to his followers in the early church (e.g., 7:17; 9:28, 33). It also presupposes Roman and not Jewish law when it considers the possibility of a woman's initiating divorce procedure against her husband (10:12), thereby reflecting the situation of the church as it moved out into the Greco-Roman empire. The very fact that the matter needed to be explained further suggests that cases of divorce had arisen. It is as if early Christians said among themselves, "We know that God's will is a permanent marriage between one man and one woman. But when that simply does not work out, and divorce does in fact occur, is remarriage all right?"

The word of the Lord in response to this question is clear and uncompromising. If remarriage follows divorce, it is an act of adultery against the abandoned first partner. The statement is not prescriptive; that is, Jesus does not reply, "If you divorce, do not remarry." It is descriptive; that is, it assumes that remarriage after divorce does occur and describes it as a violation of the relationship created by the first marriage. It is not a new law of either permission or prohibition. It is rather a principle which recognizes the primordial will of God for human marriage as well as what happens to the human psyche when that gracious purpose is not achieved. Jesus' word recognizes the legal dimensions of marriage by using the legal term *adultery*. However, by adding "against her" (v. 11) and by speaking in turn of each partner who initiates a divorce and another marriage (all

177

the verbs are active), the text deals with the issue in personal rather than legal terms.

A divorce may revoke a legal contract, but one cannot un-live the vital ties created by life together in marriage, however painful they may be. Jesus does not legislate by saying "No remarriage," but he recognizes what divorce and remarriage do to the residual relationship with a former partner and insists that his disciples understand that the problem cannot be avoided by legal means. The answer was—and is—shocking. As absolute as Jesus' teaching on selling all one's goods and giving to the poor or denying oneself and taking up one's cross, this word, like those, was heard literally by a church that expected the end of history within the span of their current generation. It set the early church counter to easy and selfish views of the marriage relationship in the surrounding culture. For whoever has ears to hear, it still does.

About Children (10:13–16)

The gospel material on Jesus and the children appears primarily in two places: as part of the second passion prediction unit (Mark 9:33–37; par. Luke 9:46–48 and Matt. 18:1–5, the latter in the Matthean discourse on the church) and here in the discipleship teachings just before the story of the rich young man (Mark 10:13–16; par. Matt. 19:13–15 and Luke 18:15–17). Of all these versions of similar scenes, the most familiar is probably the one in Mark 10:13–16. Only in the Marcan account is Jesus described as "indignant" with his disciples for hindering the approach of the children. Furthermore, only Mark says that Jesus *blesses* the children. Mark's is the fullest and most warmly human version of the traditional story, and it has had a quiet but steady influence on the life of the church through the centuries.

The unit appears in the form of a "pronouncement story"; that is, a vignette composed of a brief setting and an authoritative saying of the Lord. The setting (vv. 13–14a) involves persons (parents? relatives? friends? the text does not say) bringing children for Jesus to touch and disciples who rebuke them. Jesus in turn rebukes the disciples. Because the significant interaction is between Jesus and his disciples, rather than opponents, the story is clearly designed to function within the community of faith for the instruction of subsequent followers of Jesus.

That instruction appears in the "saying" part of the story, which in fact includes two sayings. The first (v. 14b) shows Jesus'

178

positive attitude toward children and affirms a positive relationship between children and the Kingdom of God. The latter part of this first saying, "to such belongs the kingdom of God," can be interpreted to mean either, "to these children and to other children like them" or "to persons who are similar to these children." The latter meaning is presupposed by the second saying (v. 15), and the former meaning is underscored by the conclusion of the story (v. 16) in which Jesus takes these actual children in his arms and blesses them by placing his hands on them. The two levels of the story, literal and figurative, meet in verse 14*b*, which functions in both ways.

The second saying (v. 15) is introduced by "truly, I say to you," which underscores its special importance. It appears in a different context in Matt. 18:3, so it could stand alone. Here in Mark, it is related to the preceding saying in a way that constitutes a progression from Jesus' attitude toward children to the attitude of the children themselves and finally to the attitude of disciples toward the Kingdom of God. The disciples hinder children who are being brought to Jesus for a blessing; Jesus says that rather than hinder the children, disciples need to learn from them how to be blessed. The dependence of children, who cannot support themselves but expect and receive their support from parents, becomes a metaphor for entering the Kingdom of God. The essential point in this text is not humility as in Matt. 18:3–4, nor innocence as in the Shepherd of Hermas 27:1 and 106:1–3. The key phrase here is "recieve . . . like a child." This is the climax of the unit's figurative meaning.

Verse 16, the conclusion of the incident, is visually evocative. The expression translated "took the children in his arms" can either mean that he picked them up in his arms (AV) or that he put his arms around them (JB, NEB). The word used for "children" is too imprecise to offer a clue about how large or how old they were. If Jesus, like other rabbis, taught in a seated position, we can imagine him drawing the children close in whatever way best suited their size and disposition. (See parallel wording in 9:35–37.) The blessing may or may not include saying something, but it surely includes the gesture of "laying his hands upon them," and it explains the meaning of the clause, "that he might touch them" (10:13). Only Mark notes that Jesus did, in fact, bless the children, fulfilling the desire of those who brought them. This warm, human note is the climax of the unit's literal meaning: Jesus likes and blesses children.

179

SIGNIFICANCE

The primary significance of 10:2–12 for our time lies in its strong affirmation of permanent heterosexual union as part of God's good plan for humankind established in creation. That such unions are to be heterosexual is presupposed in the text and implicit in its terms. That they are to be permanent is explicitly stated in Jesus' answer to the Pharisees and further elaborated in his answer to his disciples. This understanding of marriage offers a fixed point of reference in a time of experimentation and confusion in the field of sexual relationships.

The text is significant as a clear and unambiguous affirmation of fidelity in marriage as God's gracious plan and a worthy human goal. Though the presenting question in the text, and often in life, is divorce, Jesus shifts our attention to marriage. His teaching calls us to look beyond the complexities of particular problems and situations to what is given in creation. The union for which we yearn sexually and which we need psychically is best achieved and sustained by fidelity to one mate in a life-long union. No one in the text—Pharisees, disciples, Jesus—is unaware of the thousand ways this divine plan is thwarted and male-female relationships corrupted. They and we know that the relationship between a particular woman and a particular man often fails to meet the sexual and psychic needs of the partners and may be a cruel parody of the divine intention. By focusing more on the plan than the problems, this text guards against the corrosion of values by human failure. The text insists upon the seriousness of marriage for those considering it. It assures God's blessing on all who, with varying degrees of success and failure and against whatever odds, work at building and maintaining their marriage.

The text is relevant to the way we cope with fear of marriage or failure to achieve its high goals. With regard to our failures, we, like the Pharisees, use the law as a way to avoid the higher demands of God. Our legitimizing a lesser standard allows us to feel righteous relative to our culture. In this matter as in others, we wish to be saved by our good works rather than admit that we have fallen short and must be saved by grace. Though Jesus here recognizes the necessity of law and even makes a prescriptive statement in 10:9, he relativizes the law, deplores legalism, and insists on the priority of God's will on the one hand and interpersonal relationships on the other.

180

Fear of marriage sometimes springs from a legalistic reading of the present text. Some individuals, perhaps influenced by texts like I Cor. 7:8 and Matt. 19:10, opt for celibacy. Some couples, thinking to avoid Jesus' strictures on divorce as well as the legal obligations of a civil marriage, decide to live together outside of marriage. The text gives no clear answer to the sometimes vexing question, "When is marriage?" or "Has God joined *us* together?" It does, however, suggest that in the natural union of man and woman, ties are created without regard to law, ties which the law cannot obliterate. One does not, therefore, by avoiding legal marriage, avoid the demands of a deep, human relationship, including fidelity.

Fear of marriage may also spring from taking its obligations so very seriously that one despairs of being able to measure up. To anyone paralyzed by this kind of fear the text offers the assurance that the natural order itself is on the side of the marriage of men and women, and the following context offers gospel that is applicable to marriage as well: "All things are possible with God" (10:27).

The text in all three Synoptic Gospels speaks for marriage and fidelity, against divorce and legalism. One peculiarly Marcan contribution to the text's significance lies in its setting. Only Mark includes the travel note of 10:1, which reminds the reader that this teaching occurs while Jesus is on his way to Jerusalem to die. It is bracketed by passion prediction units in which Jesus seeks to teach his disciples the way of the cross. Jesus in his own person and by his teaching offers to Christians the model of dying in order to live. Nowhere is that model more applicable or more necessary than in the intimate, long-term relationship in which two persons become one. Nor does any element in the gospel challenge more profoundly the usual understandings of self-actualization and self-fulfillment of an egocentric culture.

The foregoing remarks have sought the significance of the text for today along lines that reflect on intention and commandment, law and grace. The way not taken here but which the interpreter might profitably pursue is to reflect on what the text says to various groups of people: to young people contemplating a first marriage, to married couples struggling with a difficult marriage and considering divorce, to divorced persons considering remarriage, to persons wrestling with a decision about a liaison outside of marriage, about homosexuality, about celibacy. Anyone taking such an approach should consider

181

whether the issue is one to which the text speaks directly or only indirectly. Since these approaches deal with specific cases, they are more likely to grip the hearer or reader. They also fall more easily into the legalism with which Jesus is in controversy, a danger which these notes are intended to help the interpreter think through and avoid.

The juxtaposition of the teaching about children (10:13–16) with that about marriage (10:2–12) makes us confront not only what divorce does to an abandoned partner but also what it does to the children whom God gives and whom Jesus loves and blesses. The juxtaposition is important in another way. "Whoever does not receive the kingdom of God like a child shall not enter it" (v. 15) stands as a further warning against legalism in our relationship to God and consequently in every aspect of life. If we are to enter the Kingdom of God, we must receive it as a child does. That means, for instance, that we do not achieve the kingdom by keeping any law against divorce or by living up to legal obligations within a marriage. We can, by rigorous determination, keep enough of the law to feel self-righteous; but this will no more guarantee achievement of the goal of marriage than it will assure entrance to the Kingdom of God. We are to work at marriage, and yet, paradoxically, it is a gift . . . as is the Kingdom of God in all its aspects. One way the gracious rule of God becomes a reality in human life is as wife and husband openly receive each other in their life together, and as both receive gladly the children God gives. Perhaps this kind of receiving is the greatest gift we can offer each other. To such as receive in this way belongs the Kingdom of God.

Mark 10:17–31
Teaching About Riches

The story of Jesus' encounter with one traditionally known as the "rich young ruler," together with the ensuing teaching, strikes a jarring note in a world of "haves" and "have-nots." These very categories evoke the struggle of those who have possessions to keep them and of those who lack possessions to get them. Jesus' word cuts into such a world in an unexpected way. He expresses no outrage and makes no denunciations. Rather, he feels love for the man who loves his possessions. In love, Jesus calls; and in calling, he makes a radical demand.

TEXT

The first words of the text remind us that Jesus is still on his journey to the cross. This is the context in which a rich man hears his call and disciples hear his teaching about riches.

The story of Jesus' encounter with a man who asks about eternal life is found in all three Synoptic Gospels. Only Matthew says the man was young; only Luke says he was a ruler. All three say that he was rich (v. 23c and parallels), and in Mark this is the only description given. The point of the story and of 10: 17–31 as a whole is the relationship of discipleship to riches.

The passage unfolds in three parts with a conclusion:

Jesus and the rich man	17-22
Jesus and the disciples	23-27
Jesus and Peter	28-30
Concluding saying	31

Jesus' encounter with the rich man is essentially a call story. It is the only such story in Mark in which the person called responds not by following, but by going away (see 1:16–20; 2:14; 10:46–52). Not only does this negative outcome strike a note of realism; it also attests the special power of possessions to hinder Christian discipleship.

The rich man's concern is to "inherit eternal life." "Eternal life" (vv. 17, 30), so characteristic of the fourth Gospel, is a synonym for the "kingdom of God" (vv. 15, 25) which is the usual term in the Synoptics, and also for "being saved" (v. 26). The verb "inherit" would come naturally to the lips of a man of wealth. Even as an heir must meet certain conditions and fulfill certain obligations, so this rich man asks what he must *do* to inherit life. The contrast with the uncalculating dependence of a child (v. 15) is striking.

Jesus' first reply is surprising to the reader. He challenges the man's unusual form of address, "Good Teacher," by saying, "No one is good but God alone." Jesus is testing the man's sincerity, not only by deflating his fulsome address but also by calling him to account before the second table of the law. "Do not defraud," though not in the decalogue, substitutes for "do

183

not covet." The man's life-long observance of these commandments assures Jesus of his sincerity, so that Jesus "looking upon
him loved him."

Jesus' second and more profound reply is surprising to the
rich man. It consists of a series of five imperatives which fall on
the man's ears like hammer blows: go, sell, give, come, follow.
These are not five separate commands, however. The series is
broken by a promise, "you will have treasure in heaven," which
separates the two movements in this word of Jesus: Go dispose
of your wealth; come follow me. For this man who had never
followed Jesus, disposal of his wealth was a prerequisite to discipleship. For later disciples who hear or read the story, disposal
of wealth may come as a consequence. The "going" and "coming" are two moments in what is essentially one command and
one decision.

In 10:23–27 Jesus turns explicitly to disciples, a Marcan
device to introduce elaboration of Jesus' teaching that has special meaning for the church of the evangelist's time and of our
own. In this text Jesus moves from a specific case (the rich man)
to a generalization about all who have riches (v. 23) and then
to an even broader generalization that embraces everyone (v.
24). The analogy of the camel and the needle's eye (v. 25)
reverts to a consideration of the rich as a class, while the final
generalization (v. 27) again applies to everyone. This alterna-
tion was troublesome to some copyists, and a number of textual
variants give evidence of their attempts to make the paragraph
flow more smoothly. The thought is not hard to follow, however, as a paraphrase will show:

> How hard, indeed, it is for *anyone* to enter the kingdom, but for
> rich people it is quite impossible. In fact, humanly speaking it is
> impossible for anyone to be saved, rich or not; but with God all
> things are possible.

Attempts to make the analogy of verse 25 more logical by
changing one Greek letter to transform "camel" into "rope," or
to make it less shocking by the hypothesis of a small door called
the "needle's eye" in the Jerusalem city gate (a fantasy not
attested before the ninth century A.D.), are misguided. By an
awkward image the text means to speak of an impossibility (as
v. 27 makes evident). To try to domesticate this language does
Jesus no favor.

Certain important patterns bind these first two parts of the

184

text together, and the unit is in fact defined as 10:17–27 in many versions of the common lectionary.

Jesus' addressing his disciples as "children" is reminiscent of his teaching about children and the Kingdom of God in the preceding paragraph, even though a different Greek word is used. The relationship between 10:13–16 and 10:17–27 is one of contrast. The principle has been established (10:15) that one must receive the kingdom like a child. In 10:17–22, not only the rich man's question but also Jesus' answer focuses on what one must do. The material in 10:13–16 seems to depict entering the kingdom as easy and deplores any hindrance to it set up by the disciples. In 10:23–27 Jesus twice says, "How hard!", and then adds "with men, impossible . . . but not with God; for all things are possible with God." These last words transform the contrast from a contradiction to a paradox. Entrance to the Kingdom of God, or eternal life, or salvation, so far from being easy, demands our best obedience and all we have. Yet all we can do is not enough to achieve the life we seek. Such life and wholeness is possible only for God, and we can receive it only as gift. Jesus' blessing of children (10:13–16) can be read as cheap grace. Jesus' call to the rich man (10:17–22) can be read as works salvation. Jesus' teaching to disciples (10:23–27) draws gift and demand together in a paradox that is astonishing but true.

Also, 10:17–27 is related as a unit to the following paragraph (vv. 28–30). What Jesus demands of the rich man, Peter, speaking for the disciples, says they have fulfilled. What is impossible with men but possible with God (v. 27) is spelled out specifically in Jesus' promise (vv. 29–30), whose "now . . . and in the age to come" echoes the present (v. 24) and future (v. 23) tenses used to speak of entering the Kingdom of God.

Besides relating to its immediate context as a unit, 10:17–27 is tied together by the repetition of the verb "look" in two intensive forms. "Look around" (*periblepō*, v. 23) is a peculiarly Marcan term (its only use outside Mark is in the Lukan parallel to Mark 3:5). It is used mostly of Jesus (five times out of six in Mark). Jesus' eyes can sweep about him in anger (3:5), appreciation (3:34), inquiry (5:32), or inspection (11:11). Here, he gathers the attention of his disciples with a glance as he begins to teach. 185 Jesus' eyes are particularly expressive when he gazes intently (*emblepō*) at someone, as at the rich man (10:21) and at the disciples (10:27). His eyes underscore his words when he says,

"Go, sell, give; come, follow" and when he says, "All things are possible with God."

The pattern of responses further links the paragraph about the rich man and that about the disciples. When he heard Jesus' demanding call, the rich man's "countenance (face) fell." The Greek participle used here can mean "be shocked" or "become gloomy, dark." "Appalled" captures both nuances, shock and gloom. Most English translations heighten the visual quality of the text by reading this emotion in the man's face. He then went away "sorrowful" or "sad," literally "grieving," for he did not want to part with his wealth.

While the rich man's reaction to Jesus' command was shock, gloom, and sorrow, that of the disciples to his teaching on riches and the Kingdom of God was first amazement and then utter astonishment, both favorite expressions in Mark. Traditionally, wealth was a sign of the blessing of God. That Jesus viewed it as a hindrance to entering the Kingdom of God was amazing. When Jesus used an analogy that made entrance of the rich into the Kingdom of God quite impossible, the disciples were "exceedingly astonished" ("astonished out of measure," AV). Though they were not wealthy, they belonged to a culture whose evaluation of wealth was fundamentally challenged by the teaching of Jesus. They were profoundly shaken.

In the third part of the passage (10:28–30), Peter, speaking for all the disciples, seeks some reassurance for those who in response to Jesus' call have abandoned all the old supports (see 1:16–20). Jesus does not rebuke their insecurity or pride, but addresses it by means of an extravagant promise introduced by a solemn assertion, "Truly I say to you" (as at 10:15). This saying of Jesus shares several qualities of a "sentence of holy law" (cf. p. 155). Like other such eschatological sayings, it is characterized by promise and blessing. It is exceptional in that it includes no threat or curse and its fulfillment begins "now in this time" in the Christian community, described as an extended family with shared possessions and undergoing persecution. Part of the fulfillment, however, is reserved for the eschatological future; ". . . and in the age to come eternal life."

186   The text is concluded by a brief saying about first and last which appears in various contexts in the Synoptic Gospels. It appropriately summarizes the teaching of verses 28–30 and of the entire passage (10:17–30) and also the entire section 9:30—

10:45 encompassing the second passion prediction and all the ensuing material, up to and including the third instruction on discipleship: "Whosoever would be great among you . . ." (10:43).

SIGNIFICANCE

This teaching of Jesus about riches has been interpreted in a variety of ways which may be classified in three main groups.

First, the literal or eschatological reading of the text was doubtless prevalent in the earliest church. It was probably the understanding of the evangelist and of the first readers of this Gospel, who anticipated that Jesus would return as Son of man in glory to meet them in Galilee (14:28; 16:7) at a time unknown (13:32) but imminent (9:1; 13:30). Even when this eschatological expectation became less urgent, as in the portrayal of the Jerusalem church in Acts, the injunction to the rich man to sell all he had and give to the poor was applied to all disciples (Acts 4:32–35). This commonality of possessions would result in something like receiving "a hundredfold . . . houses and brothers and sisters and mothers and children and lands" (no commonality of wives in Mark or Acts!). An understanding that all Christians would divest themselves of all possessions could obviously persist in practice only so long as all expected the imminent return of the Lord. The Acts account gives evidence that already the condition imposed by Jesus on the rich man was not applied as a law for everyone: "While it remained unsold, did it not remain your own? And after it was sold, was it not at your disposal?" (Acts 5:4).

Second, an ascetic or restrictive reading of the text arose partly out of practical necessity, since life went on and had to be sustained, and partly in the context of an emerging monastic movement. In this context, the passage was still read literally but was applied only to certain people in the community and not to all disciples. This reading of the text has taken institutional form in the vows of poverty of the religious orders in the Catholic tradition. It has always been taken literally by certain individual Christians, whether in orders or not, who are led by it to a life of radical renunciation of possessions and total dependence on the providence of God. They do not try to impose this pattern on the entire Christian community, however, but understand it to be the special vocation of a small minority within that community.

187

Third, a symbolic or generalized reading of the text, more common among Protestants, applies this teaching to all disciples but no longer takes it literally. On this view, Jesus' command to sell all applied to that particular man, because love of and dependence on wealth was his particular impediment to discipleship. For all disciples, however, its spiritual meaning is that we must root out of our lives whatever may hinder our following Jesus, such as lust, pride, and selfishness, together with whatever object or practices may appertain to them.

Countless variations on the latter two interpretations bear witness to the tension in this text between the ideal and the possible. In our efforts to take seriously Jesus' teaching, we institutionalize, generalize, or spiritualize the message of Mark 10: 17–31, and in the process we say many things that are true and helpful. Yet the tension of this radical text resists resolution in any way that removes its pressure on *all* disciples relative to *wealth*. After we have done our best to make this text say something less upsetting to our system of values, Jesus looks intently at us and continues quietly to affirm that life is to be had not by accumulating things, but by disencumbering ourselves. Contrary to the dominant voices of our culture, but in keeping with the entire section on discipleship in Mark, this text proclaims the good news that the way to be really rich is to die to wealth.

If this message does not take our breath away, if we are not shocked, appalled, grieved, or amazed, we have either not yet heard it or heard it so often that we do not really hear it any more.

Mark 10:32–45
On the Road: Third Passion Prediction

Jesus, the disciples, and the relationship between them, these are the three centers of interest in the entire discipleship section in Mark (8:22—10:52). Each of these motifs comes into clear focus in this third, climactic prediction of Jesus' passion (see Introduction, pp. 4–5).

188

TEXT

The structure of this passage is parallel to that of the other passion prediction units: setting (v. 32), prediction (vv. 33–34), misunderstanding (vv. 35–40), and instruction in discipleship (vv. 41–45). The setting and the prediction are the fullest and most explicit of any in the three units.

Jesus

The spotlight falls first and last upon Jesus. At the beginning Jesus and his disciples are on the road, going up to Jerusalem. Jesus is walking ahead of them. He knows where he is going, and he knows what will happen to him when he gets there (vv. 33–34); but he walks determinedly ahead.

Speculation that the second clause applied originally to Jesus ("and *he* was amazed," or alarmed) resolves the awkwardness of two descriptions of the followers of Jesus and the problem of whether one or two groups are intended. However, no known manuscript supports the proposed reading; and it flies in the face of Jesus' clear understanding of the purpose of his life of service and his death in Jerusalem, which comes to expression in verse 45. To be sure, Jesus does not go easily to his death (e.g., Gethsemane, 14:32–42), but neither does he face death with amazement, alarm, or uncertainty. He may not know just how he will die (only Matt. 20:19 has Jesus predict that he will be crucified), but it is surely to die that he goes up to Jerusalem. The goal is passion, not pilgrimage. He will be hailed as king of the Jews, but his enthronement will be paradoxical. His coronation will mean his death.

Mark does not say explicitly that Jesus knew all this ahead of time. The text, in fact, underscores Jesus' limitations rather than his divine power. He denies the request of James and John not only because it is ill-conceived, but also because "to sit at my right hand or at my left is not mine to grant." The passive construction, "but it is for those for whom it has been prepared," is a circumlocution by which Jews spoke of God without naming him. (The TEV translation and Matt. 20:23 interpret this expression correctly.) Allocating places at his enthronement is something Mark's Jesus cannot do, just as the date of his own return in glory is something he does not know (13:32).

This passage invites us, therefore, not so much to marvel at

189

Jesus' divine foreknowledge as to reflect upon his sense of the purpose of his life and death. That purpose comes to clearest expression in 10:45, the climax and conclusion of the bracketed discipleship section: "For even the Son of man (author's trans.) came not to be served but to serve, and to give his life as a ransom for many."

These words of Jesus interpret his ministry, stating the meaning of his life and of his death. The phenomenon is so rare in the Synoptic Gospels that critical scholars (Bultmann, *History of the Synoptic Tradition*, p. 144, and many others) conclude that the saying is not from Jesus himself but from the early church. The historical question of whether or not Jesus said these words is of some interest, but the deeper question is whether or not they are true. Scripture affirms that Jesus' life was one of service and that his death was for others. His life and death were of a piece, for the supreme service of Jesus Christ was the voluntary giving of his life as a ransom for many. What does this mean?

In Greek usage "many" meant "a large number, but not all." Here, however, "many" has an inclusive sense, as in Jewish usage: the multitude, in contrast to the individual. "A ransom for many" does not intend to indicate that some might not be included, though that remains a possibility. (See Jeremias, *"Polloi,"* in Kittel, TDNT, VI, pp. 543–45).

"Ransom" comes from a world in which it was possible to buy the freedom of prisoners of war, slaves, or condemned criminals. (Parallels today are seen in incidents of kidnapping and hijacking.) The sum paid was called a "ransom," a term used only here (and par. Matt. 20:28) in the New Testament. The act of setting a person free in this way was called "redemption" (used as a verb to describe the work of Jesus Christ in Luke 24:21; Tit. 2:14 and I Pet. 1:18; as a noun in Luke 1:68; 2:38 and Heb. 9:12). The person accomplishing the liberation was called a "redeemer." Only Moses is called "redeemer" in the New Testament (Acts 7:35).

As the example just given shows, it is not appropriate to try to squeeze from Mark 10:45 a complete doctrine of the atonement applicable only to Jesus Christ. After all, "service above self" may apply to the membership of a modern international service club; and the theme of the innocent dying for the guilty, expressed with such power in Isa. 53, is found in the literature of many cultures. Nevertheless, of all the statements of the

190

meaning of Jesus' life and death, this one has spoken with special power to Christians through the ages. In it countless men and women have recognized an apt description not only of the one who, somewhere in the region of Judea and beyond the Jordan, strode purposefully on the road ahead of his disciples going up to Jerusalem, but also of the Christ whom they have encountered somewhere along their own road.

The Disciples

The suffering, death, and resurrection here predicted for the third time are important not only for Jesus, but also for his disciples. The spotlight focuses upon the disciples in several ways.

First, they are pictured in verse 32 following Jesus on the road, but in contrast to his firm determination they are filled with amazement and fear. Different translations capture various nuances in the first verb: they were "amazed" (AV, RSV), "astonished" (NIV), "filled with awe" (NEB), "filled with alarm" (TEV), "their mood was one of wonderment" (NAB), and "they were in a daze" (JB, influenced by the Vulgate's *stupebant*). The second verb is plain and simple: "They were afraid." The text probably does not mean to describe two groups, one amazed and the other afraid, but one group including all who followed Jesus with fearful wonder. This description of the disciples already hints that they have at last begun to understand that Jesus will be killed in Jerusalem; but they cannot begin to understand why, under these circumstances, he is determined to go there. Like Jesus, they sense impending doom; but unlike him, they sense in it no purpose. Strung out behind Jesus, they walk the same road; but they walk aimlessly, anxiously, fearfully.

In a second, fuller vignette (vv. 35–40) the text focuses on the continuing misunderstanding of the disciples. In the earlier units they have understood neither that he must suffer nor that they must. In this unit nothing is said about their misunderstanding Jesus' suffering, but in the request of James and John their misunderstanding of their own calling and destiny stands out sharply and clearly. Matthew attenuates the apostles' density by having their mother make the request, thus calling attention to her ambition rather than theirs. Jesus' reply, however, is made directly to the two men in Matthew as in Mark. Luke omits all reference to the embarrassing request. Mark makes no effort to conceal or apologize for their obtuse-

191

ness, but holds it up to the reader's full view and invites our reflection on its inappropriateness and upon the irony of it.

Jesus had but recently set before them a child as a model (9:36). Now, instead of following Jesus in childlike lowliness and trust, James and John use a childish stratagem to manipulate him to their own advantage: "We want you to do for us whatever we ask of you." Like any prudent parent, Jesus makes them say what they want before he will reply.

A further irony is that they ask for places at the right and left of Jesus, still hoping that the trip up to Jerusalem will, despite their apprehension, end in glory. Two robbers will in fact occupy those places and it will not be in glory. Jesus will be enthroned as king, but his throne will be a cross and his crown one of thorns. Indeed, James and John do not know what they are asking.

The supreme irony, however, is that despite Jesus' rebuke of Peter and despite his teaching about denying self, taking up one's cross and losing one's life (8:34–37); despite his rebuke of the squabble over greatness by the example of the child and his words about being last of all and servant of all (9:35–36); and finally despite his threefold prediction of his own suffering and death at the end of this road, James and John are still fantasizing about the coming glory and scheming for positions of privilege.

In this cycle of passion predictions the inner three have been singled out for their denseness (8:32; 9:38; 10:35), but in this passage all the Twelve are implicated. When the other ten hear of the request, they begin to be indignant at James and John (v. 41). Their anger may masquerade as moral indignation at James's and John's ambition, but the picture of the disciples throughout Mark's Gospel leads the reader here to suspect that the other ten are angry because they want those places for themselves. Jesus' words in the following instruction on discipleship show that he so interprets the situation.

Verse 41, then, is transitional. It concludes the paragraph on misunderstanding, in which all the Twelve are implicated, and serves to introduce Jesus' third teaching on discipleship, which again turns on the nature of true greatness. The teaching is the same as in 9:35, but here it is stated more fully. Not only is it expanded into the parallelism characteristic of Hebrew proverbs:

192

"Whoever would be great among you
 must be your servant,
And whoever would be first among you
 must be slave of all" (10:43–44)

but also this pattern of life is set over against that of the surrounding culture:

"It shall not be so among you." (10:43)

The disciples have heard Jesus' words, but they have the
music all wrong. They still dance to the world's tune. The picture of this group following Jesus up to Jerusalem is like that of
an untried team trotting onto a field behind their coach. Their
uniforms are splendid, but the rules by which they are ready to
play belong to a different game.

Relationship Between Jesus and the Disciples

Besides throwing into sharp relief Jesus' steadfast purpose
and the disciples' ineptitude, this passage highlights the relationship between Jesus and his disciples. Three points may be
noted.

First, despite the inappropriateness of their question, Jesus
does not rebuke James and John. When they affirm that they are
able to drink his cup and be baptized with his baptism, he
accepts their words, but turns them right side out. They think
of his cup and his baptism as a means to share his glory. Jesus
breaks that connection, but affirms the cup of suffering (14:36)
and the baptism both of death (Rom. 6:3) and of empowerment
for mission (Mark 1:8–11) as the means of fellowship with him
and as the only way to follow him. He accepts them as they are,
but firmly points them in a new direction, in the way that he
himself is going.

Second, Jesus invites his disciples to be like him. Although
he speaks of himself in verse 45, he clearly thinks of what the
disciples should become. The RSV's "also" is misleading. The
text says, "For *even* the Son of man came not to be served but
to serve, and to give his life a ransom for many." The argument
is of the "how much more . . ." type. If the Lord Jesus was a
servant, how much more ought his disciples to be servants.

Third, although the disciples are here depicted as slow
learners, ambitious, and selfish, they nevertheless continue to
follow Jesus. Their relationship to him is imperfect, but it is

193

also unbroken. Speaking of their fear as they followed Jesus, Calvin says,

> Now, although this fear was wrong in many respects, yet their following of Christ was a sign of no common allegiance and piety. It would, of course, have been far better if they had hurried swiftly and without regrets to wherever the Son of God wanted to lead them; but their reverence deserves praise, for they would rather do violence to themselves than desert him.
>
> (*Harmony*, II, 268)

The text does not excuse the disciples, but neither does it reject them. Rather, it invites readers to identify with the Twelve as the stumbling followers of Jesus, the shaky servants of the Lord.

SIGNIFICANCE

One element of significance is discovered by comparing the terms of the three passion predictions. The first (8:31) speaks of rejection and death at the hands of Jewish religious leaders. The second (9:31) has Jesus delivered into the hands of men in general. This one (10:33) reiterates the role of Jewish religious authorities, but adds that they will deliver him to the Gentiles, meaning here the Roman political authorities. "They" in verse 34 (those who will mock, spit upon, scourge, and kill him) is ambiguous in the original text. It may refer only to the Gentiles (as in the NAB, TEV, and NIV); but in the passion narrative (chaps. 14—15) all are involved in these four actions, both Jews and Gentiles, both religious and political leaders. In the total sweep of the three predictions, all are implicated in Jesus' death; and his death is clearly for the "many" of all sorts. Every reader can identify with some party to the death of Jesus, and whoever says "Yes" to "Were you there?" is one of the "many" for whom Christ died. One significance of the text, then, is its appeal to every reader to hear the bittersweet good news: "You participated in the death of Jesus, and Jesus died for you."

A second point of significance is the text's challenge to complacency and apathy in church members. Any reader can deplore the dullness and fear of those first followers, but at least they were perceptive enough to be alarmed. Today the gospel is often presented as a no-risk offer, and persons sometimes follow Jesus in order to stay out of trouble. It is possible to understand each of these approaches in a way that is valid, but

194

the text offers a jolting challenge to any simplistic, self-centered understanding of discipleship. Getting right with God by coming to Jesus is not simply a basic factor in an orderly life. Discipleship will mean more trouble, not less. Though it may be palliative in some respects, following Jesus is likely to be disruptive in others. True discipleship is characterized by a costly pouring out of one's life for another, whether it be an aging parent, a difficult spouse, a special child, another member of the Christian fellowship who has unusual needs, or any person whose situation elicits neighborly service at personal cost. Jesus came to serve and to give his life. Anyone who contemplates following Jesus without fear and trembling has not understood true discipleship, according to Mark.

A third element of significance worthy of the preacher's or teacher's attention is its challenge to the basic value system of contemporary culture and to our standards of success. "Gentiles" in verse 42 refers again to political authorities, but in their exercise of authority they embody the prevailing norms for measuring greatness. These norms are as prevalent now as they were then. "It shall not be so among you" says the text. Theoretically, this poses a serious problem for theology and ethics, because it stands in tension with other texts (such as the image of the leaven in the loaf, Luke 13:21) which suggest that the goal of discipleship is to transform the entire culture. This text suggests a permanent minority status for disciples, a dichotomy in principle between Christians and their culture. Though a problem in theory, in practice no culture has yet emerged on the planet in which this text would be inappropriate for followers of Jesus. The task of the interpreter, then, is to isolate and articulate examples of ways in which Jesus' criterion for measuring greatness, and his standard of success, stand over against those of the prevailing culture, calling men and women to conscious and costly decisions all the way along the road.

Fourth, the text proposes the imitation of Christ as a pattern for discipleship (vv. 43–45). Discipleship means a life of service, and the text is therefore appropriate for the instruction and ordination of deacons (literally, servants), though not only for them.

Disciples cannot redeem others as Jesus did, of course; but 195 those who follow Jesus are called to pour out their lives for others as Jesus did. One follower who understood wrote:

> By this we know love, that he laid down his life for us; and we
> ought to lay down our lives for the brethren. . . . Beloved, if God
> so loved us, we also ought to love one another (I John 3:16; 4:11;
> see also I John 3:2*b*).

John in Mark 10:35–37 helps us to see ourselves as we are. The "John" of the epistle helps us to see what we may become in response to Jesus Christ: "Whoever would be great among you must be your servant, and whoever would be first must be slave of all."

Mark 10:46–52
The Healing of Blind Bartimaeus

The restoration of sight to this blind beggar at Jericho is the last healing story in the Gospel of Mark. Although not as spectacular as the raising of Jairus' daughter from the dead, the cure of Bartimaeus is climactic in the sense that its outcome marks the goal of this Gospel in the life of its readers: He followed Jesus "on the way."

TEXT

Two exegetical elements offer valuable clues to the interpreter of this text: its placement in the Gospel as a whole (setting in literature) and the inner form of the unit (literary type).

With regard to its setting in literature, this passage forms the transition between the section on discipleship (chaps. 8—10) and the section on Jesus' confrontation with the religious authorities in Jerusalem (chaps. 11—13). The final words of the passage, "on the way," form an apt conclusion to the entire section of instruction to the Twelve concerning the way of Jesus. A further element linking this paragraph to the preceding material is Jesus' question, "What do you want me to do for you?" (v. 51), echoing his identical words to James and John in 10:36. The misguided request of the latter is here corrected by the enlightened desire of a blind man. On the other hand, the story points ahead in that among "those who followed (and) cried out, 'Hosanna!' " (11:9) is the healed beggar who became a follower (10:52). Bartimaeus' twice-repeated cry for help to the Son of David (10:47, 48) is echoed by the acclamations of the

196

crowd on entering Jerusalem, "Blessed is the kingdom of our father David that is coming!" (11:10). The title "Son of David" is displaced at the critical moment in the Bartimaeus story by the more appropriate *Rabbouni* ("Master"). "Son of David" does not appear explicitly in 11:10 and is challenged fundamentally, if not rejected, in 12:35–37, so that it is no more (nor less) correct a title for Jesus than was Peter's "Christ" in 8:29. This problematical title prepares the way for the controversies in chapters 11 and 12 about Jesus' identity and authority. As a transitional passage, 10:46–52 points back to a section which has as its primary focus discipleship and points ahead to one whose primary focus is Christology. Both of these elements appear in the present passage.

A second consideration about the literary setting of the passage gives priority to the concern for discipleship. The only two Marcan accounts of Jesus' restoring sight to the blind are 8:22–26 and 10:46–52 (see Introduction, p. 4). Each is transitional between major sections of the Gospel, and both form brackets that mark the limits of part 4 and interpret the meaning of discipleship. As in the other restoration-of-sight story, "see" functions symbolically as well as literally in 10:46–52. One must not push too far the idea that through his recognition of Jesus as master Bartimaeus acquired spiritual vision and became an ideal disciple. At the cross, he, with all the other disciples, will flee. Yet at this point in the story, Bartimaeus' perception as an outsider stands in vivid contrast to the blindness of the disciples as insiders. Furthermore, "he received his sight" stands in close, parallel relationship to "followed him on the way." The text is an invitation to come to Jesus and so to see; to see and so to follow Jesus.

With regard to the literary type of 10:46–52, we are obviously dealing with an extraordinary cure and therefore with a miracle story. It includes a problem (blindness, vv. 46–51), a solution (Jesus' word "Your faith has made you well," v. 52*a*), and evidence of cure (receiving sight and following Jesus, v. 52*b*). In its emphasis on the relationship of faith and healing, this text directly echoes Jesus' word to the woman with the hemorrhage, "Your faith has made you well" or "saved you" (5:34). It reinforces the appeals to faith in 2:5; 9:23–24 and (negatively) 6:5–6. Bartimaeus offers a particularly vivid case study of faith. His crying out to Jesus, even with a less than perfect perception of who Jesus is, his persistent refusal to be

197

silenced, his bold and eager response to Jesus' call, mediated through anonymous third parties, and his clear focus on the one thing he wanted most in all the world, together with his keen anticipation that Jesus could and would grant it, are the attitudes and actions which Jesus calls "faith." Its genuineness is demonstrated by the fact that Bartimaeus, having received his sight, followed Jesus on his way.

Though the text can be interpreted fruitfully as a miracle story, in it the miracle story form is radically modified. The description of the problem dominates the scene (vv. 46–51); the actual healing and its results are reduced to a single verse (v. 52). Furthermore, the cure is effected without any word or gesture of Jesus. Jesus' word is presented simply as a dismissal of the man; the major emphasis is on the man and his faith. These considerations, coupled with the fact that "call" is repeated three times in verse 49, suggest that this passage belongs also, and perhaps more fundamentally, to the category "call story." It lacks the element of resistance common to the call narratives of the Old Testament and to that of the apostle Paul in Acts. In this regard, it is more like the call narratives earlier in Mark (1:16–20; 2:13–14). It tells how a particular individual whose name is given (quite uncharacteristic of miracle stories) became a disciple of Jesus Christ.

An even closer analogy to the story of Bartimaeus is found in Luke 5:1–11, in which the call of Peter and his companions is linked with a miracle story: the astonishing catch of fish. (For a detailed comparison, see P. J. Achtemeier, " 'And he followed him': Miracles and Discipleship in Mark 10:46–52" in *Semeia* 11:115–45 [1978].) To be sure, certain elements in the present story are unique among examples of this type. Here it is Bartimaeus who takes the initiative, both by crying out first and by choosing, without any explicit invitation, to make Jesus' way *his* way. Uniquely in this narrative the call is mutual: Bartimaeus cries out to Jesus and Jesus calls Bartimaeus. But the issue of the encounter is that of most call stories: "He followed him on the way."

SIGNIFICANCE

198   The healing of Bartimaeus is especially significant for those who sit outside the church. Because interpreters deal most often with persons who are at least nominal disciples, they may

tend to overlook the fact that Bartimaeus was an outsider who stands in sharp and favorable contrast to the insiders in Mark. The text calls attention to persons who, though lost in the crowd, may be ready and eager for some vital contact with Jesus Christ. It is significant that, while many rebuked Bartimaeus's cries and tried to silence him, Jesus, though going steadfastly up to Jerusalem (10:32), took time to call him. (See the treatment of Jesus' response to interruptions at 5:25–34, pp. 112–13)

For either outsiders or insiders, "What do you want me to do for you?" underlines the importance of getting our deepest desires straight. James and John (10:35–37) did not; but Bartimaeus did (10:51f.). His responses, first to Jesus' question and then to his command, show that he wanted the right thing; and he wanted it the right way. He did not secretly cherish his infirmity. He really wanted to be healed. "Prayer is the soul's sincere desire, unuttered or expressed." Bartimaeus expressed his prayer persistently, plainly, and honestly, "and immediately he received his sight."

Of particular relevance to insiders is the text's instruction on the meaning of faith. Some Christians, moved perhaps by Mark's exposure of the blindness of the disciples, may come to realize their own misunderstanding of Jesus and of discipleship, but accept their condition as normal. The healing of Bartimaeus is testimony to the power of Jesus to restore (make well, save) those who know they are blind. The eager persistence of Bartimaeus in calling out and his actively springing up to come to Jesus when called serve as a model for faith.

The healing of blind Bartimaeus is not simply a vivid story with a moral for Christians; it is a witness to Jesus Christ and a call to follow him. The Old Testament lesson accompanying this Gospel pericope in the common lectionary is Jer. 31:7–9, an oracle of salvation and restoration. In it the Lord promises to gather his people from the farthest parts of the earth, "among them the blind and the lame." Perhaps the framers of the lectionary have seen in Bartimaeus a particular example of the fulfillment of that promise as Jesus goes up to Jerusalem to seal, by his death and resurrection, the new covenant foretold in Jer. 31:31–34. Participation in that new covenant is open to the house of Israel and the house of Judah, but also to all who, knowing their blindness, want to see; and to all who, seeing, follow Jesus on the way.

199

INTERPRETATION

Whatever approach is adopted, the interpretation should take into account that this passage in Mark constitutes both a bracket and a transition; it speaks of both Christology and discipleship, and it is appropriately understood as both miracle and call.

PART FIVE

Jesus in Jerusalem

Mark 11:1—13:37

Mark 11:1-11
The Entry into Jerusalem

On Palm Sunday the minds of those charged with preaching, teaching, or worship in the church turn almost inevitably to this passage and its parallels (Matt. 21:1–11; Luke 19:28–40; John 12:12–19). Though John's is the only account that mentions palm branches, it is not included in the common lectionary. Each of the Synoptic accounts appears in certain of the three-year lectionary cycles as the Gospel reading for Palm Sunday. What suggestions does the text offer to interpreters who encounter the passage so regularly in the life of the church?

TEXT

The passage falls into four parts: setting (v. 1), procurement of the colt (vv. 2–6), acclamation approaching Jerusalem (vv. 7–10), and conclusion (v. 11).

Setting (11:1)

"And when they drew near to Jerusalem" marks the beginning of the Jerusalem ministry of Jesus toward which the narrative has been moving since the first passion prediction at Caesarea Philippi (8:27—9:1). Though the entry scene has many hints of an enthronement procession, its reticence at several points recalls the preceding teachings about rejection and fore-

201

shadows the coming confrontation with the Temple and its authorities which will dominate chapters 11—13. Jesus' kingship is ambiguous and his entry into the royal city ironic.

The setting on the Mount of Olives is important, for according to Zech. 14:4 the Lord would appear on the Mount of Olives "on that day," and there contemporary messianic hopes were focused (e.g., Josephus, *Antiquities* XX. 169).

The Colt (11:2–6)

Verses 2–6 contain two related problems of interpretation. First, had Jesus previously made an arrangement with the owner of the colt, which would explain what the disciples were to say and why the objectors let them go (11:3, 5–6)? That is, are we to read the story according to the normal historical canons of cause and effect or as a wonder-story involving supernatural powers on Jesus' part? Second, does "Lord" *(kyrios)* in verse 3 refer to God, to Jesus, or to the colt's owner (see TEV note: "Its owner needs it")? The issue here is whether it is possible for Jesus to refer to himself as Lord, which he does nowhere else in Mark (though 12:36 comes close). Commentators who tend toward a historical reading of Mark (e.g., Taylor and Lane) prefer the idea of a prior arrangement and the translation "owner." The intention of the text, however, seems to be to present another instance of Jesus' remarkable power and authority, evidenced in this case by his clairvoyance. "Lord," at the level of the narrative, refers to God: Jesus tells the disciples to say that the colt is needed for a sacred purpose. At the level of the evangelist's communication with the readers, however, we are to understand that Jesus is the Lord who needs the colt.

The note that no one has ever sat on the colt (11:2) might point to the sacred use to which it will be put (cf. Num. 19:2; Deut. 21:3; I Sam. 6:7). It is more likely a veiled allusion to the foal on which the messianic king would enter Jerusalem according to Zech. 9:9, an allusion which is made explicit in Matt. 21:5.

Subsequent interpreters stressed various details in the story. The phrase "a colt tied" (11:2) was pressed by patristic interpreters into a reference to the blessing of Judah in Gen. 49:8–12. Justin Martyr went so far as to say, contrary to Mark 11:4, that the colt in the Gospel was tied to a vine. This is but the beginning of patristic extravagances concerning the colt, which became central in various allegorical interpretations of the text on into the medieval period. A current example of similar allegorization is that which sees the colt as a symbol for any disciple whose help the Lord needs.

Calvin, who warned against allegorization, pointed rather to the example of the disciples themselves who, despite their puzzlement, "went away" (v. 4) in obedience to the Lord's command. This does no violence to the text, but it still places the weight of interpretation on a secondary detail rather than on the central thrust of the passage as a whole.

The main point of the narrative about the colt is that Jesus took the initiative to arrange the following acclamation and that every step of the preparation occurred through divine foreknowledge and according to plan.

The Acclamation (11:7–10)

The heart of the passage lies in verses 7–10. Once again, there is a veiled allusion to Scripture. The spreading of garments on the colt and on the road may refer to a coronation custom (II Kings 9:13).

The chief Scripture reference, however, is quite explicit. "Hosanna! Blessed is he who comes in the name of the Lord!" is a quotation from Ps. 118:25–26. This is the last of the Hallel (praise) psalms sung by pilgrims approaching the Temple. It is also a royal psalm. In its original context (Ps. 118:25), "Hosanna" retains its literal meaning of a prayer for salvation: "Save, now" or "Save, I pray." On the lips of the pilgrims, however, it became a shout of praise, as it is in Mark 11:9. In the psalm, "Blessed be he (sing.) who enters in the name of the Lord!" is pronounced by the priests, who immediately add, "We bless you (pl.) from the house of the Lord" (Ps. 118:26). The latter blessing clearly applies to the entering pilgrims; the former could apply either to the pilgrims or to the king.

This ambiguity is removed in part when the text is quoted by the clamoring crowd in Mark. To the scriptural "Hosanna! Blessed . . ." they add in chiastic (a, b: b, a) order, "Blessed is the kingdom of our father David that is coming! Hosanna in the highest!" (11:10). This makes the acclamation a royal one, yet, unlike the accounts in Matthew and in Luke, the crowd in Mark does not explicitly call Jesus either "King" or "Son of David." This is an enthronement procession, yet the text shows a remarkable reticence with regard to Jesus himself. No crowds come out from the city to meet him; the manifestation is by those who accompanied him on the way. This includes Bartima-

203

eus (10:52) who had called Jesus "Son of David" twice, but whose final address was changed (corrected?) to "Master." Similarly here, though Jesus is clearly connected with the coming kingdom of "our father David," he himself is not called "Son of David." Jesus, in fact, rides on in enigmatic silence according to Mark. Luke 19:41–44 tells of his weeping over the city and predicting its destruction, but not Mark. Mark depicts an entry which is triumphal only for Jesus' followers who have not yet understood his destiny as Son of man. For Jesus, it is an entry into suffering and death. He enters Jerusalem as a pilgrim, and as more than a pilgrim. He makes no response to a royal acclamation, but his silence seems to suggest, "I am Messiah, and I will save; but not as you expect." The irony of this rag-tag procession is that its enthusiastic participants are wrong in their expectation that Jesus will immediately restore the fortunes of Jerusalem, and yet they are right in their hope that he is Messiah. He is no less King than their words suggest, but his kingdom is other and more than they dare to think.

Conclusion (11:11)

Unlike the Synoptic parallels (Matt. 21:1–17; Luke 19:28–46), in Mark Jesus does not immediately drive the merchants and money changers from the Temple. He does, on entering the city, go straight to the Temple; but there he only looks around and returns to Bethany with the Twelve for the night. This brief note underscores the centrality of the Temple for the entire section that will follow. Deferral of the act of authority over the Temple until the next day allows its placement within the episode of the withered fig tree, a characteristic interpretive device in Mark (see comment on following passage).

SIGNIFICANCE

The significance of Jesus' entry into Jerusalem is differently understood in each of the four Gospels. In John 12:12–19 the procession is altogether triumphant, complete with palm branches and the acknowledgement of Jesus' opponents that "the world has gone after him." Matthew, like John, quotes the messianic text in Zech. 9:9 but lays greater stress on the paradoxical nature of Jesus' kingship: "Your king is coming to you, humble . . ." (Matt. 21:5). In Luke, though the crowds hail Jesus as King and the Pharisees call him "Teacher," the evangelist depicts Jesus as the prophet who foretells the destruction of the city and weeps over it (Luke 19:41–44). In Mark, this latter trait is deferred to chapter 13. Jesus is not shown as the king who, though glorious, is nonetheless lowly. Rather, Jesus enters as the lowly one, hero only to a motley rabble, but he is ironically more of a king than they think.

The challenge to the interpreter is to preserve the peculiarly Marcan force and thrust of the text, especially when interpreting it amid the pomp and circumstance with which the church often tries to invest Palm Sunday. When those efforts are humble ones, the interpreter's task is easier, for the worshipers' identity with those first celebrants is more evident; and the focus of attention can be more readily shifted to the silent figure on the ass's colt.

With attention fixed on him, the interpreter can point to the authoritative lowliness of God displayed in Jesus Christ. That lowliness is, of course, seen elsewhere in Jesus' life and ministry; but here its quiet dignity and hidden majesty come to the fore. Lowliness is a quality all too seldom associated with God, even by those who hold that God is most fully revealed in Jesus Christ.

To be clear about the grandeur of the divine lowliness is important because we tend to become like the God or gods we worship. It is easy enough to join the crowds that sing "Hosanna" fore and aft of Jesus. Jesus makes no objection to these demonstrations, but his silence in their midst is striking. For those who look and listen intently, his silent presence may become compelling. Some will follow in his way, acknowledging that they know him but in part. They will know failure, as did that first, fickle crowd. But by the grace of a crucified and risen Lord, those who continue to follow him may come also to share, in some measure, his lowliness and his strength.

Mark 11:12–25 (26)
The Temple and the Fig Tree

The story of the cleansing of the Temple appears in all four Gospels, the cursing of the fig tree in two; yet no account of these incidents is included in the common lectionary. Each raises serious questions in the mind of the common reader, and

205

both have in some circumstances proved to be embarrassing to Christians. What is the interpreter to make of them?

TEXT

In Mark the two incidents are so closely interwoven as to form a single unit in which the cleansing of the Temple is bracketed in typical Marcan fashion (e.g., 5:21–43; 6:7–32; 14: 53–72) by the cursing of the fig tree and its attendant teaching. The entire unit appears immediately after the triumphal entry and introduces the theme of conflict which will govern all the days in Jerusalem, thus setting the tone for chapters 11—13.

A close look at the structure of this composite passage offers a key to its understanding.

Cursing of fig tree: beginning	12–14
Cleansing of Temple	15–19
Action	15–16
Teaching and reaction	17–19
Cursing of fig tree: conclusion	20–23
Tree withered	20–21
Teaching on faith	22–23
Teaching on prayer	24–25
Believe	24
Forgive	25

Only in Mark do Jesus' deeds and words in the Temple appear as a story within the story of the fruitless fig tree. This placement is a strong clue to the interpretation of the text. The fig tree is a symbol for Israel, embodied in the Temple and its leaders. Each appears to be thriving; neither is bearing the desired fruit; both are condemned by Jesus.

Jesus' judgment on the tree and the Temple continues through verse 20. In 11:21 Peter evidently speaks for all the disciples, since Jesus' reply in the plural introduces a series of sayings addressed to disciples in general. The first of these, on faith (vv. 22–23), concludes the Marcan sandwich about the Temple and the fig tree. Two additional sayings are attached by catchwords: "Believe," which links verse 24 to verse 23, and "pray," which links verse 25 to verse 24. The first part of the passage (vv. 12–21) is directed against a sterile religion and its leaders. The latter part (vv. 22–25), directed to Jesus' disciples then and now, is instruction about faith, prayer, and forgiveness.

Verse 26 is a copyist's addition, imported from Matt. 6:15, and is properly eliminated from consideration.

The meaning of Jesus' action in 11:15–16 is interpreted not only by the acted parable of the withered fig tree (vv. 12–14, 20–21) but also by Jesus' teaching addressed to Temple leaders (v. 17) and to the crowd at large (v. 18), in which he makes significant use of two Old Testament texts. Jesus quotes Isa. 56:7 ("a house of prayer for all the nations"), which announces that faithful proselytes will worship in the restored Temple—a prophecy that can also refer to an eschatological temple in which all the Gentiles ("nations," "peoples") will come to worship the God of Israel (see comment on 14:58). Jesus' reference to "a den of robbers" alludes to Jeremiah's Temple sermon (Jer. 7:11) which attacks the use of religious observances to cover up sinful practices and predicts the destruction of the Temple (Jer. 7:12–15).

By combining these texts, Jesus not only attacks the use of a place of prayer for commercial purposes, but also denounces the national and religious exclusivism which denies Israel's call to be "a light to the nations [Gentiles]" (Isa. 49:6). The quotations convey a strong hint that God will punish these sins by destroying the Temple. The chief priests and scribes understand the implications of Jesus' words. He does not attack the Temple *per se*, but their way of running it, their leadership and teaching. That the fig tree withers next day "from the roots up" (11:20, Greek) reinforces the idea that the fate of the Temple is due to the moribund spiritual leadership which was at the root of Temple worship. The leaders react to Jesus' words in fear and determine to destroy him. The crowd, however, is "astonished at his teaching."

Read as history, the text poses problems which interpreters have attempted to answer in various ways. The general problem of miracle (see Introduction, p. 20) takes a special form here. Jesus uses his powerful word in a way that is not only destructive (it is a "curse," v. 21) but apparently unjust ("it was not the season for figs," v. 13). Some grasp this nettle firmly and see in it a quite human, if less than admirable, expression of irritation. A prominent actor, whose readings of Mark's Gospel attracted crowds in Britain and America in the 1970s, had Jesus glance around nervously to see whether the disciples had heard his hasty, spiteful words. Some historical critics read more literally, "May no one ever eat fruit from you *into the age*," (that is, the new age of God's perfect reign) and understand it to be not a curse but a prayer for the Kingdom of God to come before the first figs are ripe. On this reading, the historical Jesus was a thoroughgoing eschatologist who fully expected the inauguration of the messianic age within days of his entry into Jerusalem; then fruit trees would bear fruit all year round. Verses 20–21 would be a legend, in that case, added by early Christians who knew that the kingdom did not come as Jesus expected and who had seen the Temple destroyed in A.D. 70.

However, the problems posed by reading the text as history and the answers given to them tend to obscure rather than to illumine the point of the passage. A better way is to recognize the symbolic use of language here and then to listen to the text in the setting of the earliest church which remembered the sayings of Jesus and in the setting of the evangelist and his community as reflected in the text's written form.

That the sayings in 11:23–25 appear in a variety of forms and contexts in the Gospels (e.g., Matt. 6:14–15; 17:20; Luke 17:6; John 14:13–14; 15:7; 16:23) suggests that the earliest church included these teachings of Jesus in its training (catechesis) of new Christians. In the setting of the earliest church, the point was the power of faith and the necessity to believe and to forgive if prayer is to be effective.

The prominent role of the Temple throughout chapters 11 —13, coupled with the apparently symbolic cursing of the fig tree, invites reflection on the possible setting of this text in the life of the evangelist's community at the time of writing. A church engaged in bitter conflict with the synagogue might well have heard in Jesus' words the condemnation of a Judaism viewed by Christians as barren and also a promise that God would remove this obstacle which, like a mountain, was blocking the path of the church. Christians, however, must believe God's power to do so and must forgive their Jewish opponents, even while they prayed that God would move them out of the way.

SIGNIFICANCE

Of the various possible meanings of the text considered thus far, two are suggestive for its significance today. From the time of Jesus through the time of the evangelist, the text served to denounce a sterile religion and its leaders. Tragically enough, Christians continued to use it to attack Judaism long after the

208

synagogue ceased to be a threat to the spreading institutional church. It is this text's potential for encouraging anti-Semitism and hindering ecumenism which makes it embarrassing to many and which may account for its omission from the lectionary.

In our time, however, it is surely against the spiritual barrenness of us who pride ourselves on being the new temple, the extended Israel, the church, that the Lord's words in Mark 11:12–21 ring most tellingly. His adversaries today are likely to be those of his own household. Jesus took specific physical action against the evidences of sterility in Temple worship. Interpreters of the text, while aware of the limits of their authority, should weigh equally carefully and specifically the extent of their responsibility for a fruitless church. While this line of interpretation is particularly appropriate for gatherings of church leaders and meetings of church courts or councils, it can also apply to a local congregation, whose members share the responsibilities of leadership as disciples of Jesus Christ.

A second significant dimension of the text lies in the sayings of Jesus addressed explicitly to disciples whom he urges to believe, to pray, and to forgive. The earliest church remembered these sayings because they were basic to the creation and maintenance of a Christian community. They still are. The church is a community of faith or else it is an empty shell. Interpretation can focus on the relation to each other of faith, prayer, and forgiveness and of each to the life of the individual Christian and of the community.

Human experience attests that the saying on faith (11:23) is figurative; those who wish to remove literal mountains resort to earth-moving equipment, not to prayer. The context in Mark and theological reflection suggest that the figure is hyperbole: an arresting exaggeration, similar to that about the camel and the needle's eye in 10:25. Unless it is understood as hyperbole, even in its figurative sense the saying runs the risk of making the fulfillment of prayer depend ultimately upon human faith rather than on the power of God. Such an understanding can produce only frustration and guilt when the pray-er does not get what he or she wants. Hyperbole is not literally true, but it is far from a lie. That there is remarkable power in positive thinking is true, with or without reference to God. But this text speaks of faith in God (v. 22) as the channel whereby we open our lives to the power of God (vv. 23–24), and this principle is

209

profoundly true here. Although in the Bible faith often signifies trust in spite of doubt, faith is used here in its common acceptance, meaning absence of doubt. The interpreter who wishes to explore these dimensions of faith could well limit consideration to 11:22–24 and the related sayings in Matt. 17:20 and Luke 17:6.

Since church members today embody elements of the foes and the followers of Jesus in the text, interpretation might draw together the denunciation of spiritual sterility and the promise made to those who pray, believing and forgiving. It is not hard to see how denominational headquarters, middle-judicatory offices, and local church staffs resemble the chief priests and scribes of Jesus' day; nor is it hard to see how our busy, prosperous churches are like leafy, fruitless fig trees. It may be more difficult to acknowledge that some flourishing programs stand condemned and therefore doomed by the word of Jesus Christ.

Even if we hear that stern word, we have not yet fully heard the text whose last word is gospel as well as demand. The power of God that withered a fig tree and moves mountains can also bring new life to a church and its leaders, though they be dry from their roots up. The text calls us to believe that and to pray for it in faith. As we pray, we are to forgive those very leaders whom we more often excoriate than lift up to God in prayer, so that we, too, may be forgiven.

Mark 11:27–33
The Question About Authority

The question about authority is the first of five controversies between Jesus and Jewish religious leaders in chapters 11 and 12 (see Introduction, pp. 2–3). It is intimately tied to the fig tree/Temple episode which introduces the whole series. While that introductory passage focused on Jesus' adversaries and disciples, this one goes to the heart of the matter by raising a question about Jesus himself.

210

TEXT

"By what authority are you doing these things?"
Those who raise this first question are described as "the

chief priests and the scribes and the elders." This is precisely the combination of persons who had figured in the first passion prediction (8:31), who stand behind the arrest of Jesus (14:43) and before whom Jesus will be tried (14:53; 15:1). Mark does not present them as the Sanhedrin itself, but they are the three main groups from which the seventy-one members of that council were drawn. Jesus is not confronted in the present passage by a formal investigation, but by an informal yet potent attack on the part of a religious establishment that had already determined to destroy him (11:18).

"These things," repeated four times in the Greek text of this passage, may allude remotely to earlier events in Galilee (2:1—3:6); but the expression refers primarily to the cleansing of the Temple in 11:15–17. The chapter division at the end of the present text recognizes how closely it is bound to 11:12–26. The chief priests, scribes, and elders see Jesus' actions in the Temple as a challenge to their authority. The reader sees the cursing of the fig tree also as an extension of that challenge.

The basic question is indeed one of authority. If authority generally means a combination of right and power (see comment on 1:21–28; 2:1–12), here the accent is on right: "What right do you have to do these things? Who gave you such a right?" (11:28, TEV; see also 29 and 33). Yet power also comes into play, especially the power of Jesus' word. That power is evident in Jesus' reiterated "Answer me!" in the imperative (11:29–30).

Yet they do not answer him, except by an evasion: "We do not know." Jesus, therefore, does not answer their initial question. He knows the source of his authority, but he says, "Neither will I tell. . . ." This move produces the unusual phenomenon of a pronouncement story without a clear pronouncement. The form of the passage sets the stage for an authoritative saying of Jesus about his own authority. That form is broken, however, by Jesus' reiterated "Answer me!" which shifts to his interlocutors the burden of an incomplete story.

Jesus' counter-question appears first as a shrewd ploy which exemplifies his authority by showing that his wits are sharper than those of his opponents. However, his question about the baptism of John is more than a dodge. It forces his adversaries to remember John's call to repentance, his offer of forgiveness, and his announcement of a Coming One (1:4–8). It also reminds the reader of Jesus' own baptism, at which his authority is estab-

211

lished by a voice from heaven: "Thou art my beloved Son; with thee I am well pleased" (1:11). By demanding a response to the word of God through John, Jesus confronts his interlocutors (and the evangelist confronts his readers) with a personal decision which alone can answer the question about the authority of Jesus. His reply by a counter-question, then, is not an evasion but a serious theological statement.

Jesus knows full well where his authority comes from, as does the reader, but he will not tell these religious leaders who have already rejected him. What good would it do? If they did not recognize God's word in John's testimony to one who was coming, how could they recognize it in Jesus' testimony to himself? The power of God's word is not one of external compulsion, but one of inner demand. That is the meaning of Jesus' "Answer me!" And that is why, in the absence of any willingness to respond in faith and action, there is no way to hear the word of God though it be announced by Jesus himself.

SIGNIFICANCE

"By what authority . . . ?"

If the Kingdom of God had to do with assent to an authoritative structure, then Jesus could tell his opponents—and his disciples—where that authority is based. He would say "God!" and demand that we say, "Amen!" But the Kingdom of God has to do with hearing, repenting, believing, accepting, and following, so Jesus can but speak and live God's message, then await our response. Entrance to the kingdom is by faith, and the Marcan Jesus speaks in a way that elicits faith. He does not say the creed for us. There are, to be sure, other legitimate approaches in the Scriptures; but the reticence of Jesus in Mark is surely consonant with this evangelist's understanding of the Kingdom of God.

The story is our story. Modern translations obscure Mark's historical present tenses of the verbs in 11:33—"Answering they say to Jesus . . . and Jesus says to them, 'Neither am I telling you. . . .' " The text perennially springs to life when we recognize in it our present dialogue with Jesus. Throughout 8:22—10:52 the Marcan Jesus has laid heavy demands upon his disciples. We suspect that we are addressed, but we demur. "I really do not know if that means what it says, or if it still applies today, or if you are really speaking to me. After all, I have my life to live, my talents to use, my personhood to express, even my

212

proper obligations to fulfill. What right have you to ask me to deny myself and bear a cross?" Then Jesus says, "I am not telling you . . ." and moves steadfastly away through passion week to his own cross and tomb and Easter morning. His silence is more eloquent than many answers. By his action he claims ultimate authority in our lives. Through this text he cuts through our self-serving questions and our evasive answers with his sovereign command: "Answer me!" It is the hearer who must provide the missing pronouncement on the authority of Jesus.

Mark 12:1–12
The Parable of the Wicked Tenants

"Who's in charge here?" is a form the question of authority often takes in our time. It can be asked in a tone of dismay if one is confronted by chaos, of irritation if one is faced by insubordination, or of straightforward inquiry if one is looking for a chief executive officer. Mark 12:1–12 suggests that among the people of God a better way to frame the question of authority is, "For whom am I in charge?"

TEXT

The passage is closely linked to the preceding paragraph (11:27–33) in which the question of authority is put to Jesus by a hostile group of chief priests, scribes, and elders. Their attack on him ended in a draw (11:33). Now Jesus takes the offensive against them (12:1; "them" refers to the chief priests, scribes, and elders) in a parable whose terms are unavoidably clear: "They perceived that he had told the parable against them" (12:12). He acknowledges their authority (they *are* in charge here), but charges them with abuse of it and warns that as a result their authority will be stripped from them and given to others. (See similar teaching in Ezek. 34.)

"Parable" *(parabolē)* is used in the Synoptic Gospels to refer to a considerable range of literary types, from proverb (7:15–17; compare Luke 4:23) to metaphor (3:23–27; 4:21–22) to brief similitude (4:26–29, 30–32; 13:28–29, where *parabolē* is translated "lesson") to developed narrative (4:3–9 and many Lukan parables) to allegory (4:13–20; 12:1–12). For more on

213

"parable," see notes on 4:1–34 (p. 89). The present passage is unusual in that allegory is built into the story itself by a series of equivalents that neither the hearers in the story nor the reader today can fail to understand:

Owner of the vineyard	— God
Vineyard	— Israel
Tenants	— Religious leaders
Servants	— Prophets
Son	— Jesus

Behind the image of Israel as a vineyard lies the Song of the Vineyard in Isa. 5:1–7, whose hedge, pit, and tower are echoed in Mark 12:1. Early Christian interpreters, drawing on earlier Jewish traditions, extended the allegory to include these details, understanding the hedge or fence to be the Law, the tower to be the Temple, and the pit or winepress to be the altar. However, whereas in Isa. 5 the problem is a fruitless vineyard, in Mark 12 the wicked vinedressers or tenants are the problem. For this reason it is not appropriate to press the details about the vineyard, nor to ask what fruit the owner of the vineyard sought. This question is quite appropriate for the Isaiah passage, which gives the answer: justice and righteousness. The parable in Mark, however, assumes that the fruit was there; but the tenants wanted it for themselves. The concern here is the tenants and their improper exercise of authority.

The story unfolds in four stages. In the first stage, the tenants rebel against the owner by rejecting, beating, and killing a succession of servants sent to get some of the fruit of the vineyard. The pattern of three successive individuals is common to Luke and Mark; the sending of other servants ("many others") is common to Matthew and Mark. The verb for "wounded in the head" appears here only in the New Testament, and it may be an allusion to the decapitation of John the Baptist whose murder plays so large a role in Mark. The point is that throughout the history of Israel the leaders of God's people rejected the prophets God sent, preferring to exercise their authority independently of God's authoritative word.

The second stage (v. 6) depicts God's initiative of grace in Jesus Christ. It is not the normal response to rebellion, nor the action expected of a wronged property owner. It is, however, a moving expression in story form of the gospel of God's beloved Son, which John 3:16 states in a propositional nutshell.

214

The third stage shows the rejection of God's grace in Jesus Christ by Israel's leaders (vv. 7–8). The reasoning of the tenants about gaining the inheritance by killing the son is no more logical than was the initial rebellion or the owner's gracious response to it. It is, however, a clear picture of the religious leaders' self-serving abuse of the authority entrusted to them by reaching for ownership rather than exercising stewardship: "The inheritance will be ours." Their casting the son's dead body out of the vineyard is further evidence of their contemptuous rejection of the rightful owner's authority and of his gracious initiative. (Matt. and Luke both reverse the order to read "cast out" and then "kill," to sustain and extend the allegory of Jesus' crucifixion "outside the gate," as does Heb. 13:12f.)

The fourth stage, introduced by a rhetorical question whose answer on Jesus' lips is the main point of the story, tells of God's rejection of Israel's leaders and of God's giving the vineyard to others. Israel (the vineyard) is not rejected in this story; its leaders are. The multitude is evidently favorable to Jesus (12:12; see also 11:18 and 12:37). The issue is the way the religious leaders exercise their authority and how they respond to the mission and message of the Son of God. By rejecting the Son they ensure their own rejection. The "others" to whom the vineyard is given remains vague and is not clarified by Jesus' words. Early readers of Mark would see in it a reference to the leadership of the church which, as God's new temple (see notes on 14:58) included Gentiles (see notes on 11:17). Readers of every age will see in it the warning and the promise that no set of religious leaders is indispensable. Whenever the farmers of God's vineyard, the leaders of the people of God, exercise authority for themselves rather than for God, they will at God's appointed time be removed and their responsibility given to others.

A fifth point is made after the story is over. The quotation of Ps. 118:22–23, cited verbatim from the Septuagint in Greek and probably originating in the early church, triumphantly affirms the vindication of the Son, now viewed as "the stone which the builders rejected" (see Acts 4:11; I Pet. 2:6–8; Eph. 2:20). Here the image of the church as the new temple comes clearly into view, with Christ as its "main cornerstone" (NEB). 215 The entire parable of the wicked tenants has foreshadowed the passion narrative which will follow shortly. The closing Scripture quotation anticipates the resurrection (16:1–8) by which

God vindicates the Son and answers definitively the question of authority.

SIGNIFICANCE

The parable of the wicked tenants challenges the notion of proprietary rights over the church on the part of any human being at any level of the church's life.

The text speaks most directly to those who enjoy positions of formal leadership in the church, whether at congregational, regional, or denominational levels as administrators, pastors, or teachers. These are the functional equivalents of the chief priests, elders, and scribes (teachers or doctors of the Law, TEV, NIV, NEB) in our own time and situation. To all in any position of authority in the church this parable addresses a warning about the dangerous tendency to carve out "our" domain, to forget whose the vineyard is, or, most insidious of all, to refer piously to "the Lord's work" at precisely those times when we are enlisting others to help build our own petty empires. Through this word the Lord of the vineyard confronts all workers with the question of whose interests are served by any plans they may have.

In the local congregation, this text places a question mark after the statement, "This is my church." As an expression of personal involvement and dedication, the statement is appropriate. But when it leads any individual or group on the ground of proprietary interest to circumscribe the church's membership, dictate its aesthetic tastes, or determine its social policy, then "this is my church" sounds very much like ". . . and the inheritance will be ours."

At the level of denominational life, the text challenges every tendency to appropriate the word "church" for our particular manifestation of it. Any confessional group that lays exclusive claim to the rich heritage of the gospel is condemned to hear in this parable the echo of its own voice, ". . . and the inheritance will be ours."

The relationship between Christians and Jews has changed radically from the time of Jesus and the early church, but the word of warning is still the same: Be careful lest in clamoring for your place in the vineyard you reject the Son whose way is service and a cross. This warning originally addressed to arrogant Jewish leaders applies equally to arrogant Christian leaders today.

216

The positive thrust of the parable is to call religious leaders and all Christians away from the behavior of wicked tenants to that of good stewards. We are challenged to respond to the boundless grace of God, manifested in the Son whom he loved and sent . . . and who is coming.

Mark 12:13–17
The Question About Paying Taxes to Caesar

"For God and country." The motto elicits in some a fervent glow of loyalty combining patriotism and religion. In others it arouses negative feelings ranging from unease to disdain. What is a Christian to do when religious conviction conflicts with civic duty? Several passages elsewhere in the New Testament are pertinent, but only a few in the teachings of Jesus. Of those few, Mark 12:13–17 is perhaps the most obvious and best known. What does it say? And what does it mean?

TEXT

This is the second of a series of four questions put to Jesus by his adversaries (see Introduction, pp. 5–6). Several elements in the text are important for understanding the significance of this particular encounter.

The Adversaries

Pharisees, or "separated ones," were a party within Judaism noted for strict observance of the written law. They also insisted on the validity of the oral law. Herodians are totally unknown except for their mention here (par. Matt. 22:16) and at Mark 3:6. These texts imply that they were attached in some way to the court of Herod and were therefore involved in civil government. They also represent the power that killed John the Baptist. Representatives of both these groups were sent by the priests, scribes, and elders ("they" in 12:13), who were the adversaries in 11:27—12:12.

217

The Question

Both Pharisees and Herodians had reason to be interested in the question of paying taxes to Caesar. "Is it lawful?" phrases the question according to the Pharisaic interest in *halakha,* the legal side of Judaism embracing all its practices and observances; that is, the way in which one is "to go" *(halakh).* "Should we pay . . . or should we not?" puts the question in the practical terms that deeply concerned the Herodians. Not only did their livelihood depend on the Roman treasury, but their political position would be seriously threatened by any massive refusal by Jews to pay the tax. Jewish tradition classifies questions in four categories: points of law *(hokhma,* or wisdom), contradictions in Scripture *(haggadha),* vulgarity *(boruth),* and principles of conduct *(derekh 'eres).* This question is of the wisdom type, in which a sage is queried about some point of law. (See D. Daube, *The New Testament and Rabbinic Judaism,* pp. 158–61.)

The question was a trap, because it was a burning issue at the time. The head tax, or "census" as it is designated in the text, had been imposed by the first Roman governor after the deposition of Archelaus in A.D. 6. The extreme nationalists or Zealots, led by Judas the Galilean, had refused to pay it and instigated a short-lived revolt against Rome. The tax continued to be highly unpopular among the common people, and resistance to it continued to be a sore subject with the Roman authorities. The issue, then, is whether or not one ought to obey a law imposed by an army and government of occupation. The Herodians said, "Yes," and the Pharisees went along with paying it, though they did not like it. The Zealots said, "No," and their opposition expressed at least the sentiment, if not the practice, of the people. If Jesus says "Pay," he will offend the crowds that follow him; if he says "Do not pay," he can be denounced to the Romans as a fomenter of rebellion.

The Coin

One further dimension of the issue lies in the fact that the silver denarius used to pay the tax bore the image of Tiberius with an inscription that accorded to him divine honors. To acknowledge Caesar's authority perhaps posed the question of idolatry for some of Jesus' Pharisaic adversaries, as it surely did for the early church a few decades later. Furthermore, the oral law forbade introducing any effigy of the emperor into the Temple. That the Pharisees were able so readily to produce a denarius when Jesus asked to see one is supporting evidence of their hypocrisy.

The Answer

"Render to Caesar the things that are Caesar's, and to God the things that are God's." On the one hand, Jesus' answer acknowledges that the emperor has his rights. The fact that the coinage currently in use was Roman symbolizes the many ways in which Jews benefited from the *pax romana.* The clear implication is that Jews ought to pay the denarius to Caesar, whose face and name it bore. On the other hand, Jesus does not *say* it should be paid, thereby escaping the cunningly laid trap. He forces his questioners to answer for themselves. At the same time he adds, in final and climactic position, the injunction to give back to God what belongs to God. Reference to the image of Caesar on the coin would call to the mind of any good Pharisee the doctrine of the creation of humankind in the image of God (Gen. 1:26–27). One's ultimate loyalty, one's personhood, belongs to God alone. In an ultimate sense, so does all of creation. Jesus once more turns a trick question into an occasion to teach a basic principle for ethical decisions, a fundamental guideline for "the way one should go."

The Literary Type and Setting in Life

In terms of the persons in the story and the question posed, this is a controversy story. However, as in the case of other questions put by the Pharisees to trap Jesus (e.g., the question about divorce in 10:2–9), both form-critical analysis and reflection on the use of the story in the early church reveal that the passage is in fact a pronouncement story told for the guidance of Jesus' own disciples. It is true that this story depicts Jesus outwitting his Jewish adversaries who "were amazed at him," so that early Christians might have used it in their controversies with the synagogue. The more likely setting in the life of the early church, however, is the question Christians confronted about paying taxes to Caesar, when the proper obligations of civic duty (see Rom. 13:1–7; I Pet. 2:13–17; I Tim. 2:1–4) sometimes conflicted with the idolatrous demands of the empire (see Rev. 13:1–18). This situation in the life of the early church offers an interpretive bridge from text to life in recurring analogous situations in the experience of the community of faith.

219

SIGNIFICANCE

In certain of the lectionaries Mark 12:13–17 is one of the Gospel readings for a day of civic or national significance. A national holiday such as Independence Day, Memorial Day, or Labor Day is an appropriate occasion to seek in the teaching of Jesus guidance for one's life as a citizen. Happily most users of this commentary do not face the question of whether or not to pay a tax imposed by an army and government of occupation in the name of an emperor who has divine pretensions. Most do, however, pay a substantial portion of their annual income in taxes whose use is not determined, either in theory or in practice, by the dictates of the Christian religion. Conscientious Christians, therefore, must face the question of whether or not to pay taxes to support, for instance, an arms race which many find unconscionable and possibly suicidal. Young Christians opposed to war face the question of whether or not to register for a potential draft and whether or not to perform military service if drafted. Discriminatory laws of various sorts raise in various and recurring ways the question of civil disobedience. In many issues concerning the Christian and civil authority, Jesus' answer to the question about paying taxes to Caesar offers authoritative, though ambiguous, guidance to the community of faith.

The guidance offered is not that of a quick and unequivocal answer. Rather than give a direct answer in an oracle from God, Jesus uses an object lesson from everyday life and expects us to use our disciplined common sense. He does not simply tell us what we ought to do, but suggests how we ought to think about our decision.

"Render to Caesar the things that are Caesar's, and to God the things that are God's." The saying establishes a priority of loyalty. Both the final position and the subtle allusion to the notion of the image of God convey the message that while we owe some duty to the state (even an oppressive one), our primary loyalty belongs to God.

Jesus' answer appeals to the notion that it is right and just to render to each what is due ("Pay Caesar what is due to Caesar, and pay God what is due to God" NEB). Both adversaries and disciples, then and now, recognize the justice of the proposition. The text gives no clear answer to the further question, "What is due to Caesar, and what is due to God?" However, it offers two clues for those who reflect seriously on this double question.

220

First, whatever bears the imprint of Caesar—that is, whatever manifests the labor and ingenuity of the state in the service of the common good—belongs properly to Caesar. The state is therefore due the loyalty and support of its citizens in all that belongs properly to the state.

Second, whatever bears the image of God—humankind, that is, which alone in all creation is made in God's likeness—belongs exclusively to God. God is therefore due the highest loyalty and ultimate obedience of persons, who are God's own. By pointing to the doctrine of creation, the text reminds us that all we have and are belongs ultimately to God, because God made both it and us. The doctrine of the image of God also implies a higher order of concern for persons who bear God's imprint than for things which bear the imprint of human labor and ingenuity.

The Gospel as a whole offers, in the doctrine of redemption, an additional factor to weigh in determining what is due to God. "The Son of man came . . . to give his life as a ransom for many" (10:45). If Jesus' teaching reminds us that we are God's by creation, his action proclaims that we are God's by redemption. In Jesus Christ, we belong to God (see I Cor. 6:19–20).

This line of interpretation should not be allowed to suggest that money belongs solely to the state, while persons belong solely to God. Any division into two realms (finance/faith, church/state or the like) that disbars God from some dimension of our life or excludes our civic responsibility from our obedience to God, misunderstands the teaching of Jesus. What Jesus makes clear is that our primary obligation to God includes and transcends every other duty.

Disciples of Jesus Christ must answer their own questions about the limits and constraints of civic duty, guided by their ultimate obligation to act as persons made in the image of God and redeemed by the death of the Son of man. Not all Christians will reach the same conclusions, as the history of the interpretation of this text amply attests.

Preachers and teachers today may be dismayed by the open-endedness of this word of Jesus and may face hostility from hearers who want a quick, sure answer to moral questions. Instead of an easy answer, Mark 12:13–17 offers an occasion to help Christians learn to relate Scripture to daily life by means of their own theological effort, led by the Holy Spirit and issuing in mature, personal decision.

221

Mark 12:18–27
The Question About the Resurrection

When asked about the resurrection by some adversaries who thought the notion was absurd, Jesus gave a plain and unambiguous answer: "You are wrong." But that is not all there is to it. Once again Jesus turns the question back on the questioners to make them, and us, dig deeper.

TEXT

This is the third in a series of questions put to Jesus by his Jewish adversaries (see Introduction, pp. 5–6). The opponents in this case are Sadducees, an aristocratic group of priestly families from whom the high priest was chosen. Though they figure prominently in the Gospel of Matthew, this is their only appearance as a distinct group in Mark. Only two characteristics of the Sadducees are important for understanding this text. One is that they accepted as authoritative only the written Law in the five books of Moses; they did not view either the Prophets or the Writings as scripture, and they rejected the authority of oral law. The other important characteristic, evident from the text itself, is that they denied the doctrine of resurrection which the Pharisees and others affirmed (see Acts 23:8). The latter position grows out of the first, since none of the few references to resurrection in the Old Testament are found in the Pentateuch. Jesus, recognizing their authority base, answers their test case based on Deut. 25:5 by interpreting another text in the Torah, Exod. 3:6.

The type of question the Sadducees put to Jesus is called in Jewish tradition "vulgarity" *(boruth)* because it is a scoffing question, contemptuous of the person addressed (D. Daube, *The New Testament and Rabbinic Judaism,* pp. 158–160). The Mosaic law of levirate marriage presupposes that the only persistence of personality after death is in and through the lives of one's offspring; thus the Sadducees argue. They posit an imaginary test case in which seven brothers die without issue, each having in turn taken the childless wife of the next elder brother.

222

The question, "In the resurrection whose wife will she be?" evokes the ludicrous image of an overcrowded bedroom in the afterlife. This question is neither a direct attack like that of the chief priests, scribes, and elders (11:27), nor a subtle trick question like that of the Pharisees and Herodians (12:13). It is a crass *reductio ad absurdum* of the pharisaic position, on which Jesus is challenged to declare himself.

In form, this text is a pronouncement story of the controversial type. It includes a single detailed question on a disputed issue, with a single detailed answer of Jesus. Insofar as Jesus' reply answered the Sadducees' question, the text continued to be used by Christians in debates with adversaries over the resurrection. It can still be used appropriately in polemic today. However, the counter-question of Jesus in 12:24 is as applicable to disciples as to adversaries; and the text doubtless functioned from the time it was written (or before) for teaching within the Christian community as well as in debate with outsiders. This catechetical function has dominated interpretation throughout most of church history, and it is the more likely context for interpretation today.

SIGNIFICANCE

The meaning of this passage can be read either at the level of the Sadducees' question (which is sometimes ours as well) or at the level of Jesus' answer.

The question is about the resurrection. Even followers of Jesus may sometimes doubt whether or not there is a resurrection at all or sometimes wonder what the resurrection is like and whether personal relationships persist in the life of the world to come.

The text speaks to doubts about resurrection through Jesus' unambiguous rejection of the Sadducees' position as he says twice, "You are wrong." The fact of resurrection is further grounded in Jesus' interpretation of God's self-revelation in Exod. 3:6 as God of the living, not of the dead. Abraham, Isaac, and Jacob obviously died; yet, by the power and word of God they are alive. So all who belong to God, though they die, will live by the power of the word, "I am your God." To this testimony is linked also Mark 16:1–8, where the announcement "He has risen, he is not here" stands over against all human doubts and fears in the face of death. Our hope is not only in the teaching, but in the teacher.

223

With regard to questions about what the resurrection will be like, interpretation will center on Jesus' answer (12:25), coupled perhaps with Paul's response to a similar question in I Cor. 15:35–50 and II Cor. 4:16—5:10. Neither Jesus nor Paul describes the life beyond this one. Both give reason to hope for a personal existence, like that of the risen Christ, in radically transformed circumstances.

It is important to recognize that talk of angels (Mark 12:25), of seeds (I Cor. 15:36), and of tents (II Cor. 5:1) is figurative language. The Sadducees took literally the language about resurrection, made this understanding of it look absurd, and so dismissed resurrection as untrue. The Pharisees (and Christians too) took the resurrection seriously, understanding that it is a truth too deep for common prose, a mystery best expressed in analogy and myth. To think only literally about the resurrection is to be, like the Sadducees, quite mistaken; for, like them, it is to limit the power of God to conditions such as we know them on earth. Speculation about the age of resurrection bodies, the stage of personality development when one is raised from the dead, or the conditions of life after death, misses the point of Jesus' teaching. Instead of this kind of information, the Lord offers a promise: more life, with God.

Another way to read the meaning of the passage, again in terms of Jesus' answer, moves at a deeper level. The questioners are wrong about the resurrection because they know neither the Scriptures nor the power of God (v. 24). This diagnosis, included in a rhetorical question by Jesus, comes to us as a question today. How does the Bible function in the church and in our lives?

The community of faith and each member of it ought to know the Scriptures. The observation evokes reflection on widespread biblical illiteracy in our time. But Jesus speaks of something other than knowledge of Bible content, of which the Sadducees had good mastery. They knew where to find the law about levirate marriage, what it said, and how to use it to ridicule their adversaries and support their own opinion. They also acknowledged the authority of the Pentateuch, at least in religious matters. They were proud of their conservative doctrines of inspiration and interpretation. In what sense, then, did they not know the Scriptures? They seemed not to know the Scriptures as the powerful word of the living God, a word which accomplishes what it says and sustains all who hear it.

224

To a church whose vision of the Kingdom of God is limited to the kingdoms of this world, and whose understanding of the power of God is determined solely by reality as we experience it, Jesus addresses his searching question: "Is not this why you are wrong, that you know neither the scriptures nor the power of God?" He calls us to a vision beyond our own. He opens the possibility of solutions quite other than we had dreamed.

Perhaps academicians understand the Scriptures but not the power of God, while enthusiasts understand the power of God but not the Scriptures. The text invites disciples to understand the Scriptures and the power of God in the whole and vital way that Jesus did, so that the Bible will have its rightful place in the church and in individual lives. To reach this desirable goal we must stop using the Bible to prove our points and promote our programs, as the Sadducees did, and attend instead to the living word of God.

Mark 12:28–34
The Great Commandment

Jesus' teaching on the great commandment is foundational for the life of the Christian community. It is not surprising, therefore, that one of the three parallel accounts of this teaching comes up each year in the common lectionary. This fact not only attests the importance of the passage for the church, but also may tax the ingenuity of the interpreter who annually seeks a fresh approach to the text. What in these seven verses merits such attention?

TEXT

The passage, brief as it is, contains two authoritative sayings of Jesus. The one in 34*b* ("You are not far from the kingdom of God") occupies the climactic place of the saying in a typical pronouncement story, but the fuller and weightier saying is Jesus' summary of the law (vv. 29–31).

Mark 12:28–31 has parallels in the Synoptic tradition (Matt. 22:34–40; Luke 10:25–28), while 12:32–34*b* is peculiar to Mark. The Marcan text, then, includes a pronouncement story about the great commandment (12:28–31), enlarged by a further exchange between Jesus and an appreciative scribe (12:32–34*b*), the only teacher of the Law to be mentioned affirmatively in Mark.

225

Mark 12:34c is an editorial conclusion to a series of hostile questions put to Jesus in 11:27—12:34 (see Introduction, pp. 5–6). In the Lukan parallel this verse appears after the Sadducees' question (Luke 20:40). In Matthew it follows Jesus' question to the Pharisees about how Christ can be David's son (Matt. 22:46), establishing a Matthean series of five questions. The place of the concluding formula in Mark draws attention to the great commandment as climactic in a series of controversies and foundational in the teaching of Jesus.

Jesus' function as teacher plays a large role in Mark. Three of the four hostile parties in this section address him as "Teacher" (12:14, 19, 32). In the present passage, the scribe puts a kind of question which was often used in Jewish circles as a means of capturing the essential thrust and flavor of a rabbi's mind and teaching. Hillel the Elder (ca. 40 B.C.–A.D. 10), when challenged by a Gentile to "teach me the whole Torah while I stand on one foot," replied, "What is hateful to you, do not to your neighbor: that is the whole Torah, while the rest is the commentary thereof; go and learn it" (Babylonian Talmud, *Shabbath* 31a). Similarly, Jesus, asked which is the most important of all the commandments, answers by combining Deut. 6:4–5 and Lev. 19:18.

Jesus' answer includes two noteworthy areas of meaning, the second of which will require extensive exposition.

First, only Mark's account has Jesus quote the opening words of the *Shema'* (Deut. 6:4), "Hear, O Israel: The Lord our God, the Lord is one." By quoting this confession of faith which pious Jews have repeated morning and evening since the second century B.C., Jesus affirms, in common with his Jewish heritage, the oneness of God. The point would be important for an emerging church accused by the synagogue of polytheism. Implications of this monotheistic credo can be seen throughout the New Testament (e.g., Rom. 3:29–30; I Cor. 8:6; 12:5–6; Eph. 4:5–6; I Tim. 2:5). Whenever Christians are accused of polytheism, and wherever disproportionate emphasis on "Jesus only" or on the Holy Spirit appears, recourse to Jesus' own radical monotheism is appropriate.

Second, Jesus' answer to the scribe establishes love as the ground of Christian faith and life. Asked about the one greatest commandment, Jesus answers with two; but the operative verb in both is love, stated in the imperative.

The linking of these two love commandments as funda-

226

mental teachings of the Law is not unique to Jesus. It recurs often in the *Testament of the Twelve Patriarchs* and appears in Philo and probably in the Jewish source behind the *Didache.* For Christians, however, this way of summarizing the law of God is definitive, on the authority of Jesus himself. "Love is the essence of Christian living. It is also its *conditio sine qua non,* in every conceivable connection. Wherever the Christian life in commission or omission is good before God, the good thing about it is love." (Karl Barth, *Church Dogmatics* 1/2, p. 372. For a rich exposition of Mark 12:29–31, see pp. 381–401.)

The text indicates three objects of love: God, neighbor, and self.

The first, love to God, receives the fullest treatment, as Jesus quotes Deut. 6:5. Addressed to individuals ("you" is singular here), this commandment bases service to God not on any outward compulsion of duty, but on the inner movement of love as a grateful response to God's love for us. Although Jews and Christians may differ about how we are to obey God, we agree that love is the basis of our relationship to God (see the frequency of the verb "love" in Deuteronomy).

Jews and Christians also agree that we are to love God with our whole selves. The demand is total. Kierkegaard's aphorism, "Purity of heart is to will one thing" (the title of one of his works) evokes the singleness of purpose and the integrity of person to which this word of Moses and of Jesus calls its hearers.

At one point Mark 12:30 differs from Deut. 6:5. To the deuteronomic injunction to love God with heart, soul, and might (strength), Mark adds, "with all your mind." Matthew retains "mind" but drops "strength." The inclusion of "mind" in all New Testament quotations of this commandment offers good reason to reflect on the service of God with the life of the mind. In singling out the intellectual love of God, however, the interpreter should not elevate it above other dimensions of love. The text speaks of and to the whole person.

The other two objects of love both appear in Jesus' quotation of Lev. 19:18, "You shall love your neighbor as yourself." Lev. 19 includes a number of concrete examples of how to love one's neighbor. Others may be found in Exod. 22:21–27, the Old Testament lesson accompanying Matt. 22:34–40 (par. Mark 12:28–31) in many lectionaries. As in the Old Testament, the love of Christians for both God and neighbor is to be, like that of Jesus, "not love in word or speech but in deed and in truth"

227

(I John 3:18). The most striking biblical example of neighborly love is Jesus' story of the Good Samaritan, which appears in Luke only as a transformed version of the present dialogue between Jesus and a scribe (lawyer, in Luke). Interpreters wishing to emphasize the love of neighbor, therefore, might consider working from Luke 10:25–37.

The third object of love on which interpretation has focused, particularly in recent decades, is the self. Contemporary psychology, reaching back to and continuing a line of interpretation that includes Tertullian, Chrysostom, Augustine, and Thomas Aquinas, finds in Mark 12:30–31 the commandment to love three objects: God, self, and neighbor. "You shall love your neighbor as yourself" is seen as giving a certain priority to self-love. I must first love myself rightly in order to love my neighbor rightly. Over against this interpretation, a long tradition of Protestant orthodoxy, from the Reformers on, insists that the text does not command the love of self. Calvin, followed by Barth, says that self-love can never be right or good, but must be reversed and turned into love of God and neighbor. He argues that this text gives no priority to self-love, and that "we are too much devoted to ourselves" (*Harmony*, III, 37). Barth adds that "God will never think of blowing on this fire, which is bright enough already (*Church Dogmatics*, 1/2, pp. 387–88). On the other hand, if the text does not command self-love, neither does it condemn or do away with it. Rather, the text commands that we love others in the same way that we love ourselves.

"As" is commonly misread to mean "as much as" instead of "in the same way that." Reflection on a similar sentence in Matt. 5:48 may be helpful. "Be perfect, as your heavenly Father is perfect" does not mean to be as perfect as God is, but rather to be perfect or integrated in the way that God is. So also we are to love our neighbor in the way that we love ourselves; that is, we are to be tolerant of, have time for, be interested in, make excuses for, deeply desire the welfare of our neighbor in the same way that we have these attitudes toward ourselves.

Jesus taught by precept and example how a proper self-esteem and self-fulfillment is to be found in devotion to God and service to others . . . that is, in a life of love to God and neighbor.

228

The second major portion of the text (vv. 32–34*b*), found in Mark only, contains two further elements of interpretive interest. The relativization of religion (understood as cult and ritual) is the final point of the scribe's response to Jesus (vv. 32–33). He approves Jesus' answer and adds one further idea: Love of God and neighbor is "much more than all whole burnt offerings and sacrifices."

This downgrading of the sacrificial system is all the more forceful because it is pronounced by a theologian of the religious establishment in the Temple itself, where the sacrifices were being offered. On the other hand, the scribe does not denounce these ritual practices. He simply affirms their secondary role and the primacy of love, echoing the witness of many an Old Testament prophet (I Sam. 15:22; Hos. 6:6; cf. Isa. 1: 12–17; Amos 5:21–24; Micah 6:6–8). The scribe's reply is the earliest interpretation of Jesus' summary of the law. Jesus approves it warmly; it can still guide the church's life of worship and service.

Jesus' final word to the scribe, "You are not far from the kingdom of God," has provided a springboard for many a sermon on the theme "so near but yet so far." This use of the text is questionable, since no hint is given in Mark of the outcome of this conversation. The evidence, if anything, points to a favorable result, for the progression of responses by Jesus' questioners moves from hostility (12:12) to amazement (12:17) to silence (12:27) to admiration (12:32). At the moment when "no one dared to ask him any question" (12:34*c*), this scribe at least appears to be open to the possibility of becoming a disciple.

Nevertheless, the text does not say that he followed Jesus. "Not far from the kingdom of God" hangs unresolved, as an invitation delivered but still awaiting a response. This student of Scripture has responded wisely to the teaching of Jesus. He admires Jesus (vv. 28, 32), and Jesus praises him (v. 34). Yet understanding and admiration do not make this man a Christian. He, like the first four disciples, Levi, and Bartimaeus, must take the essential step of faith: He must follow Jesus. Following him means giving everything one has, as the reader is about to learn from the story of the widow in the Temple and from Jesus on his cross.

The reader, identifying with this sympathetic scribe, is the one who will supply the response to the text's unanswered invitation.

229

SIGNIFICANCE

The preceding remarks on various elements in the text have already suggested at virtually every point some significance for today. What remains is to look at the passage as a whole to see how it relates to our present situation.

Western culture has in modern times tended increasingly toward anthropocentrism. Although we have become more modest about the place of humankind in creation and more willing to acknowledge the rights of animals, plants, and the rest of the created order, our religion has become increasingly subjective or instrumental. We use the Bible and God to achieve desired psychological states or to attain moral ends which, on a variety of grounds, we perceive to be good.

In this atmosphere the words of Mark 12:28–34 ring like a trumpet. Moses and Jesus, law and gospel, resonating together, call us to another understanding of life: God first, then ourselves and our neighbor in God; love for God with all that is in us, and love of neighbor as we love ourselves. From the theocentric perspective of the Kingdom of God, religion cannot be simply a matter of ritual, nor am I any longer the center of my universe. The significance of this text is its disturbing challenge to the basic presuppositions of Western culture and to the fundamental self-centeredness of each one of us.

The challenge is compelling not only because Jesus said it; every element in it had long stood in the scripture of Israel. It is rather compelling because Jesus *did* it. Throughout the Gospel of Mark and supremely in the passion narrative toward which these controversies move, Jesus is presented as one who loves God with his whole being and his neighbor—all of us—as himself. The answer to the question, "What is love?" is to be found in Mark's story of Jesus. It is a tough story; it is caring in action.

The challenge is disturbing because none of us measures up to Jesus' standard of love. He presents a vision of life too high for us to attain, an understanding of God's demands that we can not achieve. The text, standing alone, would create in sensitive hearts an unbearable anxiety if the cross of Jesus were only an example of how we ought to love. Only as we see in the gift of his life "a ransom for many" can we bear to hear his word about the great commandment. Yet the cross, far from obliterating the command, reinforces it as love calls forth love. How shall we respond to one who gives his life for us?

230

"Hear, O Israel . . . You shall love. . . ."

Mark 12:35–44
Of Scribes and Widows

Hypocrisy is a dirty word in the Old and the New Testaments. Both Testaments offer compelling models of genuine piety. Mark 12:35–44 is powerful because it brings these two themes together by means of a bold and shocking contrast between the scribes and an anonymous widow.

Introductory words at verses 35, 38, and 41 show that these are three distinct units, as comparison with Matt. 22:41—23:36 will confirm. In Mark (and Luke) they are held together as a larger unit by Jesus' taking the initiative (in contrast to 11:27—12:34) and by the unifying theme of religious posturing versus costly discipleship. The following remarks on the text will treat the three sub-units separately; in the section on "significance" the larger unit will be treated as a whole.

TEXT

The Question About David's Son (12:35–37)

The beginning (12:35*a*) and ending (12:37*b*) of this small unit depict Jesus no longer in dialogue with adversaries but teaching the crowd. The setting is still the Temple. The break between verses 34 and 35, marked by shifts in audience and initiative, might imply also a shift in time (JB: "later"), but this is not explicit in the text. Jesus asks the crowd about the scribal understanding of who Messiah is, challenging that understanding by the quotation and interpretation of Ps. 110:1. By affirming that David wrote these words at the inspiration of the Holy Spirit, Jesus agrees with the scribes about the authority of Scripture. By his closely-reasoned interpretation, Jesus also adopts a scribal pattern of argument. On the scribes' own grounds, he challenges the scribal concept of Messiah.

That the Christ would be the Son of David was believed, so far as the matter can be ascertained, not only by the scribes but by all forms of Judaism. Hope in a descendant of David as God's anointed king was based on many texts, such as II Sam. 7:12–16; 22:51 (par. Ps. 18:50); Hos. 3:5; Jer. 30:9. Over against

231

these texts that speak of an anointed one (Messiah, Christ) as Son of David, Jesus sets the opening words of one of the royal psalms. Jesus identifies David as the speaker.

The interpretation here of Ps. 110:1 attributed to Jesus, is so compact that its meaning is not always clear to readers today. The psalm is addressed to the king in Jerusalem; it is therefore a "royal psalm." Its first words, "the Lord," refer to Yahweh, Israel's God; the second term, "my lord," (not capitalized) refers to any descendant of David who might currently be king. The psalmist addresses the anointed king throughout, assuring him of victory over his foes and even of an eternal priestly function, because of the Lord's unchanging oath.

To this plain sense of the text Jesus adds only the assumptions, held also by the scribes, that the psalmist is David and that the exalted promises of Ps. 110 will be fulfilled in the reign of the specially anointed king of the end-time, the Messiah or Christ. Jesus (i.e., Christianity) and the scribes (i.e., rabbinical Judaism) agreed on this interpretation of Ps. 110. Jesus points out that this common interpretation resulted in David's calling one of his own descendants, the Messiah, "my Lord" (capitalized in Mark 12:36 because of the messianic understanding of the term). He then poses a question intended, at the first level, to embarrass the scribes by ridiculing their position: "David himself calls him Lord; so how is he his Son?" Seen in this light, Jesus' attack on the scribes is analagous to that of the Sadducees' attack on him in the question about the resurrection (12:18-23). Jesus would then be denying the idea that Messiah is the Son of David, and a responsible minority of scholars hold this idea to be the viewpoint of the Gospel of Mark.

It is by no means self-evident, however, that the Messiah cannot be both David's descendant and David's Lord. The question may well be one not of ridicule, but of reconciling two apparently contradictory texts (a *haggadha* question). Such questions were generally answered in the rabbinic tradition by making a "distinction" and affirming that both are right in different contexts (see Daube, *The New Testament and Rabbinic Judaism*, pp. 158-63). The scribes would have no trouble affirming with Christians that the Messiah is "great David's greater Son." The point at issue, at a second level, is, "*How* is the Christ the Son of David?" This is the level at which the text addresses us today. We are to understand that the Christ is the Son of David, but we are also to understand that the scribes' triumphalist interpretation of that title is inadequate for Jesus' person and work. We are invited to reflect on what kind of king Jesus is and how it is that God will put his enemies under his feet. The entire passion narrative in chapters 14—16 will be material for that reflection. But so will the following two paragraphs in chapter 12.

Warning Against the Scribes (12:38–40)

The key to this brief and unambiguous paragraph lies in the words that are variously translated "beware of," "watch out for," or "be on guard against the scribes." The warning against these religious authorities then unfolds in three parts. First, the scribes are depicted as loving religious show and honors: long robes, public salutations, seats up front in public worship, and places of honor on social occasions. They are "stuffed shirts." Next, their greed is exposed, its ugliness compounded by the hypocrisy of trying to hide their avarice behind ostentatious piety. They are "wolves in sheep's clothing." The saying of Jesus, like prophetic oracles of judgment in the Old Testament, ends with a hammer blow: "They will receive the greater condemnation." This functionally passive construction is a circumlocution for the action of God, who will at the end judge hypocritical religious leaders with special severity.

The imperative verb, "beware," is in the second person plural. Insofar as the warning is an attack against the scribes, it is addressed to the "great throng" in the Temple still assumed to be present in the Marcan context. Insofar as the warning is a sentence of holy law (p. 155), it is addressed particularly to the disciples, that is, to the Christian community.

Jesus does not attack Judaism or Jewish religious practices *per se*. The crowd that "heard him gladly" (v. 37) consisted of Jews who had come to the Temple to fulfill religious obligations that Jesus himself acknowledged. What Jesus does attack is egotism and avarice masked in the vestments of religious learning and practices. The form of the text shows that the attack is directed equally and perhaps primarily against this phenomenon as it began to surface in the early church. It is surely in the context of professing Christians that this word of Jesus is to be read today.

In Praise of a Poor Widow (12:41–44)

Over against the false piety of the scribes the text places the genuine piety of a poor widow who came and put into the Temple treasury "two copper coins, which make a penny" (AV: "two mites, which make a farthing;" hence the expression, "the widow's mite"). Modern translations render the total value of the two coins variously as a farthing or fraction of a penny; about a penny; or a few cents. The point is, simply, that the coin was the smallest unit of money in that time and place and that the woman, having only two, gave all she had.

Jesus contrasts her gift with those of the rich, who were placing large sums into the Temple treasury. Theirs were probably calculated gifts, guided by the law of the tithe and a long tradition of how it was to be figured. Hers surely was not: She might have kept one of the two coins but did not. Instead, "she out of her poverty has put in everything she had, her whole living." She gave this to the Temple, the extravagance and imminent destruction of which will be the subject of the very next verses. Jesus might have scolded the woman for lack of prudence in giving both coins or for lack of discretion in giving them to this decadent religious establishment. Instead, he praises her highly.

The scene is the last in Jesus' public ministry; only the Temple discourse in chapter 13 and the passion narrative in chapters 14—15 remain. The teaching, however, is directed explicitly to the church by means of the familiar Marcan formula, "he called his disciples to him, and said to them." The importance of the teaching emerges when we read it as the overture to Jesus' passion. The woman's action is praiseworthy because out of her poverty and without reservation she gave her whole living to God. But more is meant here. Her gift foreshadows the one Jesus is about to make: his very life. In Mark this poor widow becomes a type of him who, "though he was rich, yet for (our) sake became poor, so that by his poverty (we) might become rich" (II Cor. 8:9).

SIGNIFICANCE

234

Taken as a whole, this three-part text has abiding significance at two levels. First, as testimony to Jesus Christ it teaches that Messiah is not the triumphalist, military-political Son of David whom the scribes and many others (e.g., the Zealots) expected to appear and deliver Israel from her oppressors. Rather, the Messiah as embodied in Jesus Christ is a king whose power is revealed in the regal simplicity with which he gives his life and whose total obedience to the rule of God in his own life will be vindicated in a kingdom that is still coming. This testimony is borne negatively by the question about David's Son and positively by the praise of the poor widow, who functions here as a type of Christ. Mark 12:35–44 is an important part of Mark's answer to the question, "Who is Jesus Christ?" Since the answer to that question is what constitutes the church as a community of faith in every age, the preaching, teaching, and hearing of this passage is of perennial and basic importance.

Second, for the guidance of disciples in every age the text holds up as a negative example the scribes and as a positive example the poor widow. The widow is a model for all disciples ("he called his disciples to him and said to them . . ."); the scribes serve as a warning to the crowd in general, but with special application to disciples who are leaders in the church. Interpreters can readily identify how the love of long (and many-colored) robes has revived in our time. The Greek word is "stoles," but it covers academic regalia too. The scribes had salutations in the market places; we have testimonial dinners. Nor is it hard to find contemporary parallels for the best seats in the synagogues and the places of honor at feasts, though sometimes our ego-builders are more subtle. Any form of ostentatious, hypocritical religion is the target of Jesus' solemn words of warning and the antithesis of the widow's wordless example.

It is easy to spin out many modern parallels to the sins attacked in this passage. Jesus' words were few. Their power lies in the way he himself lived and died and lives again in those who really hear him.

Mark 13:1–37
The Temple and the End-time

The thirteenth chapter of Mark is a happy hunting ground 235 for persons fascinated by the end of the world. It figures prominently in books by doomsayers and in sermons by evangelists more interested in the next world than in this one. On the other hand, this chapter is largely ignored by pragmatists, activists, believers in progress, and all who dismiss preoccupation with the end of the world as a juvenile state of human development or an aberration of unbalanced minds.

Here the chapter is, in the church's Scripture. What does this word of Jesus have to say to modern Christians?

TEXT

Commonly called the "Little Apocalypse" (or "Synoptic Apocalypse," cf. Matt. 24; Luke 21), Mark 13 displays several characteristics of apocalyptic thought: a deterministic and pessimistic view of history, anticipation of the end of the world in some great and imminent crisis, a dualistic understanding of human existence, and visions of cosmic upheaval. The symbolism of the chapter is largely drawn from apocalyptic passages in the Old Testament and related literature, particularly from the Book of Daniel which is quoted verbatim three times (vv. 14, 19, 26). Mark 13 is closely related to and may in part underlie or parallel II Thess. 2 and several passages in Revelation. It must be understood in the context of the apocalyptic literature of the Old and New Testaments and of the apocalyptic movement in Judaism and Christianity which gave birth to these writings.

Careful observation of the structure of the chapter is instructive for its interpretation.

The narrative setting (vv. 1–2), a brief pronouncement story, consists of Jesus' prediction of the destruction of the Temple in response to his disciples' words of admiration as they leave the Temple in Jerusalem for the last time. The entire eschatological discourse (teachings about the end-time) is thus set in the context of the destruction of the Temple, yet distanced from it by geographical movement to the Mount of Olives "opposite the Temple" (v. 3). Verses 1–2 are therefore transitional. They mark the end of the Jerusalem ministry and the final disqualification of the Temple as focal point of the Kingdom of God.

The immediate setting of Jesus' extended discourse (the longest unbroken speech in Mark) consists of a question from four disciples on the Mount of Olives (vv. 3–4). In Mark, the expression "on the mountain," also translated "in(to) the hills" (3:13; 6:46; 9:2), designates scenes in which Jesus is alone or with a chosen few, in contrast to "by the sea" where he is surrounded by crowds. The special teaching for disciples in Mark 13 (cf. 4:10; 7:17; 9:28; 10:10) was almost surely used in the early church's catechetical teaching to pass on Jesus' authoritative revelation to the inner circle of his followers.

Andrew is included with the inner three. The first four whom Jesus called (1:16–20) have in fact followed him, however imperfectly, all the way to his farewell discourse. To the same disciples to whom he had said "Follow!" Jesus will now add the command, "Watch!"

The question of the four disciples links the destruction of the Temple ("When will this be?" v. 4*a*) and the end of all things ("What will be the sign when these things are all to be accomplished?" v. 4*b*). Jesus' answer makes a clear distinction between the two.

The discourse proper starts at verse 5*b* and occupies the remainder of the chapter. It falls into two major sections. The first (vv. 5*b*–23) is a series of three warnings against deceptive signs of the end-time: the appearance of deceivers, wars, and upheavals of nature (vv. 5*b*–8); the persecution of Jesus' disciples (vv. 9–13); and the appearance of the desolating sacrilege and of false Christs (vv. 14–23). This first section is bracketed by verses 5*b*–6 and 21–23, which are exhortations to "take heed" and not to be led astray. The gist of all the intervening warnings is that "the end is not yet" (v. 7).

The second major section of the eschatological discourse (vv. 24–37) is introduced by "but in those days, after that tribulation," which marks a basic shift in time frame. This section also has three parts: the coming of the Son of man (vv. 24–27); parables and sayings on watchfulness (the fig tree, vv. 28–31, and the absent master, vv. 32–36); and a concluding word addressed to all ("Watch!" v. 37). Every significant phrase in verses 24–27 is borrowed from the Old Testament (e.g., Joel 2:10; Isa. 13:10; 34:4; Dan. 7:13; Deut. 30:3; Zech. 2:10 LXX) and woven into a tapestry of apocalyptic images. The gist of this section is that the end is in fact coming, when the Son of man comes. The event is certain (vv. 30–31), but the time is unknown (vv. 32). The appropriate stance for disciples, therefore, is to watch (vv. 33, 35, 37).

Certain specific relationships between Mark 13 and other parts of the Gospel are instructive for interpretation.

237

The prediction of hardship and persecution for disciples in 13:7–20 echoes the predictions of Jesus' own passion (8:31; 9:31

and 10:33–34). "It is necessary" *(dei),* used of preaching of the gospel to all nations (13:10), corresponds to the "it is necessary" used in connection with the suffering and death of the Son of man (8:31); both are essential elements in God's purpose to redeem humankind. The persecutions described in 13:9–13 are precisely what the first readers of Mark were experiencing in their missionary preaching to the Gentiles. The theology of the cross underlying the discipleship section (8:22—10:52) underlies Mark 13 as well, arming disciples for the troubles they must endure and the tasks they must undertake.

Mark 13 includes specific ties to the passion narrative (chaps. 14—15). The prediction of the Temple's destruction (13:2) will be referred to at the trial scene (14:58) and at the cross (15:29), when Jesus' enemies distort his words. The prediction that they will see the Son of man coming in clouds with great power and glory (13:26) is echoed in 14:62 in a way that explicitly identifies Jesus with the Son of man (see also 8:38).

The relationship of the entire discourse to the Gospel of Mark as a whole, and to the other Gospels, is significant. This is Jesus' farewell discourse to his disciples, functioning in Mark as John 14—17 does in the fourth Gospel, as the Great Commission (Matt. 28:16–20) does in Matthew, and as Jesus' resurrection appearances in Jerusalem (Luke 24:36–49) and on the Mount of Olives (Acts 1:6–11) do in Luke-Acts. While the essential, last word for disciples in John is a command to be united in love with Christ and with one another and in Matthew and Luke the final order is to be engaged in the mission to the Gentiles, the central thrust of Jesus' last will and testament in Mark is to watch for the coming of the Son of man. This latter command does not contradict or nullify the other two. It does presuppose an acute awareness of the absence of the Lord, coupled with an intense yearning for the renewal of his presence. Mark 13 meets this yearning with a sure and certain hope founded on a solemn promise of Jesus (vv. 30f.). Heard in the context of all the Gospels, Mark 13 gives urgency to the church's sense of mission and a future dimension to her fellowship of love.

The relation of Mark 13 to history is as important as it is controversial. The text offers several clues that point to a specific historical context within which to interpret it.

238

From the perspective of Jesus and the four disciples on the Mount of Olives, all the events referred to in the discourse lie in the future. From the perspective of the evangelist and the first readers of the text, however, these events might have already happened, or be in progress, or still be future. The major shift in time frame at verse 24 suggests that only events mentioned from that point on are still in the future from the perspective of the text's first readers. The false Christs of verses 5*b*–6, 21–23, and the troubles of verses 7–20 would lie in the immediate past (or present) experience of the readers.

The setting of the discourse just after Jesus and his disciples definitively leave the Temple and in connection with his prediction of its destruction offers the strongest clue to the context in which the original readers of the Gospel interpreted this chapter: the departure of Jesus' disciples from the synagogues and the destruction of the Jerusalem Temple in A.D. 70. Readers today cannot be as certain of the reference to the "desolating sacrilege" (v. 14) as the first readers evidently were. (For various explanations see Swete, pp. 304f., and Lane, pp. 466–68). The phrase is, however, a direct quotation from Daniel (Dan. 9:27; 11:31; 12:11) where it refers to the desecration of the Jerusalem Temple in 167 B.C. by Antiochus Epiphanes. "Where it (or he) ought not to be" (13:14), therefore, probably refers to the Temple; and the "desolating sacrilege," together with all the horrors of verses 14–20, are doubtless outrages against the Jewish people committed during the Roman-Jewish war of A.D. 66–70.

In this historical context, the meaning of the chapter is clear. Contrary to popular expectations in Jewish and Christian apocalyptic circles, war and catastrophe (vv. 7–8), persecution (vv. 9–13), and the fall of Jerusalem and desecration of the Temple (vv. 14–20) were not sure signs of the end of the world. Though these things had just occurred (or were occurring), "the end is not yet." The end of history is rather to be associated with the coming of the Son of man in glory, which will occur only at the collapse of the cosmos—a combination of catastrophes for the sun, moon, and stars which will be unmistakable. Although the destruction of the Temple is not a sign of the advent of Messiah, it is a major turning point in Jewish and Christian history. From now on, for Christians, the coming of the Son of man in glory replaces the Temple as the locus of hope for the full realization of the Kingdom of God.

The intention of the text is therefore to call the followers of Jesus to hope for the coming of the Son of man. That hope will sustain Christians undergoing persecution and strengthen them to "endure to the end" (v. 13).

239

The parable of the fig tree with its associated sayings (vv. 28–31) is designed to undergird hope in the coming of the Son of man with Jesus' solemn assurance that the event is both certain and imminent ("this generation will not pass away . . ." v. 30). Although interpreting signs as saying "Here!" is rejected in verses 5b–23, attention to signs that say "Near!" is invited in verses 28–31. Hope is to be eager and expectant.

The parable of the absent master with its associated sayings (vv. 32–36) makes the point that the time of the Son of man's coming is unknown to all save God the Father (v. 32), so hope should be alert and cautious. In view of the dangers both of misguided enthusiasm (vv. 5b–6, 21–23) and of careless indifference ("lest he come suddenly and find you asleep," v. 36), the text urges disciples to *take heed* (vv. 5, 9, 23, 33), to *stay awake* (v. 33), and climactically, to *watch* (vv. 34, 35, 37). In the parable (vv. 34–36), the master is absent, even at the end of the story. This is quite like the situation at the end of the Gospel of Mark, where any appearance of the risen Lord still lies in the future (16:1–8). This Gospel addresses disciples as those who are bereft of their master, fully in charge here, and responsible to be ready at any moment to give account of their stewardship when the master returns.

Certain servants have particular responsibility to be on the watch (v. 34), but the final word of Jesus' farewell discourse (v. 37) extends that responsibility to all disciples: "What I say to you I say to all: Watch!"

SIGNIFICANCE

Our historical situation today is analogous to that of the first readers in at least one important respect: The historical signs which many people associate with the end of the world have occurred (countless times, by now), but the final coming of the Son of man still lies in the future. Mark 13 speaks whenever advent hopes are excited by calculations that conclude, "This is the time!" Wherever apocalyptic movements produce froth and fever, this chapter's word to enthusiasts is, "Take heed." In response to the contemporary apocalyptic fear of nuclear holocaust, the text acknowledges the reality of disaster but adds, "the end is not yet." In the face of extravagant claims by messianic personalities or their press agents, it admonishes, "Do not believe it."

Over against all attempts to fix a date for the Parousia (the return of Christ) or the end of the world, the Gospel says plainly that not even the Son knows the day and hour of his coming, but only the Father (13:32; par. Matt. 24:36). Besides pretending to know more than the Son does, date fixers often have little sense of responsibility for the world, whose destruction they await with fascinated detachment. In contrast to these, the Marcan Jesus speaks of responsibilities imposed by the master who left us in charge here.

In another respect, however, our historical situation is quite different from that of the first readers. The cosmos did not collapse nor did the Son of man come in clouds with great power and glory during the lifetime either of the Twelve or of those earliest readers, nor in the two succeeding millennia. Consequently, many people today have quietly dismissed the vision of any reality beyond the horizons of human history.

If Mark 13 offers correctives to apocalyptic enthusiasm on the one hand, it addresses a challenge to jaded skepticism on the other. To planners who face the future with only such guides as actuarial tables and economic indicators, this chapter announces God's intervention in history to judge and to save. To disillusioned disciples whose faith has been institutionalized and whose hope is restricted to the possibilities of human institutions, this text predicts the destruction of institutions and calls for hope in the coming of the Son of man.

This chapter not only speaks of the destruction of the building which embodied the religious institutionalism of Jesus' day; it also rejects or avoids the language of institutional theology. Although it speaks of the consummation of God's sovereign rule, it does not use the term *Kingdom of God.* Furthermore, its only mention of Christ is in connection with deceivers. Instead of either Christ or Kingdom of God, the farewell discourse of Jesus speaks of the coming of the Son of man, a term not associated with the religious establishment of that day (see Introduction, pp. 11–12). The immediately preceding story of the poor widow (12:41–44) praises one who contributed selflessly to the Temple treasury, but Mark 13 warns against confusing religious institutions with the Kingdom of God or thinking God's future is tied to their success or failure.

Over against the blandness of contemporary religious life 241
and the apathy with which many face the future, the Marcan Jesus announces an electrifying message: the good news of the end of the world. The One whom we now experience primarily

as absent will come with great power and glory. We are to watch.

What is the significance today of Jesus' command to watch?

Many still, like the first readers, understand "Watch!" as a call to expect a literal return of Jesus Christ, the Son of man, in the immediate future. Some who hold to this literal interpretation erroneously identify specific current events with various troubles spoken of in verses 5b–23 (already fulfilled at the time of the first readers) and say "Now is the time." Others, taking seriously the warning that the time is unknown (v. 32), still insist that he is coming literally (v. 31) and that he is coming very soon (v. 30). "Generation" is sometimes interpreted to mean the life span of the entire human race, but hearers or readers are led to expect the return of Jesus in their own lifetime, just as the first hearers and readers did. This interpretation of "Watch!" stresses the urgency of an immediate, future hope. It has always sustained oppressed people, like the Afro-American slaves who sang, "My Lord, what a morning, when the stars begin to fall!"

A second option is to rationalize the future hope in terms that offer pragmatic guidance for the present. An example of this interpretation is seen in the story of an eclipse in colonial New England during which state legislators panicked and several moved to adjourn. But one of them said, "Mr. Speaker, if it is not the end of the world and we adjourn, we shall appear to be fools. If it is the end of the world, I should choose to be found doing my duty. I move you, sir, that candles be brought." This understanding of "Watch!" stresses the dimension of present responsibility.

A third option is to demythologize the language of Mark 13 and to understand the coming of the Son of man as the realization of the rule of God in one's own experience. This eschatological (final, definitive) encounter with Christ might come as the resolution of some period of severe trial, as a divine invasion accompanying the collapse of one's natural self-understanding, or at the end of one's life. This interpretation of "Watch!" is individual and inward. It understands eschatology in terms of the quality of present existence, for it anticipates an encounter with the Son of man in each one's Galilee (cf. 16:7).

242   On either the literal, the pragmatic, or the existential interpretation, the vision of the future in Mark 13 serves to strengthen discipleship in the present. It arms us against the wiles of deceivers (vv. 5b–6, 21–23). It sustains us in whatever

suffering or persecution we must endure (vv. 8c, 13b, 20b). It motivates us to get on with preaching the gospel to all nations (v. 10). It both ennobles and relativizes the common round of daily life by making each moment subject to the invasion of the Son of man, who comes to judge and to save.

The common lectionary includes two pericopes from Mark 13: verses 24–31(32) for the twenty-sixth Sunday after Pentecost, and verses 32–37 for the first Sunday in Advent. Pentecost does not always include twenty-six Sundays, but the Advent reading will occur regularly every third year. The regularity of Christmas makes genuine expectancy difficult, at least for adults. Perhaps facing the unexpectedness of the ultimate divine invasion can lift believers above institutionalized expectations to a more vital watchfulness. Mark 13 speaks to those who expect too much and to those who expect too little. It is especially pertinent for those who have forgotten to expect anything at all.

RESEARCH

A resurgence of interest in apocalypticism during the past two decades is reflected in lively scholarly debate on that subject in Europe and in America, especially in the 1960s. (See essays in R. W. Funk, ed., *Journal for Theology and the Church No. 6: Apocalypticism.*) During the same period redaction criticism occupied the center of attention for growing numbers of biblical scholars. Mark studies have also enjoyed an extensive revival during this time. The convergence of these three forces has produced a substantial body of research on Mark 13 which is relevant to the exposition of this Gospel.

G. R. Beasley-Murray presented a comprehensive survey of the literature on Mark 13 prior to 1954 in *Jesus and the Future: An Examination of the Criticism of the Eschatological Discourse,* and a full account of research from 1954 to 1967 constitutes the first chapter of R. Pesch, *Naherwartungen: Tradition und Redaktion in Mk 13.* Beasley-Murray represents the viewpoint of a conservative critic prior to redaction criticism, whose early manifestations the author rejects. Pesch's work remains the most solid and thorough redaction-critical analysis of Mark 13 to date. Other major monographs on this chapter published in the 1960s are listed in the Bibliography. The most recent major monograph on the chapter is that of Lloyd Gaston, *No Stone on Another: Studies in the Significance of the Fall of*

243

Jerusalem in the Synoptic Gospels. Articles on Mark 13 have appeared much less frequently during the 1970s, and they have not made appreciable advances beyond the monographs just named.

Researchers have asked, for instance, how much of the chapter is the work of the evangelist and what his source or sources may have been; whether or not an "apocalyptic flier" (tract) underlay this chapter, and if so, whether it was of Jewish or Christian origin; which, if any, may be authentic sayings of Jesus; whether the apocalyptic message of Jesus was modified by a church experiencing the delay of the Parousia, or the non-apocalyptic message of Jesus was misinterpreted by enthusiasts excited by the events of A.D. 66–70; and whether the chapter in its final form is to be dated before or after the fall of the Temple. Predictably, critical studies arrive at different answers to these and other questions.

A broad consensus of critical scholars, however, holds that this chapter is not to be read primarily as words of the historical Jesus but as the interpretation of Jesus' eschatological teaching by some person or group in the early church. This interpretation was stimulated by the traumatic events of the Roman-Jewish War, and it incorporated and modified apocalyptic teachings that were then current in Judaism and early Christianity.

Though such a view is incompatible with the traditional view of biblical inerrancy, it actually enhances the authority and expository value of the text for each succeeding generation of believers. It shows how disciples just forty years after the death of Jesus sought guidance in the memory of Jesus' words for their response to the various pressures occasioned by the great upheavals of their time. They recognized that the word of the Lord was not simply of historical interest or relevant only to the future, but that it was for them "a very present help in trouble." They submitted all other words of guidance to the correction and control of the word of the Lord Jesus Christ.

While stating the word of the Lord to disciples of about A.D. 70, Mark 13 as part of the church's Scripture is an authoritative guide for disciples of every generation. It invites us to view the desolating troubles of our time, whether world-wide (e.g., nuclear arms) or personal (e.g., cancer), in the perspective of God's ultimate purpose revealed in the Son of man. To Christians who face such seemingly ultimate troubles, as to those who faced the

244

destruction of their nation and Temple in A.D. 70, God's word through Mark 13 has several dimensions. Despite appearances, the end is not yet: Endure. These troubles are the beginnings of the end, the birth-pangs of the new age, the sign that everything created has its term: Sit loose. The Son of man, whose word is sure and will not pass away, is near: Watch for his coming.

This chapter's rootedness in the particular events of A.D. 66–70 gives reality to the guidance it offers. The openness of its apocalyptic language assures its permanent significance.

PART SIX

The Passion of Jesus

Mark 14:1 – 15:47

Mark 14:1–11
Preparations for Jesus' Death

How should one respond to the death of Jesus?

This passage about contrasting preparations for Jesus' death not only introduces the passion narrative in Mark (see Introduction, p. 6); it also leads readers on this side of the cross to think about their own response to God's costly gift.

TEXT

The three paragraphs within this unit are a prime example of the Marcan insertion or bracketing technique, whereby one narrative is included within another so that each illumines the other (cf. 5:21–43). The account of the plot against Jesus by his enemies (vv. 1–2) is continued by the report of the complicity of a friend (vv. 10–11). The chief priests and scribes on the one hand and Judas on the other are preparing for Jesus' death by planning to kill him. Between the two parts of this conspiracy account stands the story of a woman who pours ointment on Jesus' head at a dinner party (vv. 3–9). Unwittingly, she too is preparing for Jesus' death by anointing his body for burial (v. 8). The beauty of her deed contrasts sharply with the ugliness and hostility of its setting; each reinforces the impact of the other.

The plot of the priests and scribes belongs to the motif of growing conflict which began in 2:1—3:6, was prominent in the

246

three passion predictions (8:31; 9:31; 10:33–34), and was dominant in the Jerusalem section (11:1—13:37). The collaboration
of Judas belongs to the pattern of misunderstanding and failure
that has characterized Jesus' family and friends (3:20–21, 31–35;
6:1–6), his disciples, and especially the Twelve (see Introduction, pp. 14–16). To underscore this theme, Judas is presented
explicitly as "one of the twelve" (v. 10). The verb "betray" is
used of him twice (vv. 10–11), echoing the "deliver up" (same
Greek verb) of 9:31 and 10:33.

Although the nature of Judas' opposition is different, the
same language of conspiracy is used concerning him that is used
of the priests and scribes. Both he and they are "looking for a
way" (TEV, correctly reflecting the parallel expressions in
Greek), they for a way to arrest Jesus secretly and Judas for a
way to hand him over. The declared opponents of Jesus need
the failed disciple to accomplish their purpose—not in order to
identify Jesus, but to arrest him unobserved. The behavior of
both is reprehensible, but of the two, that of the failed disciple
is the more heinous because of his special relationship to Jesus
(3:14–19).

The time reference in 14:1 is the first of a series of notes
which heighten suspense as the drama builds to crucifixion and
resurrection (14:12, 17; 15:1, 25, 33, 42; 16:1–2). This note advances the redemptive interpretation of Jesus' death by explicitly relating it to the Jewish Passover and its associated feast,
Unleavened Bread.

The central portion of the unit takes the form of a pronouncement story, with a setting (vv. 3–5) and a cluster of
related sayings of Jesus (vv. 6–9).

The setting is the house of Simon, a leper or former leper.
Readers who have ever lived in a segregated society will appreciate the shock generated by Jesus' association with outcasts, a
theme characteristic of Luke but by no means limited to the
third Gospel (see also Mark 2:15, for instance).

The woman who anoints Jesus is not identified as Mary of
Bethany (cf. John), nor called a sinful woman (Mary Magdalene?
cf. Luke), but is totally anonymous: ". . . a woman came. . . ."
The reprehensible roles in Mark 14:1–11 are played by men;
the one praiseworthy character is identified only as "a woman." 247

The "alabaster of ointment of nard" was a globular vase
made of alabaster and containing an oil extracted from the nard
plant native to India. Its pungent perfume invites the reader to

smell as well as to see and hear the scene. This imported luxury was costly: "More than three hundred denarii" means approximately the annual wages of a rural day-laborer (cf. Matt. 20:2). Nard was used to perfume the head and hair (cf. Song of Sol. 1:12; 4:13–14.) and to anoint the dead. Its use here plays on these contrasting functions (love and death) as a pun plays on words.

The indignant reproach of certain persons present does not even mention the most obvious possible use of the ointment; namely, the woman might have used it for herself. Rather, the observers contrast "wasting" the ointment on Jesus with giving to the poor (vv. 4b–5), thereby stating a basic issue for followers of Jesus.

Jesus rebukes the observers (v. 6a). The following series of sayings proposes a different viewpoint for disciples. Each part of the twofold commendation of the woman is introduced by "she has done . . ." and followed by an explanation of why her deed was good. An "amen-saying" concludes the story and affirms the enduring value of the woman's action.

"She has done a beautiful *(kalos)* thing to me." *Kalos* can mean good (morally right) or beautiful (aesthetically pleasing), but in the present context it means more than either of the above. To give to the poor is right (v. 7), but the woman's deed is of a different order of rightness. To anoint the head with perfume is aesthetically pleasing, but the woman's act is of a higher order of beauty. What she does is admirable because it is timely. The beauty of her extravagant and apparently wasteful gesture is due to the particular situation: Jesus is about to die. So we bring flowers to loved ones and friends who are sick, realizing suddenly that they will not always be with us.

A further dimension makes the woman's deed admirable: "She has done what she could," or literally, ". . . what she had." This expression, found only in Mark, suggests that what she had, she gave; or what she had it in her power to do, she did. Her act is beautiful because she has invested herself in it. She gave what she had to him who was about to give his life for her.

SIGNIFICANCE

248

The words, deeds, and attitudes of personalities surrounding Jesus in this unit can serve as a mirror for observing possible responses to him today.

Some, like the chief priests and scribes, still react to Jesus with hostility, rejecting outright both him and his message. That rejection, though categorical, may be discreet ("by stealth"). One does not wish to make a scene ("lest there be a tumult"), only to be rid of Jesus. The antipathy of the chief priests and scribes was based on fear (11:18; cf. 11:32) and envy (15:10), though they spoke of blasphemy (14:64) and many other things (15:3). Rational reasons given for rejecting Jesus today may also mask uglier, real reasons, which interpretation could probe.

Others, like Judas, protest friendship for Jesus, but in fact betray him. Judas did so, finally, in response to an offer of money. He lifted no violent hand against Jesus, but his inner disloyalty (14:10–11) eventuated in a kiss as deadly as a sword or club (14:43–46.). The indifference of rich Christians to the plight of the poor and its effect on the proclamation of the gospel in the world today is one among many of the ways Jesus' declared friends betray him.

Those who objected to the woman's extravagant act understood well the importance of giving to the poor, but they failed to see something even more important: the beauty and goodness of uncalculating love. They are paradigms of Christians who "do the right deed for the wrong reason"; examples of those who "give away all (they) have, and . . . deliver (their) body to be burned, but have not love"; exponents of "the organized charity, scrimped and iced, in the name of a cautious, statistical Christ" (T. S. Eliot, *Murder in the Cathedral,* Part 1, end; I Cor. 13:3; J. B. O'Reilly, "In Bohemia," st. 5).

Christian stewardship as a regular pattern of life is a good and challenging ideal, but this anonymous woman's response to Jesus moves on different grounds. Her deed springs from a personal love for Jesus which, on occasion, breaks all patterns, defies common sense, and simply gives. Spontaneous, uncalculating, selfless, and timely, her gift calls us to love Jesus in this way too and not to judge the way others express their love for him.

That is why "wherever in all the world the gospel is proclaimed, what she has done will be told as her memorial" (NEB). She left no name, but rather the memory of a beautiful deed. 249 Love in return for costly love is no mean memorial and no small goal for disciples.

Mark 14:12–26
The Last Supper

In Mark's account of the most frequently reenacted scene in the life of Jesus, things come together and things fall apart. The themes of communion, passion, atonement, covenant, and Parousia all come together in this passage. Yet at this moment Jesus predicts his betrayal; and from this point forward he will experience growing abandonment and isolation, culminating in a cry of dereliction at the moment of his death. How do these conflicting forces meet in the text . . . and in the life of Christian groups and individuals today?

TEXT

This passage consists of three smaller units: preparation for Passover (vv. 12–16), prediction of betrayal (vv. 17–21), and covenant meal (vv. 22–25). The three are tied together by unity of place (in the city) and of action (the last supper). Verse 26 is transitional, for it marks the end of the Last Supper passage (singing the hymn) and the beginning of the events across the Kidron.

The preceding unit (14:1–11) showed the preparations for Jesus' death by his enemies and by an anonymous woman. Now Jesus himself and his disciples prepare for the Passover. The betrayal prediction prepares the reader for the arrest scene later; it also prepares disciples then and now for shattering discoveries about their own discipleship. The supper itself prepares participants to understand the impending death of Jesus, to be sustained in their life together while he is absent, and to anticipate eagerly with him the coming Kingdom of God.

Preparation for Passover (14:12–16)

The time note in 14:12a continues the countdown toward crucifixion (p. 247). Mark, following Exod. 12:6, 18 (not Lev. 23:6 or Num. 28:17), calls the day they sacrificed the passover lamb (14 Nisan) the first day of Unleavened Bread. The finding of the room and preparation of the meal occur during the daylight hours of 14 Nisan, and all of the events reported between 14:17 and 15:42 (evening to evening) occur on 15 Nisan, the day before the Sabbath. The point of specifying the time, however, is not to enable readers to synchronize calendars; it is to draw attention to the fact that Jesus died during the Jewish feast of liberation. Though the relative historicity of this text compared with other New Testament accounts of the same event is debated (see Research below), Mark insists (by repetition) that the last meal Jesus ate with his disciples was Passover: the commemoration of God's deliverance of his people from bondage.

Certain elements in the preparations are traditional, underscoring the continuity of Jesus and his followers with their Jewish heritage. The date and basic structure of the feast is determined by Exod. 12:1–27. Eating the supper in the city of Jerusalem (v. 13) while reclining on couches to symbolize the freedom they had enjoyed since the Exodus (v. 18, literally "while they were reclining and eating") follows the religious law of Jesus' time. Also, prominent rabbis often kept Passover with their disciples, so the question in verse 12b is not a new departure.

Other elements, however, are new: the disciples gathered around Jesus as his true family (cf. 3:34f.) and the new interpretation Jesus will give to the feast (vv. 22–25). This supper lies at the heart of a movement that is both new and old.

The elaborate procedure for finding the place for the supper is significant (vv. 13–15). Although it is possible to suppose that Jesus had made prior arrangements with the unnamed householder, the more probable interpretation is that this text and the similar one in 11:1–6 are "finding stories" intended to function like I Sam. 10:1–8. All are signs that God orders these events.

Nothing is haphazard about Jesus' death nor about the meal he shares with his disciples in preparation for it. All occurs by divine appointment, coupled with careful and conscious preparation by the participants. The principle still holds true: Time and place must be prepared if this established ritual is to serve effectively as a point of intersection with ultimate reality.

Prediction of Betrayal (14:17–21)

Verse 17 marks a shift in time and place, to the evening (Thursday) which began 15 Nisan and to the place which the disciples had found and prepared. Action, which had involved "disciples" (vv. 12–16), is more narrowly focused on "the twelve." The day begins with the Passover meal. By the time the Sabbath begins at sundown, twenty-four hours later, the passion and death of Jesus will have been accomplished. Mark reports just two incidents from the meal, each introduced by "as they were (at table) eating" (vv. 18, 22). The first incident (vv. 17–21) is introduced by an "amen-saying" of Jesus, and the second incident (vv. 22–25) is concluded with another such saying.

The solemn declaration, "Truly I say to you, one of you will betray me, one who is eating with me" (v. 18), focuses attention on one of the Twelve and his relationship to Jesus. "One who is eating with me" alludes to Ps. 41:9, evoking the theme of the righteous one (here, Jesus) who suffers unjustly but will be vindicated by the Lord.

Of the three forms of failure that characterize the behavior of disciples in the Marcan passion narrative—betrayal, denial, and falling away—that of Judas is the gravest. In Mark, Judas participates fully throughout the Last Supper. His intimacy with Jesus neither prevents nor excuses his treachery, but rather exacerbates it. "Woe" (v. 21*a*) is derived from the death wail, and verse 21*b* is a type of curse.

"As it is written" (v. 21*a*) probably refers to no particular verse in the Old Testament but refers generally to the divine intention as revealed in a pattern of prophecy and fulfillment.

If God planned for Jesus to be betrayed, why does God blame the betrayer? The question has troubled interpreters throughout history. While the text teaches that God plans for Jesus to be betrayed by one of the Twelve, it does not state that God designated Judas for that purpose or made Judas do it. The text does affirm, however, both the divine ordering of events and the responsibility of each individual for his or her own infidelities to Jesus.

In literary terms, the ambiguity of Judas' position is not so much a problem as an enrichment. From his first introduction in the Gospel (3:19), Judas' role is clearly that of the "opponent." That early note has stripped all surprise from the present announcement that the betrayer is one of the Twelve, but the fact is still shocking. The most intimate insider proves to be the ultimate outsider. The despicable "opponent" is also, in structuralist terms, the essential "helper," for "the Son of man goes *as it is written* of him." By opposing, Judas helps. His evil act,

252

like that of Joseph's brothers in Genesis, is ultimately a means to good. (For this and other stimulating literary insights into the Gospel of Mark, see Frank Kermode, *The Genesis of Secrecy;* e.g., p. 85.)

Covenant Meal (14:22–26)

The second incident at table focuses on Jesus and his relationship to his disciples. While the first had to do with the betrayer, this one has to do with the host at the table. By his actions and his words at this Passover meal, Jesus interprets his impending death and points to the coming Kingdom of God.

The series of verbs, took, blessed, broke, gave, and said (v. 22), though not found in Old Testament passages on Passover, characterize each account of the institution of the Christian Eucharist (Matt. 26:26–29; Luke 22:14–23; I Cor. 11:23–26). "Eucharist" derives from the Greek word for "having given thanks" (*eucharistēsas,* v. 23) which here parallels "blessed" (v. 22). Both terms doubtless refer to the traditional Jewish benedictions pronounced over bread and wine:

> Blessed art Thou, O Lord our God, King of the Universe,
>   who bringest forth bread from the earth.
> Blessed art Thou, O Lord our God, King of the Universe,
>   who createst the fruit of the vine.
>   (Midrash *Berakoth* VI.1)

God is blessed, not the bread or wine; the blessing consists in giving thanks. These blessings, used by pious Jews at any meal including Passover, underlie the terminology of the Christian Eucharist, a thanksgiving to God for Christ's gift of his life ("Take, this is my body;" "this is my blood . . . poured out for many").

The use of "cup" instead of "wine" (v. 23) has symbolic significance, as at 10:38–39 (when James and John seek first places) and at 14:36 (in Gethsemane). In all three texts, God gives the cup; it is a cup of death. Pss. 116:13 and 23:5 also speak of a cup symbolically: "the cup of salvation." Paradoxically, the cup of 14:23–24 is a cup of death and a cup of salvation.

The cup is related to the blood of the covenant (v. 24; cf. Exod. 24:3–8). The particular formulation, *"My* blood of the covenant," interprets Jesus' death in terms of a new covenant (cf. Jer. 31:31–34) sealed by his blood shed "for many" (cf. Mark 10:45; notes p. 190) and appropriated in this new covenant

253

meal. The textual variant "new" (v. 24) makes explicit the allusion implicit in the original reading.

Mark's account of the supper ends on a note of eager anticipation of the coming kingdom. The closing "amen-saying" echoes a phrase from the blessing and expresses the idea of newness: "Truly, I say to you, I shall not drink again of the fruit of the vine until that day when I drink it new in the kingdom of God." Jesus vows to abstain from drinking wine until, in the newness of the time of consummation (Rev. 21:5), he will drink it at the messianic banquet (Isa. 25:6–8; I Enoch 62:14) in the Kingdom of God (Matt. 22:1–10; par. Luke 14:15–24). His solemn affirmation underscores the certainty of the kingdom hope and strongly suggests the nearness of the coming of the Son of man.

The same future thrust and ardent hope appear in the final phrase of the Pauline tradition concerning the institution of the Lord's Supper: ". . . you proclaim the Lord's death *until he comes*" (I Cor. 11:26). It is also found in the ancient prayer, *"Maranatha"* (I Cor. 16:22) with which the Eucharist was ended according to the *Didachē* X,6.

The hymn spoken of in the transitional verse (14:26) was probably Ps. 118, since the second half of the *hallel* (Pss. 114 —118 or 115—118) was always sung after the final blessing at Passover. If so, the words of this familiar psalm accompanied the departure of Jesus and his disciples for Gethsemane, just as they had attended his entry to Jerusalem (11:9). Its memorable affirmations look beyond present distress and give thanks to God for coming victory (cf. esp. Ps. 118:1, 17, 22–23, 29). A passage which began by preparing disciples for the death of Jesus ends by pointing them to the glory of his coming kingdom.

SIGNIFICANCE

This passage is the foundation story for the church's central liturgical act, the Eucharist. Mark 14:12–26 appears in the lectionaries as a reading for Maundy Thursday or Passion Sunday. It is appropriately preached or taught any time the Lord's Supper is observed, or in preparation for such occasions.

254

Ironically, the sacrament intended to celebrate the unity of Christians with their Lord and each other has become a source of division in the church. Interpretation might therefore focus on the themes of the Gospel of Mark that come together in this passage, for they tend to unify not only the Gospel but also Jesus' disciples who reflect on them today.

The eucharistic theme, first seen in the feeding stories of 6:30–44 (pp. 128–29) and 8:1–21 (pp. 142, 146), finds echo and fulfillment when Jesus gives bread and wine to the Twelve in the upper room. Although the presence of a betrayer casts an ominous shadow (vv. 17–21), the meal is nevertheless an expression of communion between Jesus and his disciples (v. 14*b*) that nourishes disciples individually and binds them to their Lord and to each other (". . . they all drank of it," v. 23*b*). We search Mark in vain for "Do this in remembrance of me" (I Cor. 11: 24–25). The communion depicted here is not institutionalized. Instead, the text speaks of oneness with Jesus Christ based on inward appropriation of his death for us and oneness with each other that unites those who, at great personal cost, seek to follow Jesus, thereby drinking his cup (10:39).

The theme of Jesus' rejection, suffering, and death, enunciated in the three passion predictions (8:31; 9:31; 10:33–34), is reflected and advanced in the present unit when Jesus predicts that his betrayal will be at the hands of one of the Twelve. The significance of this Marcan theme for disciples today is only too evident. To present it without being judgmental or evoking defensiveness is a challenge to the interpreter's skill and sensitivity and a measure of his or her acknowledgement of personal vulnerability in the face of this message. The passion theme which serves to unify Mark's Gospel will also unify disciples who recognize that we all cause Jesus to suffer, that we all at different times and in various ways betray him.

The death of Jesus for others, a theme first enunciated in the climactic verse of the central section of the Gospel (10:45), comes to the fore again when Jesus says, "This is my blood of the covenant, which is poured out for many" (14:24). "For many" points to the inclusive scope of Jesus' sacrificial death (see p. 190) and ties the two texts together. To the note of redemption in 10:45 the present text adds the idea of covenant. Old Testament readings accompanying Mark 14:12–26 in various lectionaries include Exod. 24:3–11; Num. 9:1–3, 11–12; and Deut. 16:1–8. These open the way to reflection on the Eucharist's continuity with Passover and the Mosaic covenant. Epistle readings are I Cor. 5:6–8 and 10:16–21. These point to Christ as

255

our paschal lamb and to the new community created by participation in the blood and body of Christ. The present passage is
significant because it helps us to understand that Jesus' death is
for us, that it sets us free, and that it secures for us a place among
the covenant people of God. Rightly understood, Mark 14:
12–26 binds disciples of Jesus to their Lord, to each other, and
to God's redemptive work in history.

Finally, the earlier announcements of the future coming of
the Son of man in glory (9:1; 13:26) are underscored by Jesus'
word at the Last Supper about drinking new wine in the Kingdom of God (14:25). This theme makes of the Lord's Supper not
only a memorial but also an anticipation. Whatever may be our
sense of the real presence of Christ in the sacrament, our communion with him in the interim between his resurrection and
his return is incomplete. Jesus' vow of abstinence points to a
fulfillment, still future for us but impending, toward which he
looks with eager anticipation. Disciples who share this hope are
united in a common yearning as they "proclaim the Lord's
death *until he comes*" (I Cor. 11:26).

RESEARCH

Mark's time notices have given rise to extensive efforts to
reconstitute the chronology of the passion narrative and to relate this chronology historically to Jewish and Christian liturgical calendars.

According to Mark and the Synoptic parallels, Jesus' last
supper with his disciples was certainly a Passover meal and by
clear implication was the historical occasion on which Jesus
instituted what Paul calls the "Lord's supper" (I Cor. 11:20).
According to John 13, the last supper was definitely not a Passover meal. It occurred one evening earlier; and the only rite
associated with it is footwashing, not the Eucharist.

Interpreters throughout the history of the church have
tried either to harmonize the accounts or to show that one
evangelist was right and the other wrong or that the actual
chronology was different from the traditional reading of either
account. The literature is voluminous and inconclusive, although particular researchers and readers may be convinced by
one or another set of arguments.

All that can be said with assurance is that Jesus died at
Passover time, and that Christians from the beginning found
theological significance in that fact. One strand of interpreta-

256

tion (John) affirmed the connection between Christ's death and Passover by saying he died at the moment the Passover lambs were being slaughtered in the Temple precinct. Another (Synoptics) affirmed it by saying Jesus kept Passover with his disciples but reinterpreted it. Another (Paul) simply affirmed, without historical allusions, "Christ our paschal lamb has been sacrificed."

The source documents, including Mark, were not intended to be read as history, but as gospel (see Introduction, pp. 17–18); hence the inconclusive and sometimes contradictory nature of historical references in the Gospels. Yet the good news is grounded in historical events, so interpreters cannot simply ignore historical questions. Those who seek guidance into the literature relative to the Lord's Supper may profitably consult: M. H. Shepherd, Jr., "Last Supper" and "Lord's Supper" (with bibliographies) in *The Interpreter's Dictionary of the Bible*, Vol. 3 (1962) (Treats both historical and theological questions.); B. Klappert, "Lord's Supper" (with bibliography) in *The New International Dictionary of New Testament Theology*, Vol. 2 (1971, ET 1976) (Focuses on theological questions.); J. Jeremias, *The Eucharistic Words of Jesus* (1949, ET 1966) (Holds that the Last Supper was a Passover meal and interprets it extensively on that premise.).

Mark 14:27–52
Gethsemane and the Arrest

Jesus and his disciples have left Jerusalem again to go to the Mount of Olives (v. 26). Three events occur before they return to the city (v. 53): the prediction of general abandonment and of Peter's denial (vv. 27–31), the struggle in Gethsemane (vv. 32–42), and the arrest (vv. 43–52). What do these accounts reveal about disciples? About Jesus? About God?

TEXT

The Marcan ordering of the three elements in this passage 257 calls attention to the theme of abandonment. This theme was introduced in the passion predictions (the Son of man will be rejected and delivered up), advanced in the plot to kill Jesus

(14:1–2, 10–11) and heightened in the prediction of his betrayal (14:18–21).

The unit opens with Jesus' scripture quotation, "You will all fall away" (v. 27) and closes with a double echo of this prediction: "They all forsook him and fled" (v. 50) and "he . . . ran away naked" (v. 52). The first paragraph (vv. 27–31) predicts the abandonment of Jesus by all the disciples and by Peter in particular, despite his protestation. The Gethsemane scene (vv. 32–42) depicts Jesus' struggle with the will of God and shows the inner circle of three disciples leaving Jesus to struggle alone. The arrest (vv. 43–50) brings to fulfillment Judas' betrayal of Jesus and the abandonment of him by all the disciples. A surprising fourth paragraph (vv. 51–52), also part of the arrest scene, tells how a nameless young man fled away naked. A closer look at each of these paragraphs will show how the theme of abandonment is developed and how it serves as a dark background for some bright good news.

Prediction of Flight and Denial (14:27–31)

The scripture on Jesus' lips in verse 27 (Zech. 13:7–9) is from one of a series of apocalyptic, eschatological ("on that day") oracles in the Book of Zechariah. In the particular oracle quoted, God calls the sword to awake "against my shepherd" (the Messiah), "against the man who stands next to me" (the Son of man). Jesus quotes this oracle with reference to his own impending arrest and death and as a prediction of the falling away of his sheep, the disciples. What follows in Mark displays a variety of human actions, behind which stands the action of God himself.

Peter's promise to remain steadfast though all fall away is reminiscent of the confident "We are able" of James and John in 10:39. Unlike that instance, however (see p. 193), Jesus here counters with a solemn prediction that Peter will deny him. Unabashed by his earlier rebuke at Caesarea Philippi (8:33), Peter again vehemently contradicts Jesus with a vow: "If I must die with you, I will not deny you." All the disciples are implicated in this rash self-confidence, for "they all said the same."

Jesus' predictions of infidelity will be borne out by the flight of all the disciples at the end of the present unit and by the denial of Peter in the next one. But that is not the last word. Immediately after the Zechariah quotation, Jesus adds (v. 28),

"But after I am raised up, I will go before you to Galilee." His death and the scattering of the sheep will not be the end. Although his resurrection will conclude the Gospel of Mark, this verse already points readers beyond the end of Mark's Gospel. "Go before" evokes the picture of a shepherd leading his flock. This prophecy alerts readers to a theme which will be decisive in the resurrection account (see notes on 16:7, pp. 284–85).

In the present passage, however, the emphasis is on the disciples' abandonment of Jesus, made all the more painful for him and for them by their good intentions and solemn vows.

Gethsemane (14:32–42)

The drama narrows to the three leading disciples on the one hand and Jesus on the other. Peter had just made two promises: "I will not fall away" and "I will not deny you." Already he breaks the first of these by falling asleep when he was asked to watch. In reproaching him Jesus does not use his apostolic surname, Peter ("Rock"), but that of his old life: "Simon, are you asleep? Could you not watch one hour?" (v. 37). One day by the sea Jesus had called these three to follow him; now in the darkness they fall away, unable to obey despite their high intentions and earnest commitments.

In contrast to their failure to follow Jesus, Jesus steadfastly follows the will of God. But, unlike later martyr stories, this account does not portray one who faces death with serenity. Jesus has no martyr complex. The text plainly sets his human will over against the will of the Father. Jesus' will is that the hour pass from him, that the cup be removed. He does not want to be put to the test. He wants to fulfill God's purpose for him (10:45), but in some other way, if possible. Yet a higher will within him, also his own, finds expression in the prayer, "Not what I will, but what thou wilt" (v. 36). Fully human, Jesus knows the inner struggle of the will. He refuses to abandon the will of God, and in this decision the die is cast. Such may be the sense of Jesus' exclamation "Enough!" or "It is all over" (JB).

The disciples and Jesus in Gethsemane offer readers two archetypes for responding to the tests of life. In one response, the weakness of the flesh dominates and the outcome is the abandonment of Jesus. In the other, commitment to the will of God dominates. The immediate consequence is arrest and crucifixion, but the final outcome lies beyond the resurrection.

259

Much of the power of this passage lies in several key terms.

Watch (v. 34) is a direct echo of the concluding exhortation in Mark 13. On that occasion Jesus told Peter, James, John, and Andrew the parable of the absent householder, then warned them to watch (*grēgoreite*, stay awake, as in 14:34) lest the master come suddenly and find them asleep. Hearers of the word but not doers, these first disciples were "like a man who observes his natural face in a mirror . . . and goes away and at once forgets what he was like" (James 1:23–24). Jesus' "Watch!" is addressed to all (13:37). Mirrored in the quick forgetting of the first three, disciples of every age behold themselves. They are summoned not to forget, but to be alert and present to the agony of Christ, in whatever person or situation, in whatever place and time.

Hour (vv. 35, 41) and *cup* (v. 36) are used metaphorically for the final agony of crucifixion. The cup was invested with symbolic meaning at the Last Supper (14:22–25, see p. 253). References to the hour at 15:25, 33, and 34 lead up to the supreme hour of anguish, the crucifixion, when Jesus feels abandoned even by God (see pp. 276–77).

The exhortation to "pray that you may not enter into temptation" (v. 38), like the prayer for God's will to be done (v. 36*b*), are Marcan equivalents of two petitions of the Lord's Prayer (not included in Mark). When he begs God to let the hour pass and to remove the cup (v. 36*a*), Jesus is in effect praying, "Do not put me to the test" (Luke 11:4, JB). He urges the three disciples to give themselves to that same prayer. When Jesus adds, in effect, "thy will be done" (v. 36*b*), he wins a decisive victory in the test now under way. The determination evident in "Rise, let us be going . . . ," echoes that of 10:32, when Jesus strode ahead of his disciples on the road to Jerusalem.

"See, my betrayer is at hand" *(eggizō)*. The word is the same Jesus had used to announce the approach of the Kingdom of God (1:15). The NIV and TEV renditions of 14:42 catch the force of an approach so imminent as to be, in fact, arrival. In his successful struggle not to abandon the will of God, Jesus has won a victory through which the Kingdom of God, God's sovereign rule, is existentially realized. "And immediately while he was still speaking, Judas came . . ." (v. 43). The Marcan "immediately" is seldom so pregnant with meaning as here. Judas arrives; but proleptically, in terms of Jesus' obedience, so does God's reign.

The Arrest (14:43–52)

Suddenly the action shifts from a lonely struggle to a mob scene which includes a crowd sent by the religious authorities, Judas, Jesus, the whole group of disciples . . . and a mysterious "young man." The authorities are identified as "the chief priests and the scribes and the elders," the groups that made up the Sanhedrin (14:53, 55). Jesus' arrest at their instigation fulfills his predictions (8:31; 10:33) and translates into action their hostile intentions (11:27–28; 12:12; 14:1, 10–11).

Unlike the three friends who failed through apathy, or the enemies who declared their opposition, Judas makes every show of friendship ("Rabbi," the kiss) while actually betraying Jesus. Judas' act is an example of human behavior almost universally condemned. (For a notable exception to the rule, and a story that serves as an extended commentary on this text, see the example of Sawi culture in D. Richardson, *The Peace Child*, Glendale, Cal., 1974). Judas' identification as "one of the twelve" underscores the baseness of his deed and calls attention to the special relevance of this text for church leaders.

In contrast to the Jesus in John 18:6, whose divine self-disclosure strikes his enemies to the ground, Jesus here behaves with fearless human dignity. The courage of his words and action (vv. 48–49*a*) contrasts sharply with the behavior of others in the scene. Jesus is a model for disciples under persecution (see 8:34), but by interpreting the arrest as the fulfillment of Scripture (14:49*b*) the text points to Jesus as more than a courageous man. The reference to swords and clubs in verse 48 and the scattering of the "sheep" in verse 50 indicate that Zech. 13:7 is the scripture intended here as well as at the beginning of this passage (v. 27). Jesus, arrested by his enemies, is nevertheless the messianic shepherd of the end-time, the man who stands next to the Lord of hosts (Zech. 13:7).

A disciple standing by strikes off the ear of the high priest's slave with a sword. The fourth Gospel elaborates this incident and attributes it to Peter, but Mark presents it only as an ineffectual gesture. The significant action of the disciples is that "they all forsook him and fled" (v. 50), breaking their own solemn vow (v. 31) and fulfilling Jesus' prediction that they would "all fall away" (v. 27). Their abandonment of Jesus is the expected denouement of the entire passage.

A startling interruption separates this climactic end of the

261

action at Gethsemane from its natural sequel (v. 53). An anonymous "young man" darts onto the stage long enough to leave his clothes and run away naked. Is this young man the apostle John (Ambrose, Chrysostom, Bede)? Or James, the brother of Jesus (Epiphanius)? Or a resident of the house where Jesus and his disciples had eaten Passover (Theophylact)? Is he the evangelist himself, who secretly signs his work in this way (many nineteenth-century commentators)? Is this incident a narrative developed out of Joseph's flight from Potiphar's wife (Gen. 39: 12), or from the prediction in Amos 2:16 of warriors fleeing naked "in that day" (C. G. Montefiore, *The Synoptic Gospels*)? Is the young man a typological figure standing for desertion, as Peter stands for denial and Judas for betrayal (Farrer, *A Study in St. Mark*)? Is this the account of an eyewitness known to, but other than, Mark, introduced here to convey the sense of reality (Taylor, *St. Mark*)? Or the remnant of a secret Gospel of Mark in which a young man comes to Jesus by night for instruction and baptism into the mystery of the Kingdom of God (Morton Smith, *The Secret Gospel*)? Is this the "young man" who will reappear in 16:5–7, sitting in the tomb and announcing Jesus' resurrection, introduced here to intimate rescue from death and ultimate reintegration (Werner Kelber, *Mark's Story of Jesus*)? Or is this "boy in the shirt," like James Joyce's "man in the macintosh" in Ulysses, an irreducible secret introduced by the author to tease the reader (Kermode, *The Genesis of Secrecy*)?

We cannot know. Perhaps the young man represents one particular kind of abandonment of Jesus, as will be suggested below, but this is only one possible line of interpretation. Whatever may have been the text's origin or the writer's intention, the effect of this young man's brief appearance has been to tease readers for two millennia, an effect which the present note is not likely to alter.

SIGNIFICANCE

Many signs of Marcan editing in the Gethsemane passage suggest that it was included here in response to some scandalous failure(s) in the early Christian community. However that may be, the passage as a whole plays out three ways of abandoning Jesus. One way is by apathy, sleeping through the critical moments of life, unaware that one's discipleship is being tested (Peter, James, and John). Another is by conscious betrayal of the

Lord under the mask of friendship (Judas). A third is by flight in a time of pressure or panic (the young man). These three patterns of forsaking Jesus are reenacted in every age by individuals and by groups of Christians for whom the text is a constantly repeated call to faithful discipleship.

Over against these bad examples stands that of Jesus in Gethsemane. His human struggle with the will of God serves as criterion and magnet for struggling disciples of every time. Readers may recognize themselves in the three failures, but they are addressed by the presence and power of Jesus at the heart of the text. He commands us to stay awake and pray that we may not be put to the test; and when we are tested, he dares us to follow him as he "walks this lonesome valley," faithful to the will of God.

Beyond its warning against the faithlessness of disciples, and beyond its exhortation to be faithful like Jesus, the text proclaims good news about God. Jesus in Gethsemane is the parable of God. His agony shows what redemption costs God. His steadfastness reflects a God who holds to his saving purpose despite all that humankind does to the contrary. Although we, through sin, do all we can to flee the divine grace, in Jesus, God moves with determination toward our salvation. At Gethsemane, as on the cross, "in Christ God was reconciling the world to himself" (II Cor. 5:19). The good news of Gethsemane is the faithfulness of God.

Mark 14:53–72
Trial and Denial

God in the Dock (Eerdmans, 1970) is the title article of a collection of essays by C. S. Lewis. Lewis says that whereas the ancients had a keen sense of sin and approached God as an accused person approaches his judge, most moderns reverse the roles. Lacking any sense of sin, humankind becomes the judge: God is in the dock. The image is apt for the trial of Jesus, but the point of the text lies deeper. In Jesus before the Sanhedrin, we see how God deals with the sins of humankind.

263

Once again the Marcan insertion technique comes into play (see 5:21–43; 6:7–32; 11:12–25; 14:1–11). The trial scene (14:55–65) is set within the account of Peter's denial (vv. 54, 66–72), so that each interprets the other. The introduction (v. 53) names the same hostile authorities who have earlier confronted Jesus: the chief priests, elders, and scribes (8:31; 11:27; 14:43).

Trial (14:55–65)

These three groups are now gathered in an official, if irregular, meeting of the highest council of Judaism, the Sanhedrin (*synedrion*, v. 55). Both the vocabulary (witness, testimony, condemned) and the procedure (two witnesses necessary, v. 59; cf. Num. 35:30; Deut. 19:15) are those of an official Jewish court. The trial is irregular, however, because the verdict is predetermined (v. 55) and the evidence is false (vv. 56, 57, 59). The language about false witnesses echoes the laments of an innocent sufferer (Pss. 27:12; 35:11; 109:2) and the whole scene fulfills Jesus' predictions of his passion (8:31 and esp. 10:33). No genuine inquiry into the claims of Jesus, this "trial" is, rather, the rejection of those claims by the official leaders of Judaism, corresponding to the rejection of Christian claims about Jesus at the time this Gospel was written. This rejection, far from discrediting Jesus' messiahship, confirms it in ways not evident to participants in the drama, but abundantly clear to the reader.

The trial turns upon two charges against Jesus: He claimed he would destroy the Temple and in three days build another not made with hands; and he claimed to be the Christ, the Son of God. The first charge brings to a head the anti-Temple polemic of chapters eleven through thirteen, and the second is a climactic moment in the developing christological theme of the entire Gospel (see Introduction, pp. 9–11). Each of these charges is false at one level but, in a deeper sense, ironically true.

Jesus' "cleansing" of the Temple (11:15–19), interpreted by the cursing of the fig tree (11:12–14, 20–25), was a veiled prophecy of the Temple's fate, and Jesus plainly predicted its destruction in 13:2. Yet at no point in Mark has Jesus claimed that *he*

264

would destroy the Temple, or that after three days he would build another not made with hands. The allegation is therefore false.

On the other hand, at the crucifixion mockers again refer to a claim by Jesus that he would destroy and rebuild the Temple (15:29), and at the moment of his death the Temple curtain is torn in two (15:38). Readers are invited to infer that Jesus' death did in some sense destroy the Temple and that his resurrection after three days will in some sense establish a temple not made with hands. Other New Testament texts suggest that the claim attributed to Jesus in 14:58 comes true in the creation of the church (cf. I Cor. 3:16; II Cor. 6:16; Eph. 2:20–22; cf. Heb. 8—9). That this truth should be uttered unknowingly by false witnesses is a prime example of Marcan irony.

The silence of Jesus in response to the first charge heightens the tension in which the high priest puts the second, crucial question: "Are you the Christ, the Son of the Blessed?" (14:61). Since "the Blessed" is a pious circumlocution for God, the question brings together the two christological titles announced in the heading of the Gospel (1:1), Christ and Son of God (see pp. 28–29). In this Jewish context, both titles refer to the Messiah (pp. 10–11). Peter, on behalf of the disciples, had finally recognized Jesus as the Christ, but was silenced (8:29–30). The demons had often recognized him as Son of God, but were also silenced (1:24–25; 3:11–12). Although the evangelist has described Jesus as both Christ and Son of God, Jesus has never claimed either title for himself. Now the question is put to him directly. And now, with the drama of his passion already underway, when there is no longer any possibility for popular misunderstanding of the meaning of his claim, Jesus answers unequivocally: "I am" (v. 62a).

This straightforward answer is not only the validation by Jesus himself of the two titles with regard to which he has thus far shown such reticence; nor is it only evidence of the courage of Jesus, who says it at the cost of condemnation to death (v. 64). It is both of these, but more. "I am" is a theophanic formula of revelation. It functions as a revelation of divine presence in 6:50 (the walking-on-water narrative, a theophany) where it parallels the basic revelation of God at the burning bush and in the Johannine discourses of Jesus (see pp. 130–31). The accusation of blasphemy attests the theophanic function of "I am" in the

265

present text; a messianic claim would not in and of itself have been considered blasphemous.

To this bold answer Jesus immediately adds a Son of man saying. The formula "you will see" constitutes a potent claim to future vindication. The Jesus who is now, from the perspective of Mark's readers, clearly seen to be both Christ and Son of God will in the future be seen as "the Son of man seated at the right hand of Power (God), and coming with the clouds of heaven" (v. 62b). This saying combines allusions to Ps. 110:1 and Dan. 7:13 in a way that could refer to the resurrection, to the Parousia, or to both. Jesus' claims, incredible to the Sanhedrin, would be initially vindicated by the resurrection. Equally incredible to the contemporaries of Mark's first readers, these claims would be finally vindicated by the Parousia. Just as "Christ" and "Son of God" are misleading designations for Jesus until interpreted by his death and resurrection, so "Son of man" must remain but partially understood until his coming in glory.

The mocking of Jesus by members of the Sanhedrin (v. 65) is doubly ironic. Having convicted Jesus in part for allegedly predicting that he would destroy and rebuild the Temple, they goad him by the demand, "Prophesy!" In the very act of doing so, they fulfill his prophecy, ". . . and they will condemn him to death . . . ; and they will mock him, and spit upon him, and scourge him . . ." (10:33–34). Furthermore, at this very moment outside in the courtyard, Peter is fulfilling Jesus' prophecy by denying Jesus (vv. 66–72). The entire scene, as fulfillment of past prophecy, is ground for expecting the fulfillment of what Jesus now predicts.

By gathering up strands from earlier themes in the Gospel (Temple, Christology), the trial narrative summarizes important elements in Marcan theology. By presenting the reasons for Jesus' condemnation, it prepares the reader for what follows and serves as a commentary on the crucifixion narrative, which will recount the event without comment. By depicting the trial of Jesus, it addresses readers undergoing trials (probably those of the Jewish wars, A.D. 66–70, in the first instance), offering a model for how they should act and a theology for understanding their sufferings (J. R. Donahue, *Are You the Christ?*, p. 236).

266

Denial (14:66–72)

The account of Peter's denial should be read in light of the experience of early Christians. The loyalty of Mark's first readers was tested not only by arraignment before powerful authorities (cf. Jesus), but more frequently in the common encounters of life (cf. Peter). The accusation brought three times against Peter by a maid and bystanders is simply that he "was with the Nazarene, Jesus"; that is, that he was a Christian. If Jesus serves as example for readers who faced the danger of death, the example of Peter is offered to the many who faced hostility, ostracism, and embarrassment.

Under that kind of pressure, Peter caves in. He first pretends ignorance ("I don't know what you are talking about"), then disclaims membership in the Christian community (he denies that he is "one of them"), and finally denies any relationship to Jesus ("I do not know this man of whom you speak"). The text presents these as three ways of denying Jesus, although Peter never speaks a word against him. Rather, "he began to invoke a curse on *himself* " (v. 71a). In this touch of Marcan irony, Peter, trying to save himself embarrassment, in fact incurs the danger of divine punishment: "May God punish me if I am not (telling the truth)" (TEV). Readers know that Peter is not telling the truth. Protesting innocence, Peter is convicted by the narrative as guilty. Convicted as guilty and deserving death, Jesus is proclaimed by the narrative to be innocent, just, and ultimately victorious.

A concise and powerful conclusion, "And he broke down and wept," leaves the story open-ended. Peter's unresolved guilt functions as an implicit appeal to the reader to try to do better than Peter. More profoundly, it depicts the human condition. If in Jesus we see how God always is, in Peter we see how we always are.

SIGNIFICANCE

The trial of Jesus before the Sanhedrin and the denial of Peter in the courtyard relate to each other like twin stars: The movement of each unit is best understood in terms of the counterforce of the other. The contrasting pair has a continuing, dual significance as exhortation and as proclamation.

As paradigms for behavior under pressure, Jesus shows what we should do and Peter what we should avoid. Jesus exemplifies courage, Peter cowardice. Jesus, while losing his life through steadfast witness, ultimately saves it; Peter, trying to save himself, in fact condemns himself. The passage is hortatory. Readers are called to follow Jesus.

267

At a deeper level, however, the text proclaims the gospel. The dark side of the message is that we do not follow Jesus, despite our high intentions and loud protestations; but, like Peter, we in fact deny him. The good news is that our salvation depends not on our petty performance, but on the faithfulness of God. Jesus' firm "I am" evokes a God who is in the dock; who, in subjecting himself to our judgment, judges us; who, not sparing his own Son but giving him up for us all, redeems even those who deny him; who, from most unlikely material, builds a church, a temple not made with hands; whose power is made perfect in weakness and whose ultimate vindication is as sure as are past fulfillments of his word.

To hear this proclamation without the exhortation is cheap grace; to hear the exhortation without the proclamation is shallow moralism. The trial and denial of Jesus call us to try to do better than Peter and to believe the gospel of God.

RESEARCH

Interpreters who wish to pursue historical questions raised by the trial narrative will find useful Ernest Bammel, ed., *The Trial of Jesus* and David Catchpole, *The Trial of Jesus: A Study in the Gospels and Jewish Historiography from 1770 to the Present Day.* The latter gives access to the vast literature generated by the trial narratives, emphasizing Luke's account.

Those interested in Jewish-Christian debate over the trial of Jesus should be apprised of Paul Winter, *On the Trial of Jesus;* Haim Cohn, *The Trial and Death of Jesus;* and an issue of *Judaism,* XX (1971), devoted to this subject. In the latter publication Samuel Sandmel aptly summarizes the results of the vast research that has approached this narrative from the perspective of history: "In short, I give up on the problem."

The present notes have depended heavily on two doctoral dissertations on this passage. John R. Donahue, S. J., *Are You the Christ? The Trial Narrative in the Gospel of Mark* takes a redaction critical approach to the narrative. Donald Juel, *Messiah and Temple* represents a broader literary approach. Both agree that "to pose the historical question of the trial narrative is to pose the wrong question" (Donahue, p. 239). We are reading gospel, and the trial narrative should be read as such. This word of caution, particularly apt for Christian attorneys who approach these texts from a legal perspective, calls all interpreters to stress what the text proclaims about Jesus.

Mark 15:1–20
Jesus Before Pilate

Jesus' trial before Pilate is parallel to that before the Sanhedrin. In each Jesus is interrogated, condemned, and mocked. This parallelism draws attention to the responsibility of both religious and civil authorities for the death of Jesus. He is rejected first by Jerusalem, then by Rome; by Jews and by Gentiles, though for different reasons.

To these two agents the present passage adds a third party: the crowd. There are no spectators pure and simple. All are participants . . . even the reader.

TEXT

Although the mocking by the soldiers (vv. 16–20) might be considered separately, it is included in the present passage because of the parallelism already noted and because all the action between verses 1 and 21 occurs at the Roman governor's official residence, the praetorium. Within this unit three distinct scenes are marked off by the formula "and they led him away (out) . . .":

Consultation of Sanhedrin	1
"and they . . . led him away . . . to Pilate."	1b
Trial before Pilate	2–15
"And the soldiers led him away inside the palace..."	16a
Mocking by soldiers	16–20
"And they led him out to crucify him."	20b

Consultation of the Sanhedrin (15:1)

"As soon as it was morning" points to the fourth watch in the night (evening, midnight, cockcrow, morning; 13:35). While the countdown to Passover was in days (14:1, 12), the passage of time during passion night is marked in watches (14:17, 30; 15:1; see Introduction, p. 6–7). Now the night is over, and the present unit marks the transition to the day (according to Roman reckoning) in which the crucifixion will occur.

"Held a consultation" means not to convene the council,

269

which was already convened (14:53, 55–65), but to make plans (TEV, JB, NEB) or to reach a decision (NIV, NAB). The plan or decision was to deliver Jesus to the civil authority and press for a death sentence (15:1*b*, 13–14). Although John 18:31 states that this was because the Sanhedrin lacked authority to carry out a death sentence, Mark, ignoring this point, seems interested only in the complicity of both Jews and Gentiles in Jesus' death, as predicted in 10:33 (". . . and deliver him to the Gentiles").

Trial Before Pilate (15:2–15)

This central section of the unit consists of two parts, the interrogation (vv. 2–5) and the condemnation (vv. 6–15).

In the interrogation Pilate immediately raises the main issue: "Are you the King of the Jews?" The question is identical in all four Gospels. The shift from the high priest's terminology (14:61) is significant. Pilate wishes to know if Jesus is a revolutionary, a usurper of Caesar's authority.

Jesus' answer is deliberately ambiguous (see NEB, TEV), another example of the Marcan penchant for two-level communication. The charge is false at surface level, for Jesus is not, in Pilate's sense, a pretender to the Jewish throne. Yet the charge is true, for at a deeper level Jesus *is* King of the Jews (Messiah), though not in the sense that either Jesus' enemies or his friends had expected. Jesus' enigmatic answer leaves readers to ponder who he is.

The chief priests accuse him of "many things" and Pilate points out that they bring "many charges" against him. Luke 23:2, 5 specifies several charges, but in Mark the single explicit issue is whether or not, and in what sense, Jesus is the Messiah, the King of the Jews.

Jesus' silence in this dangerous situation causes Pilate to "wonder" or to "marvel" (AV, v. 5). In the silence of Jesus two Old Testament themes converge: the righteous sufferer of the Psalms (cf. Ps. 38:13–14) and the suffering servant of Second Isaiah (cf. Isa. 53:7). Thoughtful readers are led to share the Roman governor's amazement at Jesus' extraordinary presence.

The condemnation (vv. 6–15) is woven into a sub-plot about Barabbas, a prisoner who had been arrested for murder committed during a recent civil disturbance. The narrative establishes that Pilate thought Jesus was innocent (vv. 9–10, 14–15*a*)

270

and that he nevertheless condemns Jesus to death (v. 15*b*). The interplay of personalities in the incident serves other functions as well. For readers who ask, "Why did they kill this remarkable man?" the text states the motives of the religious and civil authorities and of the crowd.

With regard to the religious authorities, "it was out of envy (jealousy, malice) that the chief priests had delivered him up" (v. 10; cf. Wisd. of Sol. 2:24; I Clem. 5:2–5). Jesus exercised an authority they could only claim. The crowds he attracted filled them with envy as well as fear (14:2).

Pilate sentenced a man he believed to be innocent because he wished "to satisfy (please) the crowd." The expression, awkward in Greek, is a word-for-word translation of the Latin *satis facere.* By the time of Pilate (and by the time of the evangelist, still more) Roman authorities had had considerable experience in placating restive mobs.

The crowd (in Mark only) takes the initiative to ask Pilate to follow his custom of releasing a prisoner at Passover time. In introducing Barabbas, the Marcan account stresses his involvement in an insurrection, which may suggest that the crowd wishes to have this participant (leader?) in the resistance to Roman authority restored to circulation. The explicit motivation, however, is that "the chief priests stirred up the crowd." The mob is essentially mindless and subject to manipulation. For whatever motives, twice they reject Jesus as king (vv. 9, 12), and twice, by acclamation, they call for his death: "Crucify him" (vv. 13–14).

The earliest commentary on the Barabbas incident is Peter's Temple sermon in Acts. Acts captures the irony of the Marcan passage when Peter speaks to the Jerusalem crowd concerning "Jesus, whom you delivered up and denied in the presence of Pilate, when he had decided to release him. But you denied the Holy and Righteous One, and asked for a murderer to be granted to you, and killed the Author of life, whom God raised from the dead" (Acts 3:13–15). Mark depicts this apparent miscarriage of justice in a way which, ironically, reveals "the supreme truth about Jesus. Though sinless, he dies that sinners may live" (Achtemeier, *Invitation,* p. 215).

Use of another Latin loan-word *(phragelloō)* for "scourge" (v. 15) reflects the fact that it was a Roman custom to whip *(flagellare)* condemned prisoners before execution.

271

"Scourged" and "delivered" both recall Jesus' third passion prediction (10:33–34) which, along with Old Testament scripture, will be further fulfilled in the following paragraph.

Mocking by Roman Soldiers (15:16–20)

This is the second of three mockings of Jesus in Mark. He was mocked by members of the Jewish council and its guards after the trial before the Sanhedrin (14:65); now he is mocked by Roman soldiers in the praetorium (yet another Latin loanword) after the trial before Pilate (15:16–20); he will be mocked again at his crucifixion (see 15:26–32).

One reason for the prominence given to mocking is to show how this particular form of suffering fulfills Jesus' own prediction and Old Testament prophecy. The Roman soldiers' mockery includes clothing Jesus in royal purple, crowning him with thorns, addressing him as "King of the Jews" (all underscore his paradoxical kingship), striking his head with a reed, spitting on him, and kneeling in homage to him. Although Western art and tradition have emphasized the purple cloak and crown of thorns, the only elements specifically mentioned in a passion prediction are spitting and scourging (10:34, in which Gentiles will mock, spit upon, scourge, and kill him). The spitting is reminiscent of the third servant song in Second Isaiah, where spitting occupies the climactic place in a description of mocking (Isa. 50:6). Visualizing this aspect of Jesus' passion, Calvin reflected that "the face of Christ, marred with spittle and blows, has restored to us that image which sin had corrupted, indeed destroyed" (*Harmony*, III, 168).

A further probable reason for the prominence of mockings in Mark is that this Gospel was written for Christians who were themselves undergoing ridicule and abuse for their faith. They could identify with Jesus, because Jesus had identified with them.

This unit, like the preceding one (14:72), closes with a plain, factual statement: "And they led him out to crucify him" (15: 20). Heb. 13:11–13 is an early interpretation of these words. Mark includes no theological reflection. The simplicity of the text gives it power. The crucial moment has arrived.

272

Basic Theme

A basic theme underscored throughout this unit is that Jesus goes to his death as God's anointed, the King of the Jews.

The claim is implicit in the Sanhedrin's decision to deliver Jesus to Pilate (v. 1) and the term itself is explicit in Pilate's interrogation (v. 2), in the Barabbas incident (vv. 9–15) and in the mocking (v. 18). The religious authorities do not think he is Messiah, and Pilate finds the idea of his kingship useful only to taunt the Jews (15:12). The text, however, appeals to the reader for a different verdict.

In this tumultuous scene, rival authorities vie for power. The chief priests, elders and scribes have religious authority, which they can exercise only by manipulating a Roman governor and an excitable crowd. Pilate possesses civil authority but will not act on his own judgment because, like the religious leaders (14:2), he fears the crowd. The crowd clamors for blood, but with no clear sense of purpose or direction.

The one quiet figure in the midst of this confusion is Jesus. Reticent about claiming authority, he demonstrates it by his quiet dignity. In this apparently powerless figure the reader, like the evangelist, perceives the real King.

SIGNIFICANCE

Christ before Pilate is an archetypical scene which holds a mirror up to countless situations of decision in life. Each successive movement in the scene—the interrogation, the Barabbas incident, and the mocking—can become a paradigm for human actions and reactions under pressure.

The religious leaders' determination to destroy one whose idea of the Kingdom of God challenged not only their theology but their privileged position, Pilate's overruling desire to satisfy the crowd, the crowd's mindless propensity for violent solutions, Jesus' unjust condemnation and subjection to taunting and torture are all elements which suggest to interpreters analogies in contemporary experience.

To stand outside text and situation and assign roles to persons and groups does not interpret the Scripture. Genuine interpretation demands real participation, based on the realization that each reader or hearer probably can identify with every one of the actors at different times and in various relationships. Jesus' call to take up one's cross implies that those who seriously try to follow him may be expected to identify with him in this scene. Like the first readers of Mark, who were undergoing persecution, other early Christians understood the image of Jesus before Pilate as a model for their own behavior:

273

". . . Christ also suffered for you, leaving you an example, that you should follow in his steps. . . . When he was reviled, he did not revile in return; when he suffered, he did not threaten; but he trusted to him who judges justly" (I Pet. 2:21–23; cf. I Tim. 6:13–14). However, experience suggests that in practice even serious disciples will often identify with priests, Pilate, or the crowd, rather than with their King.

Interpreters can facilitate real participation by working, in a given lesson or sermon, with one specific situation on which this text may bring to bear the light of God's word: our response to the drama of the struggling poor in one particular country; a specific case in which following Jesus instead of one's peers leads to ridicule; a critical decision in which obeying God rather than the state might entail prosecution. Such a list, to be sufficiently particular, must be completed out of the experience of the interpreter and the community being addressed.

The centrality of the term "King of the Jews" in this passage poses a special interpretive challenge. In a culture in which kings are only historical memories or decorative figureheads, the affirmation that Jesus is King of the Jews runs a double risk of being meaningless. The interpreter must somehow recover not only the notion of Messiah, but that of kingship itself. The problem is not that we have failed to recognize the kingship of Jesus, but that we make him just another of the ornamental kings of whom we read, in whom we are mildly interested, but with whom personally we have little to do.

The fundamental issue is the true nature of authority. Over against the authority imposed by force from above, this King of the Jews exercises an authority born of fidelity to the will of God. More than merely a good man, a noble example, or an innocent sufferer, Jesus before Pilate is the representative in our midst of the authority of God. Consequently, this text speaks not only of the kingliness of Jesus but of the lowliness of God. In Jesus, God identifies with the unjustly accused and the wretched of the earth. Jesus exercises power through weakness and authority through love, thereby revealing in revolutionary terms the way the ultimate Power of the universe works.

Mark 15:21–41
The Crucifixion

Crucial. The crux of the matter.

The place of Jesus' death on a cross in the Gospel of Mark and its impact on the way Christians understand God and history are attested by the common use of these terms.

Yet this event, toward which Mark's entire story builds, is narrated in only twenty-one verses, and the crucifixion itself is reported in just four words (in Greek, three; v. 24*a*). What elements are included in this lean account? Why is it so powerful? How does it speak today?

TEXT

Chapter fifteen of Mark is summarized in four affirmations of the Apostles' Creed: (He) suffered under Pontius Pilate (vv. 1–20), was crucified (vv. 21–32), dead (vv. 33–41), and buried (vv. 42–47). The two central affirmations of these four are treated in the present passage.

The drama of Jesus' crucifixion and death is heightened by time notices based on the Roman day. It was the third hour (9:00 A.M.) when they crucified him (v. 25), and there was darkness over the whole land from the sixth hour (noon) till the ninth hour (3:00 P.M.) when he cried out and died (vv. 33–34). This measurement in hours and this darkness at noon underscore the fateful significance of the event.

Its meaning is conveyed less by explicit statement than by allusions to the Old Testament and to earlier texts and themes in Mark which have prepared the reader for this concise, carefully structured account.

The most striking Old Testament influence on the text is that of Ps. 22. Jesus' cry of dereliction (v. 34) is a direct quotation in Aramaic of the psalmist's opening complaint (Ps. 22:1). Furthermore, several details of the narrative appear to be the historicization of elements in the Psalm: dividing Jesus' garments and casting lots (v. 24; cf. Ps. 22: 18 and John 19:24); wagging heads and mocking (vv. 29–32; cf. Ps. 22:7–8 and Matt. 27:43).

275

Similarly, Ps. 69:21 seems to underlie the offer of vinegar (v. 36) and perhaps that of wine mixed with myrrh (v. 23). Pss. 22 and 69 are laments of a righteous sufferer (they "hate me without cause; . . . attack me with lies," Ps. 69:4), traditionally identified as David. As divinely ordained righteous sufferer, Jesus is the suffering Son of man through whom God is working out his saving purpose. Seemingly abandoned now (v. 34), Jesus, like the righteous sufferer (Ps. 22:22–31), will be vindicated in the end.

The traditional Greek text and earlier versions (AV; cf. TEV in brackets) included as verse 28 a reference to Isa. 53:12. This is a scribal note imported from Luke where the two robbers (criminals) play a larger role. The authentic Mark includes no Old Testament reference here.

On the other hand, the three hours of darkness at midday (v. 33) is not only a dramatic pause before the death of Jesus but is also a subtle allusion to Amos 8:9, which appears in an eschatological oracle beginning with "And on that day." A recurring theme in apocalyptic literature, the darkening of the sun, suggests the eschatological import of the crucifixion of Jesus. The reference is not only to tribulation and judgment, but to the time when, after the great tribulation, the sun will be darkened (13:24) and the Son of man will come with power and glory. The darkness, like the cry of dereliction, is open to the future.

Allusions to earlier texts and themes in Mark are the second way this unit leads readers to the meaning of the crucifixion. Some are subtle, like the connection between the darkness and 13:24, or the way Jesus' death as a righteous sufferer shows that he is innocent (cf. 14:55–59; 15:14) and that he dies in accordance with God's will (cf. 14:36). Others are much more evident.

The third passion prediction (10:33–34) is fulfilled throughout chapters fourteen and fifteen in circumstantial detail. Jesus will not come down from the cross (15:30, 32, 36) because to this end he has come *up to Jerusalem* (10:32, 33). The strong Roman flavor of the present unit stresses the fact that Gentiles (10:33) finally kill him, and a Gentile first, after his death, recognizes the Son of God (15:39).

Basic Marcan themes come to a head here. The hostility of the religious authorities, introduced at 2:6–7 and building ever since, culminates when the Sanhedrin's death sentence (14:64) is carried out and the chief priests and scribes mock Jesus on his cross (15:31–32). The failure of his disciples through misunder-

276

standing, betrayal, denial, and flight reaches its nadir at the cross; in Mark, not a single disciple is present. The abandonment of Jesus, foretold in 14:27 and progressively realized throughout passion night, reaches its climax in Jesus' cry, "My God, my God, why hast thou forsaken me?"

The suffering and death of Jesus has been interpreted earlier in the Gospel by predictions which show that it is necessary (8:31; 9:12, 31; 10:33–34), by instruction which makes it the model for discipleship (8:34–35; 9:35; 10:42–44), and by the climactic verse of the discipleship section which says that Jesus dies to serve and to redeem (10:45).

Mark's witness to Jesus Christ gathers to a head at the crucifixion. The christological theme is focused in the witness of chapter 15 to the kingship of Jesus. The point is made by the repetition of key terms whose importance stands out in their relationship to the basic structure of the chapter:

Trial before Pilate	2–15
Interrogation	2–5
Barabbas incident	6–15
Mocking by Roman soldiers	16–20*a*
Transition	20*b*
Crucifixion	21–26
Transition	27
(scribal gloss)	28
Mocking by passersby, priests and scribes, robbers	29–32
Death, including . . .	33–39
Mocking by bystanders	35–36
Centurion's confession	39
Witnesses: the women	40–41
Burial	42–46
Witnesses: the women	47

Tried and mocked as King of the Jews (vv. 2, 9, 12, 18), Jesus is crucified as King of the Jews (v. 26) and mocked as Messiah, the King of Israel (v. 32), with robbers, not disciples, at his right and left hands (v. 27). Dying, he cries out in the words of a suffering David (v. 34). He is mocked as a messianic pretender (vv. 35–36) but a Roman centurion confesses that he is the Son of God (v. 39), a royal title (pp. 10–11, 265–66).

Jesus is the Messiah, King and Son of God, but his coronation is ironic. His throne is a cross, his courtiers two robbers, and his public the enemies who kill him. The only one present who

277

recognizes this suffering Son of man to be the royal Son of God is a Gentile soldier who, representative of Mark's first readers, can see the truth only after Jesus has died and the Temple curtain is split in two (vv. 37–38).

The women looking on from afar do what the disciples should do, but do not (cf. 1:31*b;* 12:41–44; 14:3–9). Having served him in Galilee, they witness his death in Jerusalem (15: 40–41). The presence of these witnesses underscores the creedal nature of the narrative. The women cannot yet understand the full meaning of the event, but because they watch, they see Jesus die. Their stance is that of the reader at this point; their silent presence afar off will tie this unit to the two following units which clarify the meaning of Jesus' death.

Such are the elements in this concise narrative. Devoid of explanation and restrained in its description, the text depends for its meaning on preparatory hints and interpretive remarks earlier in the Gospel, and in a denouement which is yet to come. The drama is gripping; but the true power of the text lies in the mystery of the death of the Son of God.

SIGNIFICANCE

While John depicts the cross as glory and Luke highlights Jesus' solidarity with the oppressed, Mark (followed by Matthew) presents the crucifixion of Jesus as the paradoxical enthronement and coronation of the suffering King of the Jews. This Gospel points to Jesus on his cross and says, "God is like that."

The power of Mark 15:21–41 lies, at least in part, in its brevity and restraint. Interpreters (and commentators!) should therefore beware of talking it to death. The text says little but evokes much. It may be better understood through meditation and contemplation than through explanation. That is why artists are sometime the best expositors of Scripture. The interpreter can set this text beside the work of an artist who has understood it and allow each to illumine the other in such a way that the text speaks anew with depth and power.

The crucifixion of Jesus Christ has been variously understood throughout history.

278   For Constantine, the Crusaders, and for nineteenth-century missions, the cross was a symbol of victory, an expression of the triumph of the gospel. "Onward, Christian soldiers . . . with the cross of Jesus. . . ."

For medieval saints and mystics, for modern romantics and pietists, and for simple Christians in every age, Jesus on his cross was and is an object of personal devotion, a call to repentance, an incentive to good works. "Jesus hath now many lovers of his heavenly kingdom, but few bearers of his cross" (Thomas a Kempis, *The Imitation of Christ*, XI, 1).

For the poor and oppressed throughout history, and particularly for movements of liberation in our time, the crucifixion is Jesus' identification in the flesh with the wretched of the earth. His death between two robbers is the sign of where his church is called to be. Pieter Bruegel's "Procession to Calvary" (1564) reflecting the Spanish inquisition in the Netherlands, Marc Chagall's "White Crucifixion" (1938) reflecting Russian pogroms and the German holocaust, and Guido Rocha's "The Tortured Christ" (1975, sculpture) reflecting the current anguish of Latin American peasants all capture Jesus' solidarity with groups who suffer.

Literature, music, sculpture, graphic art, and cinema are among the forms in which artists treat the crucifixion. A brief list of examples may suggest others to the interpreter: Kazantzakis's novel, *The Greek Passion;* Aslan's death in *The Lion, the Witch and the Wardrobe* by C. S. Lewis; the line from Venatius Fortunatus's sixth-century Passion Hymn, "God has reigned from a tree"; Studdert-Kennedy's twentieth-century poem, "Indifference"; J. S. Bach's Passions according to St. Matthew and St. John (his fragmentary St. Mark Passion is less familiar); the southern folk song, "What Wondrous Love Is This"; the medieval "Devout Christ of Perpignan" and other sculpted crucifixes, ancient and modern; Grünewald's Isenheim altarpiece; Rembrandt's etchings; painted crucifixions by Velasquez, Graham Sutherland, Philip Evergood ("The New Lazarus"), and Rouault (one in *Miserere* inscribed with Pascal's words, "Jesus will be in agony even to the end of the world"); the Byzantine "Passion" mosaic in St. Mark's cathedral of Venice, and the twentieth-century martyrs' window (1980) behind the great altar of Salisbury cathedral; the film "Parable" (1964) in which a white-faced clown, reminiscent of Rouault's clowns, takes upon himself the burdens of the lowly, the abused, and the humiliated and is put to death in a harness as a human marionette.

279

Interpreters who wish to pursue the crucifixion in art can find help in H.- R. Weber, *On a Friday Noon*, E. Newton and

W. Neil, *2000 Years of Christian Art* and J. Dillenberger, *Secular Art with Sacred Themes.* A more accessible resource is any good hymnal. "O Sacred Head Now Wounded," for example, combines words ascribed to Bernard of Clairvaux with the passion chorale melody harmonized by J. S. Bach in his St. Matthew Passion. "When I Survey the Wondrous Cross" by Isaac Watts (1707) and "Were You There When They Crucified My Lord," an Afro-American Spiritual, are examples of the breadth and depth of interpretations of the crucifixion available in many hymnals.

The task of the interpreter is to choose the expository work of art judiciously, guided by specifically Marcan emphases. Few if any artists will reflect the Marcan text exactly; attention can be called to both similarities and differences, allowing both text and art to speak with their own integrity.

Since the goal of interpretation in this mode is to lead the reader, hearer, or observer to non-verbal apprehension of the text's significance, the interpreter must first meditate carefully on text and art, then speak only as may be necessary. The "Crucifixus" from the *Credo* in Bach's B-Minor Mass is a good model. In descending cadences and a minor key, the music builds a mood of sadness as a setting for the familiar words of the Nicene Creed, rising in intensity and then sinking into silence as the hearer contemplates: *Crucifixus etiam pro nobis. . . ."*

Mark 15:42–47
Burial

"He suffered under Pontius Pilate, was crucified, dead and buried." If he died, of course he was buried. Why, then, is this detail included in the creed? And why is it important that whoever reads the Gospel be there with Joseph when they lay him in the tomb, and with the women when they see where he is laid?

TEXT

First, the account is here because the incident occurred. Jesus was buried in a certain place on a certain day by a certain person or persons. But the fact alone is not enough to justify its inclusion in the narrative, for the Gospel of Mark does not purport to include all that happened to or through Jesus. This is not a history book, but a gospel (see Introduction, pp. 17–18).

A second answer grows out of the dramatic context. The note about the evening of the day of Preparation (v. 42) establishes that Jesus was buried toward sundown on a Friday. Since his resurrection occurs early Sunday morning, the day after the Sabbath (16:1–2), the burial marks a long, dramatic pause between Jesus' death and resurrection. Similar pauses underscore other important moments in the passion narrative (14:61; 15:33), but the key event still lies ahead. The breathless silence of the tomb sets apart Jesus' resurrection as the climax of the Gospel.

Other clues to the importance of this incident are found within the passage, particularly in the Marcan treatment of the persons who appear.

Joseph of Arimathea is described as "a respected member of the council who was also himself looking for the kingdom of God" (v. 43). Mark does not call Joseph a disciple; these have all forsaken Jesus and fled. But Joseph is doing what a follower of Jesus should do; he is looking for (waiting for, looking forward to, living in hope of seeing) the Kingdom of God (cf. 1:15; 13:37). Joseph's expectancy is not merely passive. He "took courage (Mark only) and went to Pilate and asked for the body of Jesus." He does what he can (cf. 14:8) at the risk of his own reputation. Jesus has at least one courageous follower among leading members of the religious establishment that condemned him.

The interchange between Pilate and the centurion (vv. 44–45) serves to verify that Jesus is really dead, as does the account of the burial itself (v. 46). Western art has emphasized the deposition from the cross, and popular piety is fascinated by the shroud, but the only detail of the burial which has a consequence in the Marcan text is the sealing of the tomb with a large stone (cf. 16:3–4). Jesus is thoroughly dead and, in terms of human experience, irrevocably buried.

The function of the watching women (v. 47) is to attest the fact of Jesus' burial, as well as (at the narrative level) to know where to come and complete their service to him. The Jewish council member, the Roman governor and soldier, and the Galilean women all concur in the witness that Jesus was "crucified, dead, and buried."

281

INTERPRETATION

That Jesus really died became important in the christological controversies which began before the end of the first century and lasted until the beginning of the fourth. Important at the time for defining orthodox belief and establishing the theological limits which determined the shape of the church, these controversies are of lasting significance because they show us how we can appropriately relate to God in Jesus Christ, fully human and fully divine.

The significance of the present text is best appreciated when one stands beside an open grave. Jesus has been there, too, not simply as a mourner but as the corpse. Only if he really died could he give his life a ransom for many (10:45), and he did die. At the tomb it appears that Satan has been victorious, for Jesus enters the "strong man's" (3:27) house not as a liberator but as a lifeless body. This is the lowest point on his earthly journey. The way he took on our behalf has led him to the grave. There is no dimension of our mortality he has not assumed; for by the grace of God he tasted death for everyone (Heb. 2:9).

Envoi

Mark 16:1–8
The Resurrection

When is an ending not the end?

When a dead man rises from the tomb—and when a Gospel ends in the middle of a sentence.

TEXT

The first eight verses of Mark 16 report the resurrection of Jesus, and verse 8 ends in Greek with the word "for" *(gar)*, a particle which normally comes second in a clause of several or many words. No words follow *gar*, and no appearances of Jesus follow the report of his resurrection in the most reliable manuscripts of Mark. The apparent incompleteness of this ending prompted early Christians to add either a short two-sentence ending which appears as a footnote in most English versions or (in most manuscripts) a long ending designated as 16:9–20 in the traditional text of Mark (see Appendix below).

While most informed persons agree that 16:9–20 is not authentically Marcan, responsible scholars debate whether the original ending is lost or whether the Gospel in fact ended abruptly at 16:8. Recent critics have argued persuasively on literary grounds that the latter is true. (E.g., Norman R. Petersen, "When Is the End Not the End? Literary Reflections on the Ending of Mark's Narrative," *Interpretation* 34:151–66 [April, 1980].) In all probability, 16:1–8 is the original ending of Mark's Gospel.

The unit includes three movements. The women come to the tomb (vv. 1–4), a young man in the tomb gives them a message (vv. 5–7), and the women leave the tomb (v. 8).

283

INTERPRETATION

A traditional list of women in 16:1 was probably combined with the slightly different one in 15:47 to form the first, full list in 15:40. This redactional device makes the point that the same women witness the death, burial, and resurrection of Jesus. On the one hand, their witness assures the continuity of the risen Lord with the crucified Jesus. On the other, by bringing spices to anoint Jesus' dead body, these women seek to perform one last service to him. The disciples had heard Jesus talk of service (10:42–45); the women serve (see comment on 15:40f., p. 277).

The report of their arrival at the tomb that Sunday morning (very early on the first day of the week) is dominated by concern about the stone. "The stone was rolled back" is an example of the passive voice used to avoid speaking directly of God. Readers are to understand that the entire event is God's doing.

The women enter the tomb and find "a young man" dressed in a white robe. He is not Jesus (cf. v. 6), and to identify him with the young man of 14:51 is only speculation. Traditional designation of him as an angel (messenger) is quite appropriate, for the message he brings is the heart of this unit and the key to the entire Gospel.

"He has risen, he is not here." The message brings dramatic reversal to a tragic narrative which had seemed to end in the abandonment and death of the Son of God. The tragedy is stood on its head. Looking among the dead for one crucified, the women are assured that they are looking in the wrong place. "The place where they laid him" is empty. In this emptiness is expressed the futility of every effort to possess the Nazarene, the frustration of every quest of the historical Jesus. To see Jesus the women and the disciples must look ahead, as the second part of the message makes clear.

"Go, tell his disciples and Peter that he is going before you to Galilee; there you will see him, as he told you." The falling away of the disciples and the denial of Peter are not the end of God's plans for them. In this command of the angel to the women lies the promise of forgiveness and restitution, of a renewed call and a fresh start for disciples chastened by failure and empowered by the resurrection.

Jesus had told them, "After I am raised up, I will go before you to Galilee" (14:28). The promise interrupted the flow of the

284

narrative on passion night; now in the Easter narrative the same prediction has added force because Jesus' earlier predictions of resurrection have just been fulfilled. In Mark, things always occur "as he told you": the finding of the colt and of the upper room, the betrayal by Judas, the denial by Peter, and the flight of all the disciples, not to mention the rejection, delivering up, condemnation, mocking, death, and resurrection of Jesus. Through the repetition of yet another prediction, the reader is prepared for an appearance of Jesus to his disciples in Galilee.

Galilee. At the narrative level, the term functions literally and geographically. Other evangelists understood it so (Matt. 28:16–20; John 21:1–14), and Mark 13 presupposes that some such meeting must have occurred. The apocalyptic discourse reflects a life setting in which restored disciples are engaged in mission to all nations in the face of severe opposition and persecution (13:9–13). They have finally come to a true understanding of Christ in light of which they can recognize false Christs (whose understanding was formerly their own! 13:22). Mark posits a time after the promised meeting in Galilee.

Galilee functions otherwise, however, at the level of discourse between text and reader. Galilee of the Gentiles is the locus of the mission to the nations. Galilee is also the place from which the disciples and the women came: their home turf, the place of their daily routine.

The last verse of Mark's Gospel falls like a bomb on the carefully nurtured expectation that the women will always faithfully do what needs to be done and that predictions of Jesus will always find fulfillment in the story. Instead of giving the message to disciples, as they were commanded, the women flee from the tomb in astonishment, fear, and trembling and tell no one anything. And instead of reporting a glorious epiphany in Galilee, the Gospel ends abruptly with no resurrection appearance at all. The one group of faithful followers finally fails; the resurrection predictions are fulfilled, but the second shoe (appearance to the disciples in Galilee) never drops.

The crucifixion had seemed to end the story but did not. The resurrection does not really do so, either. Resurrection-with-appearances would bring closure to the narrative, a closure which characterizes the other three Gospels. Mark's ending is no end; only the reader can bring closure.

285

SIGNIFICANCE

In one sense this unfinished story puts the ball in the reader's court. It puts us to work; we must decide how the story should come out.

In a deeper sense, however, Jesus remains in control of the ball. No ending proposed by our decisions can contain him, any more than the tomb with its great stone could. Always he goes before us; always he beckons forward to a new appearance in the Galilee of the nations, in the Galilee of our daily lives. We never know where and when we shall see him; we only know we cannot escape him.

"He is going before you . . . there you will see him." This possibility and this promise makes of Mark the Gospel of expectations still unfulfilled and of a future beyond our control. It inspired in the women trembling, awe, and ecstatic dread. It still has the same impact on whoever has ears to hear.

Those who seek, in the resurrection, closure for the story of Jesus and a program for the mission of the church should turn to another Gospel. The significance of Mark 16:1–8 lies instead in its understanding of the basic life-stance of a Christian: expectancy.

Appendix

Mark 16:9–20
The Longer Ending of Mark

Mark 16:9–20 was almost surely not a part of the original text of Mark (see B. M. Metzger, *A Textual Commentary on the Greek New Testament*, pp. 122–26; W. G. Kümmel, *Introduction to the New Testament*, pp. 98–101; contra: W. R. Farmer, *The Last Twelve Verses of Mark*, p. 109). Yet these verses are part of the canon. How are they related to Mark and the other Gospels, and how can they function in preaching and teaching today?

TEXT

The three resurrection appearances (vv. 9–11, 12–13, 14–18), the ascension (v. 19), and the statement about the world mission (v. 20) in this longer ending appear to be pieced together from accounts scattered in the other Gospels and in Acts. Particularly prominent are echoes of the appearance to Mary Magdalene (John 20:14–18), to the two disciples on the road to Emmaus (Luke 24:13–35), to the assembled disciples (Luke 24: 36–38), as well as references to the universal mission charge (Matt. 28:19) and to signs that accompany the apostles' preaching throughout the Book of Acts. (For a fuller list of these relationships, see Achtemeier, *Invitation*, pp. 233–34.)

The whole, in a style other than that of any of the canonical Gospels, does not really relieve the literary tensions created by 16:1–8. No appearance to Peter is mentioned, nor do any of the three appearances occur in Galilee. The longer ending does, however, bring the disciples back onto the scene, recommissions them, and connects their story in the Gospel with the ongoing history of the church. This text is a call to faith and to mission quite appropriate to the second-century church in which it probably originated.

The call to faith appears in the repetition of believe/not believe. Christians (those who had been with him, v. 10) and their leaders (the eleven, v. 14a) repeatedly fail to believe (vv. 11, 13, 14c), even after the resurrection (cf. Matt. 28:17b), and are upbraided for their unbelief and hardness of heart (v. 14b). Non-Christians are invited to believe and be baptized, since those who do so will be saved while those who do not believe will be condemned (v. 16). Certain signs are promised to "those who believe" (v. 17), whether recent converts or Christians in mission.

The command to mission (v. 15) is followed by the promise of signs (vv. 17–18). The text concludes with the carrying out of the order (v. 20a) and the consequent fulfillment of the promise (v. 20b). "Amen" expresses the full closure which this longer ending intends to give to the Gospel.

SIGNIFICANCE

287

This unit is secondary to and dependent upon the other Gospels and Acts. It expresses an understanding of signs and miracles that stands in some tension with that of the authentic

Mark (e.g., mention of snakes and poison; use of signs to prove the truth of the message). It is, however, a valid witness to the faith of the church in the early second century, and its basic thrusts (unbelief, commissioning) are both true to the Gospel of Mark and significant for the church today.

The risen Jesus' reproach of his unbelieving disciples is consistent with Mark (4:40; 9:19) and is at least as relevant to the church today as it was to the church of the first and second centuries. The dimensions of unbelief within the church today are many: practical atheism in the common decisions of life, identification with the powerful instead of the poor, the struggle for security instead of fidelity, complicity in worldly power and fear of being crushed by it. Interpreters will recognize in their own communities the shape of unbelief, the attitudes and priorities resulting from lack of any experience of Jesus risen and alive, and from skepticism toward those who have in fact seen him.

The last word, however, is not rebuke but command. The deepest wonder in the text is not the list of extravagant signs, but that the Lord Jesus entrusts his saving message to such dense, hard-hearted messengers. To those whom he upbraids for unbelief he also says, "Go . . . preach . . ." (v. 15). The risen Lord does not wait for his faithless church to get its house in order before announcing the gospel to others. By the act of obedience to that command, faithless disciples become believers; for "those who believe" (v. 17a) are those who go forth and preach everywhere (v. 20). In the act of obedience faith is born, and in the course of the mission faith is confirmed.

What of the signs (vv. 17–18)? Taken literally these verses can lead to such aberrations as snake-handling sects and other forms of religious enthusiasm that occasionally cause death and often bring Christianity into disrepute.

Taken seriously, however, the verses promise that those who give themselves to costly, self-denying announcement of the gospel in the world today will find their faithfulness confirmed in tangible ways. The growing literature of Christian witness through identification with the poor and the oppressed bears testimony to the reality of a power that prisons and death cannot extinguish.

Can the signs be taken both seriously and literally? This question can only be answered out of the experience of readers who, acknowledging their unbelief but committing themselves to mission, translate the text into life.

288

BIBLIOGRAPHY

The following commentaries, arranged in chronological order, have proved particularly helpful in the preparation of this one. The first two titles offer stimulating expository insights; the rest explore historical, linguistic, and critical concerns which the present commentary does not treat directly.

BEDE, THE VENERABLE (died A.D. 735). *In Marci Evangelium Expositio.* In *Corpus Christianorum, Series Latina,* CXX, 427–648 (Turnholti: Typographi Brepols, 1960).

Bede collects comments of Ambrose, Jerome, Augustine, Gregory the Great, adding his own.

CALVIN, JOHN (1509–1564). *A Harmony of the Gospels Matthew, Mark and Luke,* 3 vols., D.W. and T.F. Torrance, ed. (Grand Rapids: William B. Eerdmans Publishing Company, 1972).

Calvin's comments give priority to Matthew and reflect his battle with Rome, but his sense of the theological and pastoral heart of the text is sure.

SWETE, HENRY BARCLAY. *Commentary on Mark: The Greek Text with Introduction, Notes and Indexes* (Grand Rapids: Kregel Publications, 1977). Reprint of 1913 rev. ed.; first ed. 1898.

An Anglican scholar, Swete quotes relevant patristic comments and gives attention to textual, grammatical, historical, and theological questions.

TAYLOR, VINCENT. *The Gospel According to St. Mark: The Greek Text with Introduction, Notes and Indexes,* second ed. (New York: St. Martin's Press, 1966). First ed. 1952.

Taylor, a British Methodist, incorporates the fruits of form criticism and tradition history, and takes initial steps toward redaction criticism, but still reads Mark as history written by an attendant of Peter.

BRATCHER, ROBERT G. and NIDA, EUGENE A. *A Translator's Handbook on the Gospel of Mark* (Leiden: E. J. Brill [for the United Bible Societies], 1961).

Two of the scholars primarily responsible for *Today's English Version* offer guidance on exegesis and translation for Bible Society translators; useful for all interpreters.

SCHWEIZER, EDUARD. *The Good News According to Mark,* trans. by Donald H. Madvig (Atlanta, John Knox Press, 1970).

289

Appearing first in *Das Neue Testament Deutsch* in 1967, this work by a Swiss Reformed scholar is written from the perspective of redaction criticism and with a view to use in the church.

LANE, WILLIAM. *The Gospel According to Mark: The English Text with Introduction, Exposition and Notes* (Grand Rapids: William B. Eerdmans Publishing Company, 1974).

A conservative evangelical scholar, Lane shows special interest in historical and theological questions in Mark.

ACHTEMEIER, PAUL J. *Mark*, PROCLAMATION COMMENTARIES, Gerhard Krodel, ed. (Philadelphia, Fortress Press, 1975).

The New Testament editor of *Interpretation: A Bible Commentary for Teaching and Preaching* and a prominent contributor to current form and redaction studies in Mark, Achtemeier writes clearly and concisely about basic themes and issues in Mark's Gospel.

ACHTEMEIER, PAUL J. *Invitation to Mark: A Commentary on the Gospel of Mark with Complete Text from the Jerusalem Bible* (Garden City, N.Y.: Doubleday & Company, Image Books, 1978).

A consecutive treatment of the Marcan text aimed at a lay audience, with questions for reflection on each passage.

GNILKA, JOACHIM. *Das Evangelium nach Markus*, 2 vols. Evangelisch-Katholischer Kommentar zum Neuen Testament, Band II (Zürich: Benziger Verlag and Neukirchen-Vluyn, Neu-Kirchener Verlag, 1978–79).

Gnilka, a Catholic scholar, treats Marcan research, the intention of the text, and the history of its interpretation with a select bibliography for each passage.